FEMINIST PERSPECTIVES ON CONTEMPORARY INTERNATIONAL LAW

The essays in this volume analyse feminism's positioning vis-à-vis international law and the current paradigms of international law. The authors argue that, willingly or unwillingly, feminist perspectives on international law have come to be situated between 'resistance' and 'compliance'. That is, feminist scholarship aims at deconstructing international law to show why and how 'women' have been marginalised; at the same time feminists have been largely unwilling to challenge the core of international law and its institutions, remaining hopeful of international law's potential for women. The analysis is clustered around three themes: the first part, theory and method, looks at how feminist perspectives on international law have developed and seeks to introduce new theoretical and methodological tools (especially through a focus on psychoanalysis and geography). The second part, national and international security, focuses on how feminists have situated themselves in relation to the current discourses of 'crisis', the post-9/11 NGO 'industry' and the changing discourses of violence against women. The third part, global and local justice, addresses some of the emerging trends in international law, focusing especially on transitional justice, state-building, trafficking and economic globalisation.

Oñati International Series in Law and Society

A SERIES PUBLISHED FOR THE OÑATI INSTITUTE
FOR THE SOCIOLOGY OF LAW

General Editors

Rosemary Hunter   David Nelken

Founding Editors

William LF Felstiner   Eve Darian-Smith

Board of General Editors

Carlos Lugo, Hostos Law School, Puerto Rico
Jacek Kurczewski, Warsaw University, Poland
Marie-Claire Foblets, Leuven University, Belgium
Roderick Macdonald, McGill University, Canada

Recent titles in this series

Changing Contours of Domestic Life, Family and Law: Caring and Sharing
edited by Anne Bottomley and Simone Wong

Criminology and Archaeology: Studies in Looted Antiquities
edited by Simon Mackenzie and Penny Green

The Legal Tender of Gender: Welfare Law and the Regulation of
Women's Poverty edited by Shelley Gavigan and Dorothy Chunn

Human Rights at Work
edited by Colin Fenwick and Tonia Novitz

Travels of the Criminal Question: Cultural Embeddedness and Diffusion
edited by Dario Melossi, Máximo Sozzo and Richard Sparks

Feminist Perspectives on Contemporary International Law: Between
Resistance and Compliance? edited by Sari Kouvo and Zoe Pearson

Challenging Gender Inequality in Tax Policy Making:
Comparative Perspectives edited by Kim Brooks, Åsa Gunnarson,
Lisa Philipps and Maria Wersig

For the complete list of titles in this series, see
'Oñati International Series in Law and Society' link at
www.hartpub.co.uk/books/series.asp

Feminist Perspectives on Contemporary International Law

Between Resistance and Compliance?

Edited by

Sari Kouvo

and

Zoe Pearson

Oñati International Series in Law and Society

A SERIES PUBLISHED FOR THE OÑATI INSTITUTE
FOR THE SOCIOLOGY OF LAW

·HART·
PUBLISHING

OXFORD AND PORTLAND, OREGON
2011

Published in the United Kingdom by Hart Publishing Ltd
16C Worcester Place, Oxford, OX1 2JW
Telephone: +44 (0)1865 517530
Fax: +44 (0)1865 510710
E-mail: mail@hartpub.co.uk
Website: http://www.hartpub.co.uk

Published in North America (US and Canada) by
Hart Publishing
c/o International Specialized Book Services
920 NE 58th Avenue, Suite 300
Portland, OR 97213-3786
USA
Tel: +1 503 287 3093 or toll-free: (1) 800 944 6190
Fax: +1 503 280 8832
E-mail: orders@isbs.com
Website: http://www.isbs.com

© Oñati IISL 2014

First printed in hardback in 2011. Reprinted in paperback in 2014.

Hart Publishing is an imprint of Bloomsbury Publishing plc.

British Library Cataloguing in Publication Data
Data Available

ISBN: 978-1-84946-658-5

Typeset by Compuscript Ltd, Shannon
Printed and bound in Great Britain by
Lightning Source UK Ltd

Acknowledgements

We warmly thank the Oñati International Institute for the Sociology of Law for enabling us to organise the workshop 'Between Resistance and Compliance? Feminist Perspectives on International Law in an Era of Anxiety and Terror' in May 2008. The discussions at the workshop have greatly contributed to the framework for and the chapters in this collection, and we thank all the participants for their contributions to those conversations. Thanks to Rohee Dasgupta for initial editing work. We also wish to thank the Centre for Law, Gender and Sexuality at Kent and Keele Universities and the Swedish Research Foundation for Sari Kouvo's fellowship opportunity at the Centre in December 2006. The fellowship allowed us to start planning the workshop and this edited collection.

Sari Kouvo, Brussels and Zoe Pearson, Keele
June 2010

Table of Contents

Acknowledgements v
Notes on Contributors ix

1. Introduction 1
   Sari Kouvo and Zoe Pearson

PART ONE: FEMINIST THEORY AND METHOD IN INTERNATIONAL LAW

Navigating Feminisms: At the Margins, in the Mainstreams
or Elsewhere? Reflections on Charlesworth, Otomo
and Pearson.. 13
Vanessa Munro

2. Talking to Ourselves? Feminist Scholarship in
   International Law... 17
   Hilary Charlesworth

3. Searching for Virtue in International Law 33
   Yoriko Otomo

4. Feminist Project(s): The Spaces of International Law 47
   Zoe Pearson

PART TWO: FEMINIST PERSPECTIVES ON NATIONAL AND INTERNATIONAL SECURITY

Three Feminist Critiques of Varying Feminist Capitulations
to Crisis-Hegemony. Reflections on Otto, Mertus and
Grahn-Farley.. 71
Anna Grear

5. Remapping Crisis through a Feminist Lens 75
   Dianne Otto

6. Road Blocks, Blind Spots, Speed Bumps: A Feminist
   Look at the Post-9/11 Landscape for NGOs 97
   Julie Mertus

7. The Politics of Inevitability: An Examination of Janet Halley's
   Critique of the Criminalisation of Rape as Torture 109
   Maria Grahn-Farley

PART THREE: FEMINIST PERSPECTIVES ON GLOBAL AND LOCAL JUSTICE

From the Margins to the Mainstream and Back Again:
Problems and Paradoxes of Feminist Engagement in
Global and Local Justice. Reflections on Nesiah, Kouvo,
Andersson, and Thomas.. 133
Alice Edwards

8. Missionary Zeal for a Secular Mission: Bringing Gender
to Transitional Justice and Redemption to Feminism..................... 137
Vasuki Nesiah

9. Taking Women Seriously? Conflict, State-building and
Gender in Afghanistan 159
Sari Kouvo

10. Trafficking in Human Beings: Vulnerability,
Criminal Law and Human Rights 177
Ulrika Andersson

11. Women Workers Take Over Power at the Margins: Economic
Resistance, Political Compliance 193
Dania Thomas

12. Concluding (or Beginning?) Thoughts:
Postcards to the Future 213
Sari Kouvo and Zoe Pearson

Index.. 221

Notes on Contributors

Ulrika Andersson is lecturer and researcher in criminal law at the Faculty of law, Lund University, Sweden. She has worked extensively with issues relating to sexual violence in criminal law and gender theory. Her main area of interest is legal subjectivity in relation to different aspects of power. Together with Titti Mattson she is currently working on a project on juvenile crime and delinquency issues, in connection to gang activity.

Hilary Charlesworth is an Australian Research Council Federation Fellow, Professor in RegNet and Director of the Centre for International Governance and Justice at the Australian National University. She also holds an appointment as Professor of International Law and Human Rights in the Australian National University College of Law. She has held visiting appointments at United States and European universities.

Alice Edwards is Senior Legal Coordinator, Division of International Protection, at the United Nations High Commissioner for Refugees (UNHCR) in Geneva, where she leads the Organization's core work on refugee law and policy and human rights. She has previously been on the law faculties of the universities of Oxford and Nottingham, and she remains Research Associate at Oxford's Refugee Studies Centre, Research Fellow of St Anne's College, Oxford, and a Fellow of Nottingham's Human Rights Law Centre. Her research interests are in refugee law, human rights and gender/feminist theory, and her work includes *Violence against Women under International Human Rights Law* (Cambridge University Press, 2011). She holds a PhD from the Australian National University.

Maria Grahn-Farley is an Associate Professor of Law at Albany Law School, and a Doctor of Juridical Sciences candidate at Harvard Law School, United States. Before Albany, she was the Godfrey Lecturer at the University of Maine School of Law. She held the Harvard Law School Gammon Fellowship and, before that, an Andrew Mellon Postdoctoral Fellowship at the University of California. Maria works in the area of international child rights and served on the National Board for Save the Children, Sweden. Her research focus is on international law, post-colonial theory and human rights.

Anna Grear is a relatively late entrant to academic life, having completed the Bachelor of Civil Law degree at the University of Oxford in 1999 at a mature age that will remain undisclosed! Her key interests lie in the area of legal theory, particularly human rights theory. Her interest in gender comes from a long-time passion for feminist goals, intuitively adopted in childhood. Feminist goals, intersectionally located, emerge as a concern deeply implicated by her broadly critical theoretical stance towards the legal construction of the human being. Her current projects centre on the theorisation of embodied vulnerability and its implications for human rights law and theory, and for the construction of legal subjectivitys.

Sari Kouvo is currently working as an adviser on human rights and gender at the European External Action Service, and as an executive board member of the Afghanistan Analysts Network. She has previously held the positions of Senior Program Associate with the International Centre for Transitional Justice and Co-Director of the Afghanistan Analysts Network, Human Rights Adviser to the European Union Special Representative for Afghanistan, Researcher on Afghanistan at Amnesty International, and lecturer and researcher at the Department of Law, Göteborg University, Sweden. She has held visiting scholarships, including at the Australian National University and the NATO Defence College, Italy.

Julie Mertus is a Co-Director of the MA programme in Ethics, Peace and Global Affairs at American University, United States. An authority on the Balkans, she has worked on gender and human rights issues for governmental, intergovernmental and non-governmental organizations, including UNHCR, USAID, the Norwegian Government, the Open Society Institute, Women for Inclusive Security and the Women's Commission for Refugee Women and Children. She has held a number of visiting fellowships and appointments, including at the US Institute of Peace, Harvard Law School, as Fulbright Fellow, and at Human Rights Watch.

Vanessa Munro is Professor of Socio-Legal Studies in the School of Law at the University of Nottingham, United Kingdom. She has published widely on various aspects of feminist legal and political theory, and combines this theoretical work with empirical projects examining popular and penal responses to sexual violence. She has advised the UK Parliament in relation to human trafficking and sexual offences reform. She is currently involved in a research project exploring disclosure and decision-making in applications for asylum in the UK lodged by women who claim to have been raped.

Vasuki Nesiah is Associate Professor of Practice in human rights and law at the Gallatin School in NYU. She came to NYU from Brown University, where she was Director of International Affairs and a Visiting Assistant Professor in International Relations and Gender Studies. Prior to her tenure at Brown, she was the head and founder of the gender programme at the International Center for Transitional Justice. Vasuki has also taught in different capacities at Columbia University, Syracuse University, the University of Puerto Rico Law School and Harvard University. Currently, her main areas of research include the law and politics of international human rights, with a particular focus on transitional justice.

Yoriko Otomo is a PhD candidate at the Melbourne Law School, University of Melbourne, Australia. Yoriko has worked in several government and non-governmental organisations, and is currently completing a PhD thesis while undertaking public interest litigation at a Melbourne law firm. She researches and teaches in the areas of legal theory, international law, international humanitarian law and international economic law, gender studies, and environmental law.

Dianne Otto is Professor of Law at the Melbourne Law School, University of Melbourne, Australia, where she is Director of the International Human Rights Law Program of the Institute for International Law and the Humanities (IILAH) and Programme Director for Peacekeeping at the Asia-Pacific Centre for Military Law (APCML). Her research interests include utilising feminist, post-colonial and queer theory to reveal the voices and interests that are marginalised or silenced by mainstream international legal doctrines, practices and advocacy.

Zoe Pearson currently works in the area of immigration and refugee law in New Zealand. She was formerly a lecturer in the School of Law, Keele University, United Kingdom, teaching human rights and international law. Prior to joining Keele, she worked on issues of the legal implementation of international and domestic human rights in New Zealand. Her research focuses on space, pluralism and complexity in international legal regulation, with particular reference to the participation of non-state actors in the structures and processes of public international law.

Dania Thomas is a lecturer in the School of Law, Keele University, United Kingdom, where she specialises in private law, mainly the English common law of contract, and company law. She has a particular interest in the contemporary politics of identity and sovereign debt. In her work on the private law aspects of sovereign debt regulation, she explores the political and economic roles that private doctrine plays in international finance.

1

Introduction

SARI KOUVO AND ZOE PEARSON

INTRODUCTION

FEMINIST PERSPECTIVES HAVE developed into a flourishing discourse within the discipline of international law. From the lecture theatres and conferences of academia to the corridors of international institutions frequented by non-governmental organisations, diplomats and the bureaucrats of international institutions, it would seem that gender issues have been placed firmly on the international legal agenda. However, at times this engagement has been an uneasy one for feminist scholars and practitioners. This collection represents a 'stock-take' of where feminist perspectives on international law are today vis-à-vis women of the world and the mainstream of international legal scholarship and practice. In particular, this collection analyses how feminist scholars of international law, while trying to maintain the apparent momentum of feminist discourses, have responded to critical inquiries that emerged during the last decade highlighting feminisms' blind spots and taken-for-granted truths. The collection also explores how feminist scholars have responded, and continue to respond to the hegemonies of international law that persist, particularly visible in the post-9/11 changes in international law and politics that would seem to obfuscate and threaten feminist discourses.

The collection draws on papers and discussions that emerged from the workshop 'Between Resistance and Compliance? Feminist Perspectives in an Era of Anxiety and Terror' convened at the International Institute for the Sociology of Law in Oñati, Spain. The workshop aimed to provide a forum for critical discussion about the role of, and changes in, feminist perspectives on international law post-9/11. The debates surrounding the 'War on Terror' and the terrorist attacks in New York, Madrid and London, have centred on a perceived 'clash of civilisations' between the Western world and the Islamic world, dusting off Imperial imagery of 'the civilised' and 'the native', of men as agents either on the side of good or on the side of evil, and of women as mourners and victims. Feminist international law scholars seem to have engaged in these debates somewhat ambivalently: while feminists have criticised the gendered imagery and protectionist discourses of the United States (US) and its allies vis-à-vis Afghan and Iraqi women, feminist scholars have remained loyal to peace- and state-building and democratisation agendas.

The publication of this collection is timely: the peak of the global economic crisis and the change of administration in the US do—although no victories should be planned in advance—suggest a possibility for a renewed and more reflective commitment to international law and multilateral action. In this context, the contributions to this collection offer, first, considerations on the progress made for a feminist voice in international law in the post-Cold War era and the challenges to this in the post-9/11 era; and second, a critical and self-reflective questioning of the feminist canon about hard won successes for women's rights in the 1990s, followed by a re-assertion of Western hegemonic and patriarchal values after the millennium.

In keeping with feminism's critical, self-reflective and, at its foundation, emancipatory project for international law, this collection seeks to examine the present and future contributions of feminist scholarship and practice to international law by considering a number of fundamental questions: the 'what, why, who, where and how?' of feminist perspectives on international law. Is there a core normative project for feminism in international law, and if so, what is this? Why is feminist engagement with international law relevant? Or, is it? Who is feminist scholarship speaking for and who are feminist scholars speaking to? Where does feminist scholarship situate itself? Do feminist scholars remain at the margins or have we become mainstream? How does (or should) feminist scholarship situate itself within the broader framework of international law scholarship?

THREE DECADES OF FEMINIST SCHOLARSHIP ON INTERNATIONAL LAW

While it is impossible to give a comprehensive overview of the breadth and depth of feminist explorations on international law in only a few pages, a brief sketch of some of feminism's landmark publications in the area of international law and some of the key themes is useful to contextualise the discussions in the collection.

The late-1980s and early-1990s' feminist scholarship on international law was largely inspired by feminist legal studies and cross-disciplinary women's studies (later gender studies). Early publications such as Hilary Charlesworth, Christine Chinkin and Shelley Wright's article 'Feminist Approaches to International Law' (1991) and Karen Engle's 'International Human Rights and Feminist: When Discourses Meet' (1992) explored both the potential of feminist analysis of international law and international law's emancipatory potential for women.[1] This early work carefully approached questions about if and how feminist theories and methods could be adapted for an analysis of international law, and to what extent the political, legal and institutional frameworks of international law could be sensitised to women's concerns and needs. The focus on feminist scholarship on international law and international law's emancipatory potential is dominant in this early scholarship: feminist engagement in international law is worthwhile insofar as international law can be a useful tool for promoting women's rights. Nevertheless, no clear answer to this question is articulated: it was argued that international law and its institutions were male biased and dominated by men and that women's rights and women were marginalised within the overall system. At the same time, international law and the international institutional arena was a new arena for feminist scholars and the broader cadres of women's rights advocates, and consequently the 'international' had an allure of novelty and possibility for women.

The end of the Cold War and the relative success of women's rights advocacy at the World Conference for Human Rights (1993), the International Conference on Population and Development (1994) and the World Conference for Women (1995) inspired increased feminist scholarship especially in the area of international human rights law. Edited collections such as Dorinda Dallmeyer's *Reconceiving Reality: Women and International Law* (1993), Rebecca Cook's *Human Rights of Women: National and International Perspectives* (1994) and Kelly Askin and Dorean Koenig's trilogy *Women and International Human Rights Law* (1999–2001) challenged the political, legal and institutional frameworks of international law for their failure to acknowledge and address violations suffered by women such as sexual violence and used, where possible, international human rights law as a tool to challenge discriminatory national laws and practices.[2] The link between feminist scholarship and actual progress for women continued to be strong in the 1990s' scholarship: the (arguably limited) political successes such as the adoption of the United Nations (UN) *Declaration on the Elimination of Violence Against*

---

[1] H Charlesworth, C Chinkin and S Wright, 'Feminist Approaches to International Law' (1991) 85 *The American Journal of International Law* 613 and K Engle, 'International Human Rights and Feminism: When Discourses Meet' (1992) 13 *Michigan Journal of International Law* 517.

[2] DG Dallmeyer (ed), *Reconceiving Reality: Women and International Law* (Washington, The American Society of International Law, 1993); RJ Cook (ed), *Human Rights of Women. National and International Perspectives* (US, University of Pennsylvania Press, 1994); KD Askin and DM Koenig (eds), *Women and International Human Rights Law, Volume 2* (New York, Transnational Publishers, Inc, 1999); KD Askin and DM Koenig (eds), *Women and International Human Rights Law, Volume 1* (New York, Transnational Publishers, Inc, 2000); and KD Askin and DM Koenig (eds), *Women and International Human Rights Law, Volume 3* (New York, Transnational Publishers, Inc, 2001).

Women (1992),[3] the establishment of the office of the UN Special Rapporteur on Violence against Women, its Causes and its Consequences (1993) and the recognition of select gender-based crimes as war crimes in the International Criminal Tribunals for the Former Yugoslavia and Rwanda did, however, make feminist scholars more prone to defend international law's and the international arena's emancipatory potential for women.

A more critical strand of feminist scholarship on international law also developed in the 1990s, and has continued to flourish in the first decade of the new millennium. Inspired by post-colonial and post-structural scholarship, this later scholarship, including that of Dianne Otto and Anne Orford, takes a more sceptical standpoint, asking if and how feminism has really had an effect on international law and how international law has affected feminism.[4] This exploration is continued in Hilary Charlesworth and Christine Chinkin's *The Boundaries of International Law* (2000) and Doris Buss and Ambreena Manji's edited collection *International Law: Modern Feminist Approaches* (2005).[5] Hence, at the turn of the millennium and during the first years of the new millennium, international law and the international institutional arena have lost their allure or novelty and possibility for women. At the same time, engaging in international law and with international institutions has exposed Western feminist scholarship especially to its own blind spots and biases: well-meaning Western feminisms 'speaking for' Others results in misrepresentations and criticisms. However, for feminist scholarship, realising the shortcomings of the international sphere and being exposed to criticism is, as is shown in this collection, not a negative, rather it is what fuels continued feminist debate.

BETWEEN RESISTANCE AND COMPLIANCE?

After the turn of the century, it became increasingly clear that feminist and other 'alternative' perspectives on international law had been invited to join

---

[3] *Declaration on the Elimination of Violence Against Women*, UN General Assembly Resolution 48/104, 20 December 1993, A/RES/48/104, 23 February 1994.

[4] A Orford, 'Muscular Humanitarianism: Reading the Narratives of the New Interventionism' (1999) 10 *European Journal of International Law* 679; A Orford, 'Feminism, Imperialism and the Mission of International Law' (2002) 71 *Nordic Journal of International Law* 275; D Otto, 'Nongovernmental Organizations in the United Nations System: The Emerging Role of International Civil Society' (1996) 18 *Human Rights Quarterly* 107; D Otto, 'Subalternity and International Law: The Problems of Global Community and the Incommensurability of Difference' (1996) 5 *Social & Legal Studies* 337; D Otto, 'Rethinking the Universality of Human Rights Law' (1997) 29 *Columbia Human Rights Law Review* 1; and D Otto, 'Rethinking Universals: Opening Transformative Possibilities in International Human Rights Law' (1997) 18 *The Australian Yearbook of International Law* 1.

[5] H Charlesworth and C Chinkin, *The Boundaries of International Law: A Feminist Analysis* (Manchester; Manchester University Press, 2000); and D Buss and A Manji (eds), *International Law. Modern Feminist Approaches* (US, Hart Publishing, 2005).

with the predominantly Western and liberal international law scholarship in legal and political debates and in policy-making. As we have observed above, this is evident in the apparent integration of concepts of gender and issues of women's rights in international legal practice, and the ostensible acceptance of feminist legal scholarship into the discipline. This 'invitation' was, however, conditional: feminists were asked to be the 'women's voice', but not to challenge the foundations of international law and its institutions. Willingly or unwillingly, feminist perspectives on international law have come to be situated between 'resistance' and 'compliance'. That is, feminist scholarship aims at deconstructing international law to show why and how 'women' have been marginalised; at the same time feminists have been largely unwilling to challenge the core of international law and its institutions, remaining hopeful of international law's potential for women.

The tension between resistance and compliance is, in fact, built into the heart of the feminist project within international law. Charlesworth and Chinkin have in their landmark work on feminist perspectives on international law defined this as a two-stage project: first, feminists need to deconstruct the explicit and implicit values of the international legal system, challenging their claims to objectivity and revealing the blind spots of international law and its exclusions as concerns women and women's experiences. Secondly, feminists need to reconstruct an international law that does not support men's oppression of women.[6] They note that the dual commitments of feminist scholarship coexist uneasily. In her early article, Karen Engle noted that feminist international legal scholars sense that 'their work at the periphery can only succeed if they can save the core' and so, for the most part, they defend this core. Engle stresses 'No matter how hard we push on the core, though, we never attack its essence. We are afraid that if we push too hard, it might dissolve and become useless to us'.[7] The uneasiness of feminist scholarship with questioning the foundations of international law in order to ensure that international law remains (potentially) useful for women has led to criticism. As a result, minority and postcolonial feminists have argued that feminist scholarship on international law runs the risk of reproducing old themes of 'white women saving black women from black men'.[8] Others have noted that feminism, by focusing primarily on the category of gender, misses opportunities to challenge, and runs

---

[6] Charlesworth and Chinkin, above n 5.

[7] Engle, above n 1, 605.

[8] See, eg, GC Spivak, 'Can the Subaltern Speak?' in P Williams and L Chrisman (eds), *Colonial Discourse and Post-Colonial Theory: A Reader* (New York, Colombia University Press 1994), previously published as C Nelson and L Grossberg (eds), *Marxism and the Interpretation of Culture* (Basingstoke, Macmillan Education, 1988) 271–313.

the risk of facilitating, other global-scale inequalities and injustices.[9] The tension between resistance and compliance remains a core area for reflection for feminist international scholarship and, as will be shown below, it is at the heart of this collection.

FROM SELF-REFLECTION TO SECURITY TO JUSTICE

The chapters in the three Parts of this collection seek to engage with the core themes of this collection from different perspectives. First, where and how do feminist perspectives on international law situate themselves on the trajectory between 'resistance' and 'compliance'? The chapters seek to consider this question through using feminist methods of self-reflection, analysing how feminist scholars situate themselves in relation to the emancipatory project of feminism on the one hand and to mainstream international law scholarship and practice on the other hand. Second, how have feminist scholars of international law reacted to and approached the post-9/11 changes of international law? How does feminist scholarship withstand the challenges that the post-9/11 era has posed for international law—and how are our projects affected by the discourses of 'clash of civilisations', 'crisis', 'emergency', '(in)security' and 'terror'? How do feminists relate to the equally dominant discourses of 'democratisation', 'justice' and 'rule of law'? The chapters seek to answer these questions through challenging the relative feminist silence on the one hand, and by drawing alternative maps of the current developments and challenging the language that frames the current debates on the other hand. In doing so, the Parts move from reflections on theory and method, to challenging current discourses of national and international security, and to analyses of diverse conceptions of global and local justice.

The first Part, 'Feminist Theory and Method of International Law', explores how feminist theories and methods of international law have evolved over the past decades and what the blind spots and stumbling blocks in our feminist endeavours might be. Making particular use of feminist methods of self-reflection, the chapters in this Part attempt to analyse whether feminist scholarship on international law still draws its energy from feminism's emancipatory project, and if so, how feminist scholars should tackle the increasingly complex and multi-layered understanding of gender and sites of women's oppression and resistance. While continuing to commit to the emancipatory

---

[9] See eg, C Mohanty, '"Under Western Eyes" Revisited: Feminist Solidarity through Anticapitalist Struggles' (2002) 28 *Signs: Journal of Women in Culture and Society* 499–530; Odim-Johnson, 'Common Themes, Different Contexts, Third World Women and Feminism' in C Mohanty, A Russo, and L Torres et al (eds), *Third World Women—the Politics of Feminism* (Bloomington Indianapolis, Indiana Press, 1991).

project, the authors of the chapters seek alternative methods for dealing with the complexities of gender and engagement with the law. In 'Talking to Ourselves: Feminist Scholarship in International Law', Charlesworth challenges and draws on Janet Halley's argument that we should 'Take a Break from Feminism' in attempting to develop a deeper feminist engagement with the contemporary peace- and state-building agendas. She concludes that feminist messages must be accompanied by feminist methods of engagement if they are to be productively used in the many varied contexts of women's lives. In 'Searching for Virtue in International Law', Yoriko Otomo analyses the potential for post-structuralist psychoanalytical theory for understanding the foundational biases of international law. She argues that feminist scholars must retain a grasp of both resistance and revolution as feminist telos, distinguishing between resistance to institutional structures of international law and the spaces created by the failures of masculinist international law discourse 'which we can fill with revolutionary readings, writings, speakings and beings'. In 'Feminist Project(s): The Spaces of International Law', Zoe Pearson, using contemporary theories and methods of feminist geography and notions of cartography, seeks to uncover the complex spatialities of norm production in international law, and in doing so, highlights opportunities for feminist analysis and critique to engage with such spaces as part of a resistive approach aimed at transcending the hegemonic binaries inherent in international law.

The second Part, 'Feminist Approaches to National and International Security', seeks to explore what feminist analysis can bring to the current discussions about national and international security. Exploring the relationships between feminism, international law and security has become increasingly urgent at a time when the advances made by women's advocates during the 1990s are being challenged and when the foundations of international law seem to have been under attack. Feminist scholarship and activism on international law has both adapted to and challenged the post-9/11 discourses of crisis, emergency and terror. In 'Remapping Emergencies through a Feminist Lens', Dianne Otto tackles the current language of 'crisis' arguing against feminist appropriation of this terminology. Julie Mertus, in her chapter 'Road Blocks, Blind Spots, Speed Bumps: A Feminist Look at the Post-9/11 Landscape for NGOs', analyses how the 1990s' international women's rights movement and major non-governmental organisations have adapted to the changing discourses of the post-9/11 and learnt to accommodate security discourses. She argues that the dominance of security agendas threaten to co-opt both feminist and human rights interventions in international law, presenting a key concern for feminist work in navigating a path between resistance and compliance. In 'The Politics of Inevitability: An Examination of Janet Halley's Critique of the Criminalisation of Rape as Torture', Grahn-Farley challenges Halley and what Grahn-Farley calls 'liquid feminists', who, in their efforts to challenge the mainstream's victimisation of women end up defending not women's free choice but facilitating the oppression of women. We must, Grahn-Farley argues, beware the 'politics of inevitability' that seemingly accepts institutional oppression of individuals as inevitable.

The third Part, 'Feminist Perspectives on Global and Local Justice', takes a different perspective on the post-9/11 changes of international law. This Part shifts from the theoretical and methodological self-reflection of the first Part, and the feminist challenges to contemporary mainstream discourses on security in the second Part, to analysing the consequences of the gender mainstreaming discourses of the 1990s. This Part casts a critical eye over some of the apparent feminist success stories of international law, and analyses the compromises that have been necessary for these successes. In 'Missionary Zeal for a Secular Mission: Bringing Gender to Transitional Justice and Redemption to Feminism', Vasuki Nesiah takes a critical look at how gender has been mainstreamed in transitional justice discourses. She argues that gender mainstreaming has ensured recognition of violations suffered by women and women's participation only in a very narrow way and at a superficial level. In 'Taking Women Seriously? Conflict, State-Building and Gender in Afghanistan', Sari Kouvo argues that although the saving of Afghan women was one of the legitimising arguments for the international intervention that sought to oust the Taliban regime in Afghanistan, the international community has failed to take Afghan women seriously. The interveners sought to liberate the image of the timid and oppressed *burqa*-clad woman oppressed by a brutal, medieval and misogynist Taliban regime; much less effort, however, was focused on attempting to understand the conflict-induced differences amongst Afghan women and how Afghan women with all their multiplicities wished to see their rights ensured. In 'Trafficking in Human Beings: Vulnerability, Criminal Law and Human Rights', Ulrika Andersson tackles a similar issue. Her analysis focuses on the construction of the woman trafficked for sexual purposes, showing how the need to define this woman as a 'deserving victim' actually ends up excluding many women from protection under current trafficking legislation. In 'Women Workers Take-Over Power at the Margins: Economic Resistance, Political Compliance', Dania Thomas utilises a feminist framework to explore the dominant framing of contemporary sovereign debt regulation, using a case study of women workers in the Brukman factory in Argentina. She shows that local resistance against the neo-liberal economic order is possible, but that no resistance comes without compromise.

CONCLUDING REMARKS

This collection draws on three decades of feminist scholarship on international law; it critically engages with feminist theories and methods, challenges the feminist canon and seeks to break new ground for feminist analysis. The chapters provide reflection on the many different methods and sites from which feminists negotiate the tensions between resistance and compliance that seem inherent in our work, and in doing so, illustrate the necessary open-endedness and unfinished nature of feminist projects in international law. While recognising the dangers of both resistance and compliance, particularly stark in the contemporary, crisis-driven hegemonies of international law in this 'era of anxiety and terror', the chapters argue for attention to the different methods and sites of feminist engagements with international law as a means to negotiating the simultaneous occupation of feminist international law scholars and practitioners on the margins of the discipline, as well as in the mainstream, in sites of resistance at the same time as sites of compliance.

The final words in the collection are given to the participants from the Oñati workshop, in a series of 'postcards to the future', an attempt, as one of the participants encouraged us all, to 'think beyond the full stops'. These postcards, like the chapters in the collection, illustrate the necessity and the potential of feminist theorising and practice for imagining and working towards a world that sees beyond structuring binaries, and can accommodate diversity. The postcards leave this collection with a sense that feminist perspectives on international law in an era of anxiety and terror are full of possibility.

Part One

Feminist Theory and Method in International Law

Navigating Feminisms: At the Margins, in the Mainstreams or Elsewhere?

Reflections on Charlesworth, Otomo and Pearson

VANESSA E MUNRO

T HE CHAPTERS INCLUDED in this Part speak in diverse ways to the relationship between feminism, law and resistance. They offer a critical stock-take, born of frustration at the impenetrability of the discourses of knowledge and the structures of power to which the authors believe feminists have failed to secure access in international law. Explicitly, for both Hilary Charlesworth and, to a lesser extent, Yoriko Otomo, and implicitly, for Zoe Pearson, this appraisal is undertaken in a context in which commentators, most notably Janet Halley, have invited us to 'take a break from feminism'[1]—or at least from overarching analyses of systemic female injury and omnipresent patriarchal privilege.

Each author risks rebuke from those who argue that highlighting women's disenfranchisement trivialises the influence wielded by (certain genres of) feminism in national and international legislative processes. While Pearson highlights the paradoxical nature of international law's central sites, Charlesworth insists—and Otomo accepts—that feminism is still in a 'scholarly ghetto'.[2] Concepts like 'gender-mainstreaming' may have gained prominence in regulatory discourses and (some) 'card-carrying' feminists may have secured access to the institutional corridors of the international legal regime, but this has yielded only partial gains, and rarely without attendant costs. Echoing the now well-established scepticism that greets feminist models grounded in gender assimilation, the authors—in their

---

[1] JE Halley, *Split Decisions: How and Why to Take a Break from Feminism* (Princeton, Princeton University Press, 2005).

[2] Charlesworth, below, this collection.

different ways—thus emphasise that women's mere presence and formal inclusion has not, and cannot, ensure genuine gender equality.

This insistence that, official appearances notwithstanding, feminism remains on the peripheries in international law raises the spectre of token-ism in the socio-political landscape. Drawing on experiences of post-conflict state-building in Iraq and East Timor for illustration, Charlesworth points to popular, but superficial, concessions to concepts and processes that are substantively vacuous without further sustained and critical engagement. But this, in turn, poses further dilemmas: for example, can one criticise rhetorically powerful strategies that have secured reformist currency (such as rights discourse) without being relegated as a perpetual outsider?; can one, as Audre Lorde puts it, dismantle the master's house with the master's tools?;[3] can one successfully navigate the increasingly acute tensions between feminist theory and politics?; and can normative, feminist utopias meaning-fully co-exist with deconstructive, critical methodology?

Otomo draws on Anne Orford's insight that each attempt to read, speak or write differently inevitably imposes a new form, and signals the disap-pearance of another.[4] To the extent that the mandate to take a break from feminism involves writing a new form, the authors in this Part beg the question of what might thereby be eclipsed, such that it can never quite be reclaimed. Halley and her followers concede that there *are* risks—of demor-alisation, demobilisation, co-option by regressive forces and the legitima-tion of women's injuries. But in the following chapters, each author raises issues central to our assessment of whether, in the context of international law, these are risks that those concerned with women's lives can afford to take. And at whose cost are they taken?

Together, these chapters also illustrate the benefits of inter-disciplinary insights for feminist reform. Pearson draws on critical legal and feminist geographies to engage with the myriad porous and pluri-potential spaces in which local, regional and global norms are constructed and enforced in complex, mutually defining and yet distinguishing patterns. Charlesworth explores insights derived from international relations and political theory on democratisation and state-building, and in so doing—like Pearson—highlights the inevitable tensions between the global and the local, as stan-dards that purport to ensure women's rights are imposed upon local cultures with competing conceptions of how to achieve this ideal. Meanwhile, Otomo relies on psychoanalytical theory to re-cast the notion of female hysteria which, amongst other things, foregrounds the so-called 'injury triad' that Halley identifies as integral to feminism. But to the extent that, as

---

[3] A Lorde, 'The Master's Tools Will Never Dismantle the Master's House' in *Sister Outside: Essays and Speeches* (Berkeley, The Crossing Press, 1984) 110–14.

[4] A Orford, 'Beyond Harmonization: Trade, Human Rights and the Economy of Sacrifice' (2005) 18 *Leiden Journal of International Law* 179, 211.

Charlesworth points out, Halley's call to 'take a break' insists that feminism peer round the corners of its own construction, Otomo takes this mandate further, invoking the imagery of mad women in the attic (note again the spatial symbolism) marking the corners of Law's cardboard walls in order to remind us that legal discourse and legal reform are themselves also constructions; and highly complex ones at that.

Each chapter, in different ways, raises the dilemma of how to engage with law (as a flawed normative and coercive system) without becoming co-opted by it. To the extent that law manages its own excesses by permitting certain transgressions, it polices the integrity of its claim to authority through the type of superficial and non-threatening capitulations that Charlesworth identifies. At the same time, the power of the transgressive remains parasitic on a respect for law and authority that can only ever allow itself to be partially undermined by criticisms, including feminist ones, that seek to deconstruct its foundations. For Otomo, this perpetual tension is refracted through Julia Kristeva's insight that the possibility of revolt is endangered by the existence of an 'easy fit' between law and transgression.[5] Meanwhile, for Pearson, it is located in her use of Gillian Rose's concept of 'paradoxical spaces' in which positions that appear mutually exclusive when charted two-dimensionally are occupied simultaneously, thereby disrupting—without necessarily dismantling—the dualism that frames their construction.[6]

As Martha Fineman has noted, the extent to which it is possible, simultaneously, for law to be an *object* of feminist inquiry and for law reform to be its *objective* remains contested.[7] Each of the authors in this Part reflects personally, politically and ideologically upon the inevitable fluctuation between reconstruction and deconstruction, searching as Pearson puts it for 'an elsewhere' that will enable candid engagement with legal feminism's precarious occupation of sites of both resistance and compliance.

Each of the chapters, while acknowledging the complexity and duplicity of feminism's engagement with law, thus rejects the inevitable constraints of binary logic. The paradoxical nature of spaces (and in particular, the multiple 'small spaces of law and politics'), which is highlighted by Pearson, is transposed to the scale of international law by Otomo who emphasises that its permanently subversive nature—its inevitable falling short of the imagined legal ideal of a sovereign subjectivity with enforceable and indivisible authority over a defined territory—ensures its perpetual potential to provide a site for resistance, and even revolution. In a similar vein,

---

[5] J Kristeva, *The Sense and Non-Sense of Revolt: The Powers and Limits of Psychoanalysis* (New York, Columbia University Press, 2001) 25.

[6] G Rose, *Feminism and Geography. The Limits of Geographical Knowledge* (Minneapolis, University of Minnesota Press, 1993).

[7] M Fineman, 'Challenging Law, Establishing Differences: The Future of Feminist Legal Scholarship' (1990) 42 *Florida Law Review* 25, 43.

Charlesworth's call to reconnect feminist messages with feminist methods, through techniques such as 'world travelling', underlines a transgressive and reformist potential that can be muted or mimicked by international institutions, but never entirely repressed. Meanwhile, the flow invoked by this notion of 'world travelling' is reflected in Pearson's descriptive insistence on the fluidity of socio-political and legal spaces, which in turn finds a prescriptive articulation in Otomo's notion of 'hosting' as a model that acknowledges both the instability of borders and the inevitability of transitional trespass.

The focus on space(s)—for inclusion, for resistance, for reflection—that animate these chapters is mirrored, moreover, in the self-consciously situated nature of each author's contribution. Pearson's opening and closing observations regarding the local and normative spaces of Ankara, Otomo's deliberate reflections from the vantage point of a Japanese-Australian girl in a glass office in central Melbourne, and Charlesworth's experience of a split and splintered identity as academic and activist inform the experiential locations from which their respective engagements are made.

The chapters in this Part, in subtle but compelling ways, traverse and transcend the present dichotomy in much feminist commentary between sustained allegations of a systemic and entrenched patriarchal privilege that is impervious (in law and beyond) to challenge and celebratory endorsements of international law's adoption (or co-option?) of feminist language and core concepts in setting its institutional agendas. Highlighting the paradoxical, fluid, complex, and multi-faceted nature of the spaces of international law, the authors make a collective call for caution in the face of suggestions that it is time to 'take a break from feminism'. At the same time, they reject monochrome visions of gender, or legal, power relations, and insist upon the reconstructive potential—for feminism—of international institutions and doctrines. Though not purporting to chart a detailed map, the authors offer hope for an elsewhere between resistance and compliance. Their chapters provoke a critical re-appraisal of feminist theory in general, and in relation to international law in particular; and promise to re-invigorate reformist politics therein.

2

Talking to Ourselves? Feminist Scholarship in International Law

HILARY CHARLESWORTH*

INTRODUCTION

FEMINIST SCHOLARSHIP IN international law has generated debate between feminists, but little engagement from the disciplinary mainstream. This chapter addresses one strand of the internal debate, Janet Halley's argument that feminism has come to exercise considerable power in international law and its institutions; and that it does so with little self-reflection, indeed denying its own influence by asserting an inauthentic underdog status. After describing the place of feminist theorising in international law, and then Halley's critique, the chapter considers feminist scholarship and its oscillation between resistance to and compliance with international law in the context of state-building and democratisation. It argues that feminists have been successful in bringing the language of women's empowerment into international law but less adept at identifying methods to give this language life on the ground.

FEMINIST CONVERSATIONS IN INTERNATIONAL LAW

Much feminist international legal scholarship presents itself as being in conversation with the mainstream of international law. We ask the mainstream to consider women's lives when applying or developing the law; we critique the assumptions of international legal principles; and we argue for an expanded referential universe. This conversation is, however, almost completely one-sided; a monologue rather than a dialogue. It is very hard

* Many thanks to the editors of this book for their comments on earlier drafts of this chapter. I also thank Karen Engle and Ann Genovese for their valuable comments on the chapter and Susan Harris Rimmer for her research assistance.

to find any response from international legal scholars to feminist questions and critiques; feminist scholarship is an optional extra, a decorative frill on the edge of the discipline. This lack of engagement by the academy contrasts with the approach taken in international institutions, as I describe below.

Some critical and progressive scholars use the occasional footnote to feminist scholarship to signal that they have kept up with their reading, and mainstream international law texts sometimes feature women's lives, especially in discussions of universalism and relativism. Feminist ideas are however almost never treated seriously; they are not acknowledged, debated or refuted. Similarly, international law casebooks often include a paragraph or two from a feminist article in the 'overview' or 'theory' section to show that they have broadminded authors, but feminist critiques usually appear as token offerings as they are not carried through to all areas of inquiry. In short, feminist theories are in a scholarly ghetto in international legal scholarship.

Although feminist international lawyers are often grouped under the umbrella of 'New Approaches to International Law', feminist ideas are in some tension with those of critical theorists. For example, David Kennedy's work has excavated the dark sides of international law. He understands the law largely as a method of ducking responsibility for ethical and political choices.[1] On this account, international law is worth studying for its contradictions and obfuscations but it can deliver only fleeting or illusory benefits. Martti Koskenniemi recognises a realm for international law that is distinct from politics—'the regulative idea of universal community' which directs us beyond the interests of particular groups.[2] However Koskenniemi indicates his political commitments only in the most general terms—rejection of imperialism and totalitarianism—and is wary of a broader suite of causes.[3] Feminists, by contrast, embrace normative projects—in particular achieving equality for women—with alacrity. Feminists lawyers tend generally to assume that the right sort of international law will achieve women's equality, or at least get them part of the way.

Feminist international legal writings often draw on a range of theoretical positions that can sit uneasily together; for example the idea that women have distinctive attitudes, interests and experiences may be combined with an argument that a reconstructed international law can deliver a truly impartial form of justice. This has led to charges of theoretical incoherence or impurity. Thus Nathaniel Berman has pointed out that feminist international

---

[1] See, eg, D Kennedy, *The Dark Sides of Virtue: Reassessing International Humanitarianism* (Princeton, Princeton University Press, 2004); and D Kennedy, *Of War and Law* (Princeton, Princeton University Press, 2006).

[2] M Koskenniemi, 'The Fate of Public International Law: Between Technique and Politics' (2007) 70 *Modern Law Review* 1, 30.

[3] M Koskenniemi, *From Apology to Utopia* (Helsinki, Finnish Lawyers Publishing Company, 1989) 497.

lawyers critique the doctrines and structure of international law and yet also rely on the expansionist spirit of *après-guerre* internationalism to campaign for improvements in women's lives.[4] Such a critique illustrates Elizabeth Grosz's observation that feminist theories generally rest on a deep tension between their role in analysing the thoroughgoing masculinity of disciplinary knowledges and their role as a response to political feminist goals; they often incur the wrath of the traditional academy because of their overtly political ends; and the ire of feminist activists because they can become immersed in the male-dominated world of theory.[5]

As in other areas of knowledge, most of the debate and engagement with feminist ideas in international law comes from other feminists. It seems that one needs to be a card-carrying feminist to use or discuss feminist ideas.[6] So, while the rest of the discipline ignores us, feminists have created a veritable industry of internal critique, pointing to the problematic assumptions and approaches of other feminists. Examples of such critiques include those of Third World and postmodern feminists. Take Ratna Kapur's scrutiny of what she terms the 'victimisation' rhetoric used by the international human rights movement when discussing the situation of Third World women, particularly in relation to violence and trafficking. Kapur argues that the assumption of a common international women's victimhood operates to keep women in their place by presenting them as both vulnerable and ignorant.[7] She criticises a focus on sex as the locus of women's oppression and urges a more complex understanding of women's lives through considering factors such as race, wealth, class and religion. Karen Engle has taken on one of the apparent success stories of international feminist activism, the criminalisation of rape in the International Criminal Tribunal for the Former Yugoslavia.[8] She suggests that this strategy is built on a view of women as passive victims of sexual violence and political and military agency, and that it presents a one-dimensional view of the suffering of women in the conflict in Bosnia-Herzegovina. Engle argues that the strategy of prosecution has had the practical impact of reifying ethnic differences and the legal and moral effect of denying the possibility of sexual agency in times of conflict. She seems suspicious of the utility of any claims made

---

[4] N Berman, 'Power and Irony, or, International Law after the Après-Guerre' in E Jouannet, H Ruiz Fabri, and JM Sorel (eds), *Regards D'Une Génération de Juristes Sur Le Droit International* (Paris, Editions A Pedone, 2008) 79.

[5] E Grosz, 'A note on essentialism and difference' in S Gunew (ed), *Feminist Knowledge: Critique and Construct* (London and New York, Routledge, 1990) 332.

[6] A critical international law scholar once told me that he did not consider feminist ideas in his work because there were no books on feminist theory in his university's library.

[7] R Kapur, 'The Tragedy of Victimization Rhetoric: Resurrecting the "Native" Subject in International/Post-Colonial Feminist Legal Politics' (2002) 15 *Harvard Human Rights Law Journal* 1.

[8] K Engle, 'Feminism and its (Dis)Contents: Criminalizing Wartime Rape in Bosnia and Herzegovina' (2005) 99 *American Journal of International Law* 778.

in the name of feminism and implies that change will depend on economic reforms such as redistribution of wealth.[9]

To some extent, the internal debates about feminist scholarship map onto a divide between scholars and activists. Academics seem much more willing to scrutinise the premises of feminist theory and to attack impurity and inconsistency; people working in non-governmental organisations (NGOs) or international institutions with feminist agendas, by contrast, are generally keen to work with a big picture, and associate feminism with getting more women involved in decisions, or using international law to help women.[10] Generally, academics are more concerned to identify the flaws and faultlines of feminist analyses of international law, while feminists in NGOs or international institutions are less critical.[11]

The tension between critical approaches to international law, which are concerned with identifying the politics of international law, and feminist approaches, which analyse the law to improve the position of women, is often acute. I find myself one day discussing with colleagues and students the dark sides of international law and the way that the discipline puffs up its own importance. On such days, I counsel modesty and restraint. On other days I find myself talking to community groups about the value of international law in framing arguments about injustices. On such days, I counsel enthusiasm and hope. My inconsistencies trouble me but are unresolved. So, in this uneasy situation, Janet Halley's book, *Split Decisions: How and Why to Take a Break from Feminism*, with its snappy title and clear prescriptions, seems to offer a way ahead. Is taking a break from feminism a useful strategy in international law?

TAKING A BREAK FROM FEMINISM

Halley's arguments about feminism derive in large part from her experience of left of centre American sexual politics.[12] She describes feminism as essentially 'a subordination theory set by default to seek the social welfare of women, femininity, and/or female or feminine gender by undoing some part or all of their subordination to men, masculinity, and/or male or

---

[9] K Engle, 'International Human Rights and Feminisms: When Discourses Keep Meeting' in D Buss and A Manji (eds), *International Law: Modern Feminist Approaches* (Oxford and Portland, Hart Publishing, 2005) 47.

[10] See H Charlesworth, 'Are Women Peaceful? Reflections on the Role of Women in Peace-Building' (2008) 16 *Feminist Legal Studies* 347.

[11] See further Mertus' chapter, below, this collection. There are of course disputes about transnational feminist agendas: see, eg, B Ackerly, '"How Does Change Happen?" Deliberation and Difficulty' (2007) 22 (4) *Hypatia* 46.

[12] JE Halley, *Split Decisions: How and Why to Take a Break from Feminism* (Princeton, Princeton University Press, 2005) 4.

masculine gender'.[13] Halley summarises the three basic conditions for feminist argument pithily: drawing a distinction between male/masculinity/men and female/femininity/women (m/f); positing a relationship of subordination between m and f (m>f); and opposing the subordination of f to m—in Halley's words 'carrying a brief for f'.[14] Many feminists, she argues, are also committed to the 'Injury Triad'—female injury + female innocence + male immunity. Halley describes 'governance feminism' as the institutionalisation of feminist ideas in law and other sites of formal power. For Halley, feminism has now achieved considerable clout in many areas—governance, society and culture—and refusal to acknowledge and manage this is a form of bad faith.[15] She presents a draft of the terms of such an acknowledgment:

> Yes, feminism wields power; ratifies as well as critiques the experience of feminine injury; cares not whether its famous plaintiffs are telling the truth; seeks to impose itself with vigour and sometimes with violence on the social world; rules across the board, not case by case; and so, overall will necessarily generate male road kill, male scapegoats, and male objects of retributive vigour. So be it.[16]

Other feminist commitments identified and criticised by Halley are the belief that feminism is integral to any theory of sexuality and the idea that one theory is better than many.

Halley has the 'late' work of Catharine MacKinnon in her sights in particular, describing MacKinnon's work in the 1990s and 2000 as dogmatic, totalising and so focused on male power that it is unable to recognise the power of women and feminism.[17] Robin West's work on cultural feminism[18] is also attacked by Halley for failing to explain 'women's erotic yearning for men'.[19] Halley associates feminism with an almost punitive, or joyless, approach to sex. MacKinnon and West are 'anti-sex' while Halley describes herself as 'sex-positive'.

Although the title of her book may imply a rupture with or discarding of feminist theory, Halley emphasises that she respects the traditions and contributions of feminism and is seeking simply to draw attention to its blind spots and limitations. She explains her mission as getting feminism 'to see around the corners of its own construction',[20] while resisting any substantive feminist program, such as sex equality. In this sense Halley's interest in sexuality rather than social justice is deeply influenced by queer theories. Halley advocates Taking a Break from Feminism (her capitalisation) so that

---

[13] Idem.
[14] Ibid 17–18.
[15] Ibid 341–44.
[16] Ibid 342.
[17] She is enthusiastic about the 'early' MacKinnon, which she sees as radical and uncertain.
[18] See, eg, R West, *Caring for Justice* (New York, New York University Press, 1997).
[19] Halley, above n 12, 65.
[20] Ibid 321.

we can let go of being committed to an overarching explanation for the places in which women find themselves and the problems they encounter. In this way, Halley presents herself as breathing new life into feminism. She argues that 'the very vitality and usefulness of feminism as a social theory seems to have waxed when the commitment to its omnipresence wanes, and vice versa'.[21]

Halley's work has prompted a range of responses. It has been criticised for presenting a narrow account of feminism, glossing over different feminist forms, with their diverse and often contradictory goals and methods.[22] Critics have also attacked Halley's generalities and broad brush.[23] But the clarity and energy of Halley's critique make it hard to dismiss quickly. It usefully draws attention to some of the assumptions that feminists rely on in the international arena.

TAKING A BREAK FROM FEMINISM IN INTERNATIONAL LAW

What implications do Halley's arguments have for feminists working in international law? Although Halley does not identify as part of the 'invisible college' of international lawyers,[24] and is concerned mainly with the United States (US) feminist academy, her work has increasingly engaged with international legal issues.[25] In demonstrating the bad faith of feminist argument, she inverts its second condition: rather than m>f, we regularly find that in fact f>m. Thus, Halley claims that feminism 'is running things' in 'the European Union, the human rights establishment, even the World Bank'.[26] 'Sex harassment, child sexual abuse, pornography, sexual violence, antiprostitution and antitrafficking regimes ... have moved off the street and into the state'.[27] Feminist activism directed at the ad hoc international criminal tribunals, she writes, has had a major effect on the development of international criminal law and, she concludes '[b]y positing themselves as *experts* on women, sexuality, motherhood, and so on, feminists walk the halls of power'.[28]

---

[21] Ibid 6.

[22] AP Romero, 'Methodological Descriptions: "Feminist" and "Queer" Legal Theories' (2007) 19 *Yale Journal of Law and Feminism* 227.

[23] See, eg, M Hawkesworth, 'Book Review' (2007) 5 *Perspectives on Politics* 608.

[24] O Schachter, 'The Invisible College of International Lawyers' (1977) 72 *Northwestern University Law Review* 217.

[25] See J Halley, P Kotiswaran, H Shamir and C Thomas, 'From the International to the Local in Feminist Legal Responses to Rape, Prostitution/Sex Work, and Sex Trafficking: Four Studies in Contemporary Governance Feminism' (2006) 29 *Harvard Journal of Gender and Law* 335.

[26] Halley, above n 12, 20.

[27] Idem.

[28] Ibid 21. See also J Halley, 'Rape in Berlin: Reconsidering the Criminalisation of Rape in the International Law of Armed Conflict' (2008) 9 *Melbourne Journal of International Law* 78.

Halley's diagnosis of feminism's great power and its inevitable 'male road kill' has little resonance in international law. Halley's examples of the feminist takeover of 'the human rights establishment' or the international criminal tribunals, for example, seem exaggerated in light of the evidence. Some international institutions have to some extent absorbed the vocabulary of women and gender, but they have reduced feminist ideas to ritualised incantations. Despite all the talk of women, gender and gender mainstreaming, women's lives remain on the periphery of international institutions.[29] Halley seems to have been dazzled by the inclusive language, but she has not looked beneath the surface. As I discuss below, at the international level, feminist concerns have been translated in a very limited way as simply a head count of women; even so, numerical equality always seems out of women's reach. And some central institutions, such as the World Trade Organisation, have never taken on even the vocabulary of women or gender. In the academy, as I have noted above, the fact we are usually over in a corner talking to ourselves makes most feminists feel powerless. The fact that feminists wear a label allows the masculinism of the mainstream to become an unremarked backdrop in our work and lives. Halley's claim of the triumph of feminism and feminists on the international stage also overlooks the way that hierarchies based on gender continue to influence the development of international law.[30]

But Halley's overstatement of the power of feminism in international institutions should not obscure the value of her other insights. One important aspect of Halley's critique is its attention to the crusading and emotional dangers inherent in feminist international legal discourse. The seductive possibilities for international lawyers of using other people's disasters for their own consolation are ever present. Halley's challenge to peer around the corners of the construction of feminist projects in international law is also useful, although it is very hard to do. Almost all feminist writing in international law neatly replicates Halley's tripartite feminist pattern, and the Injury Triad is omnipresent in the literature. We have assumed that women and men are always in different situations in the international order; that women always do worse than men; and that our task is to insist on women being taken seriously. The first two steps in this argument are often simply asserted—for example, the differential, and worse, impact

---

[29] See the discussion of gender mainstreaming below; and in Kouvo, below, this collection. Also S Kouvo, 'The United Nations and Gender Mainstreaming: Limits and Possibilities' in D Buss and A Manji (eds), *International Law: Modern Feminist Approaches* (Oxford and Portland, Hart Publishing, 2005) 237.

[30] See D Otto, 'Disconcerting "Masculinities": Reinventing the Gendered Subject(s) of International Human Rights Law' in D Buss and A Manji (eds), *International Law: Modern Feminist Approaches* (Oxford and Portland, Hart Publishing, 2005) 105, 125.

of conflict on women.[31] We should be wary of these blanket statements and present more contextualised and nuanced accounts of women's lives. However the third condition of feminist argument identified by Halley, 'carrying a brief for women', is hard to avoid precisely because it is the political edge of feminist projects.

Halley's work resists identifying a central feminist project. Earlier scholarship about diversity in feminism typically searched for a unifying thread; for example Denise Réaume proposed an account of feminist jurisprudence as 'an analysis of the exclusion of (some) women's needs, interests, aspirations, or attributes from the design or application of the law'.[32] This account does not require a thick substantive conception of the aims of feminism. In other words, it assumes a broad commitment to the equality of women, without defining what equality actually is. Réaume's notion of feminist jurisprudence also builds on the sense that the injustice women face is structural and systemic; it is sceptical about the justice of traditional power structures. Halley's work, by contrast, suggests that any attempt to locate an overarching theory of feminism is on the wrong track; we are too concerned with finding a theory and sticking to it, integrating alternative theories as best we can.[33] We should acknowledge instead the partial and imperfect insights of feminism.

Halley's focus on MacKinnon as the embodiment of legal feminism overlooks feminist work in law that focuses on specific situations and acknowledges the limits of legal mechanisms.[34] Like many academic feminists, Halley is suspicious of the category 'women' and political claims based on it.[35] She does address the complex interaction of feminism's political aims and its theories; can they be separated out, or would feminism lose its point if it had no political agenda? The politics and power of feminist messages, such as the equality of women, comes precisely from their generality, although they require careful translation in specific contexts. In the next section, I suggest that feminism remains useful in the international context in bringing women's lives onto the agenda, but that feminist messages without feminist methods are unlikely to bring change.

---

[31] See, eg, RC Carpenter, *'Innocent Women and Children': Gender, Norms and the Protection of Civilians* (London, Ashgate, 2006); Charlesworth, above n 10.

[32] D Réaume, 'What's Distinctive About Feminist Analysis of Law?' (1996) 2 *Legal Theory* 265, 271.

[33] Halley, above n 12, 5.

[34] See, eg, V Nikolic-Ristanovic, 'Sexual Violence, International Law and Restorative Justice' in D Buss and A Manji (eds), *International Law: Modern Feminist Approaches* (Oxford and Portland, Hart Publishing, 2005) 273; J Krishnadas, 'Global De-Valuing of Local Capacities to Care: From Rights of Redistribution to Revaluation in the Post-Earthquake Reconstruction Process, Maharashtra' (2007) 58 *Northern Ireland Legal Quarterly* 376.

[35] Margaret Thornton connects this type of postmodern feminism with neoliberalism in the academy. See M Thornton, 'Neoliberal Melancholia: The Case of Feminist Legal Scholarship' (2004) 20 *Australian Feminist Law Journal* 7.

STATE-BUILDING: WHAT DOES FEMINIST ANALYSIS ADD?

State-building is often presented as an opportunity to improve women's lives and thus provides a fruitful context to assess the role of feminism at the international level. International institutions have become deeply implicated in state-building since the end of the Cold War, particularly in the wake of 11 September 2001, and the advancement of women has been accorded considerable prominence in these projects. For example, the United Nations Development Fund for Women (UNIFEM) defines its role in the project of reconstruction after the conflicts in Afghanistan and Iraq as 'advanc[ing] gender equality by supporting new legislation, backing women's leadership and equal representation, and widening the space for women's participation at peace tables'.[36] The international state-building industry also has embraced the language of women's human rights, supporting women's capacity 'to take their rightful and equal place at the decision-making table in questions of peace and security'.[37] A different type of feminist engagement with international intervention can be found in Catharine MacKinnon's arguments that there is a direct parallel between the violence against the US of 11 September 2001 and global violence against women and that both forms of violence merit international intervention. She has asked:

> What will it take for violence against women, this daily war, this terrorism against women as women that goes on every day worldwide, this everyday, group-based, systematic threat to and crime against the peace, to receive a response in the structure and practice of international law anything approximate to the level of focus and determination inspired by the September 11th attacks? … Why, with all the violations of international law and repeated Security Council resolutions, was [Afghan women's] treatment alone not an act of war or a reason to intervene (including, yes, militarily) on any day up to September 10, 2001?[38]

How can we 'peer around the corners' of these different feminist prescriptions? Both seem unsatisfactory: the first is a focus on women's presence at decision-making tables alone, while the second advocates military intervention in pursuit of women's human rights. While both strategies rest on a feminist commitment to women's equality, their methods do not taken into account the specificity of the situations they are addressing and are unlikely to achieve their goal.

---

[36] Available at www.unifem.org/gender_issues/governance_peace_security/at_a_glance.php.

[37] United Nations. Press Release from the Secretariat on the Secretary-General's address to the special meeting of the Security Council meeting on women and peace and security. UN Doc SG/SM/7598 (24 October 2000).

[38] C MacKinnon, *Are Women Human?* (Cambridge, Harvard University Press, 2007) 271–72.

State-building is often regarded more generally as a process that has the capacity to deliver a new dispensation for women. Simona Sharoni has observed that 'while in some instances, political conflict may complicate women's lives and set back their struggles for gender equality, in a different context and under different circumstances, a heightened political conflict may become a springboard for gender equality'.[39] She notes, for example, that in Northern Ireland 'far from being mutually exclusive or irrecon-cilable, feminism and nationalism are presented as two complementary movements wh[ich] seek to radically transform existing social and political relationships and structures as a stepping stone for the future envisioned nation'.[40] However, other cases of international state-building and democ-ratisation suggest that these projects are more usually conceived in a limited way and produce asymmetrical power relations between women and men. The language of 'women's rights' may have rhetorical power, but women's claims are usually not met. For example, to take two recent cases of state-building, women's groups in East Timor and Iraq express great frustration with their inability to affect the post-conflict settlement.

In East Timor, gender roles assigning men to a public world of politics and employment and women to a private world of home and family pervade social and economic relations. They are supported by religious doctrine, low levels of education and traditional practices.[41] The situation in Iraq is more complex. Despite the oppressive nature of Saddam Hussein's regime, Iraqi women generally benefitted from its secular approach to personal status laws.[42] The United Nations Arab Development Report noted in 2002 that Iraqi women rated highest among Arab women on United Nations (UN) measures of 'gender empowerment' because of their significant political participation.[43] The 2003 invasion of Iraq, among other things, has allowed an assertive masculine traditionalism to re-claim authenticity and authority and this has not been challenged by international state-builders.

One significant issue in both countries has been the association of talk of women's rights with imposed, international standards, inevitably in tension with some local cultures. Thus the East Timorese resistance (and now political) leader, Xanana Gusmão, complained in 2001 of the 'obsessive

---

[39] S Sharoni, 'The Empowering and Disempowering Effects of Conflict and Violence' (paper presented to the Gender, Armed Conflict and Political Violence conference, The World Bank, Washington DC, 10–11 June 1999) 1.

[40] Ibid 7.

[41] See S Harris Rimmer, *Gender and Transitional Justice: The Women of East Timor* (New York, Routledge, 2010).

[42] G Tabet, 'Women in Personal Status Laws: Iraq, Jordan, Lebanon, Palestine, Syria' SHS Papers in Women's Studies/ Gender Research, 4 (Paris: UNESCO, July 2005) 11–12.

[43] United Nations Development Program, *Arab Human Development Report: Creating Opportunities for Future Generations* (New York, United Nations Publications, 2002). In 2002, women held almost 20% of parliamentary seats in Iraq compared to the 3.5% average for Arab states.

acculturation to standards that hundreds of international experts try to convey to the East Timorese, who are hungry for values'.[44] He implied that the right of women to determine their own lives had no natural affinity with East Timorese culture. This type of argument has been strongly resisted by women's groups in East Timor, but has continued to undermine women's rights campaigns.[45] In Iraq also there has been considerable local hostility, particularly from religious groups, to international pressure for the involvement of women in public life.[46] The international community has often tolerated these culturally-based rejections of women's rights to prevent alienating local leaders. In this way very specific, male, cultures have been made generally applicable in both East Timor and Iraq through the state-building process.

The cultures of the international communities involved in state-building do little to promote women's equality. Very few women hold senior positions in agencies concerned with state-building, an absence that sends a strong message in post-conflict societies. Including more women in the state-building process will not automatically lead to changed practices, but it signals a greater willingness to pay attention to identity and diversity. Evidence from the last decade of state-building also shows an institutional insouciance or forgetfulness about the position of women, with mistakes being repeated in subsequent missions. One recurring issue in this respect is the lack of funding for initiatives that focus on women's lives.[47]

A second concern for women in state-building is the way that relevant international human rights standards are defined. Representation of women has been the major concern addressed, albeit superficially and inadequately, by the international community, with intense debate about the legitimacy and impact of quotas for women. Other problems women face in particular contexts tend to be obscured. For example, Sumie Nakaya points to the lack of attention paid to the effect of the ethnic partitions model used in state-building in Bosnia-Herzegovina and Kosovo where women who had married across ethnic lines faced both sex and race discrimination.[48] Moreover the right to equality in international law invoked in state-building has essentially remained tethered to a limited, procedural, account of non-discrimination

---

[44] Available at www.pcug.org.au/~wildwood/JanNewYear.htm.

[45] See N Hall and J True, 'Gender Mainstreaming in a Post-conflict State: Towards Democratic Peace in Timor-Leste?' in B D'Costa and K Lee-Koo, *Gender and Global Politics in the Asia-Pacific* (New York, Palgrave Macmillan, 2009) 159.

[46] S Hunt and C Posa, 'Iraq's Excluded Women' (July/August 2004) *Foreign Policy*, 40.

[47] H Charlesworth and C Chinkin, 'Regulatory Frameworks in International Law' in C Parker, C Scott, N Lacey and J Braithwaite (eds), *Regulating Law* (Melbourne, Oxford University Press, 2004) 246; T Smith 'Post-War Bosnia and Herzegovina: The Erosion of Women's Rights under International Governance' (2005) 38 *Critical Half* 2, 3.

[48] S Nakaya, 'Women and Gender Equality in Peacebuilding: Somalia and Mozambique' in T Keating and WA Knight (eds), *Building Sustainable Peace* (Tokyo, UN University Press, 2004) 143, 146.

which has had minimal effect on improving women's lives. It may be more useful to investigate alternatives to discrimination paradigms, such as those identified by Rosemary Hunter in national legal systems. She proposes the language of 'undervaluation' in the context of pay disparities for women rather than that of 'equal pay', which immediately implicates a male comparator. Another alternative to the language of discrimination is that of 'policy neglect' in the area of resource allocation, which draws attention to groups that end up disadvantaged by apparently neutral policies.[49] These ideas have resonance in the context of state-building; for example the concept of policy neglect could be used to capture the effect of international monetary institutions' policies on women's lives.

A related problem is the tendency in state-building to emphasise civil and political rights over economic, social and cultural rights.[50] This is of course an issue for men as well as women, but existing discrimination against women in areas such as access to land or inheritance of housing and property makes it particularly acute for women.[51] If the empowerment of women is understood to depend simply on the inclusion of women in various spheres of public life, there will be inadequate attention to the gendered nature of the rules of the game that women are required to play. We need to rethink traditional structures of public and private life, such as ideas of economic activity and value, to accommodate women's lives. We also must consider the effects of the unequal balance of domestic labour which limits the capacity of women to operate in the public, political sphere.

State-building relies on the human rights concept of self-determination. In international law, self-determination accords a people the right to autonomy, freedom from alien oppression and the right to choose an economic, political and social system 'free from outside intervention, subversion, coercion or constraint of any kind whatsoever'.[52] Once external self-determination has been achieved and internal self-determination is guaranteed, it is assumed that all members of the group will equally benefit, in other words that the terms 'self' and 'peoples' are homogenous. Individual and group aspirations and goals, both before and after the achievement of self-determination, are subsumed within those of the self-determining unit. This assumption of

---

[49] R Hunter, 'Alternatives to Equality' in R Hunter (ed), *Rethinking Equality Projects in Law: Feminist Challenges* (Oxford and Portland, Hart Publishing, 2008) 82–83.

[50] I Muvingi, 'Sitting on Powder Kegs: Socioeconomic Rights in Transitional Societies' (2009) 3 *International Journal of Transitional Justice* 163; H Charlesworth, 'Human Rights and the Rule of Law After Conflict' in P Cane (ed), *The Hart-Fuller Debate in the Twenty-First Century* (Oxford, Hart Publishing, 2010) 43.

[51] See N Niland, 'Rights, Rhetoric and Reality: A Snapshot from Afghanistan' in ND White and D Klaasen (eds), *The UN, Human Rights and Post-Conflict Situations* (Manchester, Manchester University Press, 2005) 322; C Chinkin and H Charlesworth, 'Building Women into Peace: The International Legal Framework' (2006) 27 *Third World Quarterly* 937.

[52] The wording is taken from a General Assembly Resolution on Afghanistan after the Soviet invasion in 1979. GA Res ES-6 2 (14 January 1980).

group identity and commonality is open to challenge. The notion of a self-determining unit collapses many forms of diversity, but most particularly that of sex. The consequences of this limited definition are evident in the fact that apparently successful claims to self-determination typically fail to deliver the same level of personal freedom and autonomy for women as for men. Indeed, in many cases achievement of national self-determination has led to deterioration in the position of women.[53]

A third problem for the protection of women's human rights in state-building is its relationship to the flawed 'gender mainstreaming' enterprise promoted by some women's organisations and endorsed by international institutions. Gender mainstreaming projects in state-building typically achieve little change in women's lives.[54] But more significant is the inadequacy of the concept itself.[55] The notion of gender mainstreaming is both too broad and too narrow in the international arena. In one sense, it has become an almost meaningless term. Most commitments to gender mainstreaming draw on the definition adopted by United Nations Economic and Social Council (ECOSOC) in 1997:

> Mainstreaming a gender perspective is the process of assessing the implications for women and men of any planned action, including legislation, policies or programmes, in all areas and at all levels. It is a strategy for making women's as well as men's concerns and experiences an integral dimension of the design, implementation, monitoring and evaluation of policies and programmes in all political, economic and societal spheres so that women and men benefit equally and inequality is not perpetuated. The ultimate goal is to achieve gender equality.[56]

This definition is so wide and inclusive that it is hard to implement. If gender mainstreaming is 'the process of assessing the implications for women and men of any planned action', how can we define what it means in any particular context and how it is different from a standard policy consideration of impact?

On the other hand, the ECOSOC definition is also a very narrow one: it reads as if animated by an idea of equality as equal treatment of women and men, assuming symmetry of position between women and men. It does not address the complex ways that gender is created and sustained by

---

[53] See, eg, the discussion of Bougainville in Charlesworth, above n 10, 352–54.

[54] L Handrahan, 'Rhetoric and Reality: Post-Conflict Recovery and Development—the UN and Gender Reform' in ND White and D Klaasen (eds), *The UN, Human Rights and Post-Conflict Situations* (Manchester, Manchester University Press, 2005) 404, 414–18; compare Hall and True, above n 45.

[55] See further H Charlesworth, 'Not Waving but Drowning: Gender Mainstreaming and Human Rights' (2005) 18 *Harvard Human Rights Journal* 1. See also S Kouvo, *Making Just Rights? Mainstreaming Women's Human Rights and a Gender Perspective* (Sweden, Iustus Publications, 2004).

[56] United Nations, *Platform for Action, ECOSOC Agreed Conclusions* 1997/2 (1997) at www.un.org/ womenwatch/osagi/pdf/ECOSOCAC1997.2.PDF.

social and power relations.[57] Treating women and men as though they face similar obstacles will perpetuate existing disparities between them. In some accounts of gender mainstreaming, the strategy has become simply a head count of women in particular positions, a modest variation on the 'equal opportunity' agenda.[58] While increasing women's participation in institutions is important, it does not itself change institutional agendas.

Moreover, the definition of gender mainstreaming in international institutions contemplates a limited sphere for its operation. It is regarded as primarily relevant to policy development in particular areas, such as development, human rights and some aspects of labour markets. Other fields appear immune to gendered scrutiny. For example, the European Union has not extended gender mainstreaming to competition policy.[59] Within the UN, most areas of law have been treated as if they were impervious to concerns of gender: gender mainstreaming mandates have not been given to either the International Law Commission or the International Court of Justice. The Statute of the International Criminal Court refers to 'gender' in the definition of some of the crimes within the Court's jurisdiction, but defines it in a curiously restrictive way as 'the two sexes, male and female, within the context of society'.[60]

Perhaps the most fundamental problem with the strategy of gender mainstreaming is that it rests on an insipid and bland concept of gender that has little cutting edge. In some contexts, the UN has followed the second wave of feminist thought in drawing a clear distinction between the concepts of 'sex' and 'gender'.[61] It has thus defined sex as a matter of biology and gender as the constructed meaning of sex, the designation of social roles. This distinction has now come under scrutiny from feminist scholars, who have questioned whether the category of 'sex' can be regarded as natural and uncontentious.[62]

In the case of gender mainstreaming, however, the sex/gender distinction has been elided. UN gender mainstreaming policies assume that 'gender' is a

---

[57] E Reid, 'Transformational development and the wellbeing of women' (2004) 64 *Development Bulletin* 19.

[58] A Woodward, 'Gender Mainstreaming in European Policy: Innovation or Deception?' Discussion Paper FS 101-103 Wissensschaftszentrum Berlin fur Sozialforschung October 2001, 22.

[59] M Pollack and E Hafner-Burton, 'Mainstreaming Gender in the European Union' (2000) 7 *Journal of European Public Policy* 432, 446.

[60] United Nations, *Rome Statute of the International Criminal Court*, ICC-ASP/2/Res.3, 12 September 2003 Article 7 (3). Available at www.icc-cpi.int/library/about/officialjournal/ Rome_Statute_120704-EN.pdf.

[61] Eg Report of the Expert Group Meeting on the Development of Guidelines for the Integration of Gender Perspectives into Human Rights Activities and Programmes UN Doc. E/ CN.4/1996/105 (1995) available at http://daccess-dds-ny.un.org/doc/UNDOC/GEN/G95/ 144/87/PDF/G9514487.pdf.

[62] N Lacey, 'Feminist Legal Theory and the Rights of Women' in K Knop (ed), *Gender and Human Rights* (Oxford, Oxford University Press, 2004) 13.

synonym for women. This is evident in the influential ECOSOC definition, quoted above. This elision causes a number of problems. First, it links gender with biology, implying that gender is a fixed, objective fact about a person. It does not capture the ways that gender is constructed in society to make some actions seem natural and others controversial. It reaffirms the 'naturalness' of female/male identities and bypasses the performative aspects of gender. Understanding gender as essentially about women does not capture the relational nature of gender, the role of power relations and the way that structures of subordination are reproduced.[63] It allows problems facing women to be understood as the product of particular cultures, lack of participation in public arenas or lack of information or skills and obscures the way that gender shapes our understanding of the world. Most significantly, the association of the term 'gender' primarily with women leaves both the roles of men and male gender identities unexamined, as though they were somehow natural and immutable.

CONCLUSION

The legitimacy and legality of international state-building projects have become widely accepted in the twenty-first century. However, they have been mixed experiences for both the women and men who have been their objects. Oppressive regimes may have been overthrown, but there have been tough prices to pay. State-building is a nice example of feminist positioning between resistance and compliance. Feminist analysis can identify some of the dark sides of state-building projects by examining how women have fared in the rebuilt state. While the vocabulary of women's rights is now a staple of state-building packages, women's rights are often traded away in the search for stability and strong leadership. Moreover, as the story of gender mainstreaming shows, even where feminist concepts are invoked in state-building, their radical edge is often lost in bureaucratic translations.

Janet Halley argues that feminism fails to acknowledge its power; the case of state-building illustrates however the complexity of feminist success in the international arena. While some feminist vocabulary has become part of state-building packages, feminist projects have had limited success in empowering women and improving their lives, and carrying a brief for women remain important. Halley's critique of feminism is focused on its manifestation in law, but feminist goals and methods extend far beyond the law. In the international arena international law may not be more useful than other forms of regulation. It is partial and porous and can create groups of insiders and outsiders, based on wealth and power.

---

[63] S Baden and AM Goetz, 'Who Needs [Sex] When You Can Have [Gender]?' (1997) 56 *Feminist Review* 3, 7.

Feminist commitments, such as the equality of women, have influenced the development of international law, but they have been incorporated only in a partial manner and implemented without regard to context or with empathy for their intended beneficiaries. This underlines a distinction between feminist messages and feminist methods in international law. The former have been influential in rhetorical terms, while the latter have been ignored. Feminist messages however are likely to be productive only if they are deployed through feminist techniques such as 'world travelling'.[64] This involves being explicit about our own historical and cultural background, trying to understand how other women might see us, and recognising the complexities of the lives of other women.[65] Feminist methodologies suggest that prescriptions of women's equality must respond to the needs and desires of the women we think we are helping. Understanding these needs is not always easy and requires patience and empathy, particularly in post-conflict situations. So the challenge is to devise practical and responsive feminist methods to support feminist political projects.

---

[64] The term was introduced by Maria Lugones in 'Playfulness, "world-traveling", and loving perception' (1987) 2 *Hypatia* 3.

[65] I Gunning, 'Arrogant Perception, World-Traveling and Multicultural Feminism: The Case of Female Genital Surgeries' (1991–92) 23 *Columbia Human Rights Law Review* 189, 191. See also A McNevin, 'Confessions of a Failed Feminist IR Scholar: Feminist Methodologies in Practice in Peshawar' in B D'Costa and K Lee-Koo, *Gender and Global Politics in the Asia-Pacific* (New York, Palgrave Macmillan, 2009) 115.

3

Searching for Virtue in International Law

YORIKO OTOMO

INTRODUCTION

WE FEMINISTS, INTERNATIONAL lawyers—are called to find ourselves in an era of anxiety and terror. What is this anxiety, this terror? What is virtue, and where are our revolutions? The writings of feminist legal theorists are torn between the impulse to resist[1] and the drive to comply[2] with the Law. To withhold or to fill up. Are these really our two poles of inhabitation?

Hilary Charlesworth, in responding to Janet Halley's provocation to 'take a break from feminism'[3] points out that vis-à-vis international law, both as an academic discipline and as a platform for imperialist state-building operations around the world, feminism still lies 'in a scholarly ghetto', and calls for renewed attention to feminist theories within the discipline. Charlesworth does nuance this call, however, with an acknowledgement of a core tension between feminism's embrace of normative projects that aim to improve the lives of women, and critical theory's concerns with identifying the politics of law itself.[4]

I agree with Charlesworth's call to engage feminist theory in the work towards real and necessary social change, and even more so in light of Halley's

---

[1] 'Resist': c.1374, from O.Fr. *resister*, from L. *resistere* 'to resist, standing back, withstanding'. Resistance is attested from 1417, from O.Fr. *resistence*, from L.L. *resistentia*, from L. *resistentem* (nom. resistens), prp. of *resistere*. Sense of 'organized covert opposition to an occupying power' first recorded 1940 in reference to French opposition to Nazi rule.

[2] 'Comply' from the early 14c., from O.Fr. *compli*, pp. of *complir*, from L. *complere* 'to fill up'. Originally 'to fulfill, carry out,' sense of 'consent' began c.1600 and may have been a reintroduction from It., where *complire* had come to mean 'satisfy by "filling up" the forms of courtesy'.

[3] J Halley, *Split Decisions: How and Why to Take a Break from Feminism* (Princeton, Princeton University Press, 2006). Also see discussion of Halley's work in Grahn-Farley, below, this collection.

[4] Charlesworth, above, this collection.

depiction of the woman 'taking a break' from feminism on the cover of her book: the image shows an older, darker, faded, unsmiling Hindu woman looking directly *at* the viewer, while in the foreground the head of a younger, whiter, prettier, woman without a bindi is transposed onto the body of the other woman, smiling and looking *away* into the distance. Taking a break from feminism, indeed, has never been a more ambiguous proposition.

This chapter seeks to respond both to the editors' thematic and undertake a sustained engagement with the tension between the feminism and critical legal theory identified by Charlesworth. Both are now well-established 'marginal' discourses within the academe of international law, and yet, both shuffle uneasily (and sometimes antagonistically) beside one other. I propose that the divergence between what I argue are first- and second-wave feminist approaches, and critical theory, can (and must) in fact be strategically realigned, by relying upon the non-essentialising feminism of the 'third wave'. Common to both of these strands of thought are feminist post-structuralist thinkers such as Julia Kristeva and Luce Irigaray, upon whose work I will draw for this analysis.

My point of departure, then, is to rethink our opening reflection. We, feminist international lawyers, do not find ourselves trapped between resistance against, and compliance with, international law. The feminist telos has firmly been defined as responding to masculinist hegemony, and compliance with the existing discourse is not usually entertained. Rather, I argue, we find ourselves impelled towards resistance against the existing structures of an international law with its normative discourse of emancipation, while at the same time being seduced by the possibilities of revolution:

> If the basis of a popular government in peacetime is virtue, its basis in a time of revolution is virtue and terror—virtue, without which terror would be barbaric; and terror, without which virtue would be impotent.
>
> (Robespierre, speech at the French National Convention, 1794)

Over 200 years ago a French man speaks of virtue, barbarism, terror and impotence. Navigating the hook-turn, littered streets of Melbourne's central business district, I contemplate whether any of these terms still hold meaning for a Japanese-Australian girl trying to understand the meaning of international law in a post-9/11 world. The summer's desert air scorches the city's bitumen and its few remaining trees. I sit in an air-conditioned glass office.

'The Terror,' declares Robespierre, 'is nothing save justice, prompt, severe, inflexible. It is an emanation of Virtue', and virtue, he says, 'is nothing more than love of the fatherland and of its laws.' Robespierre's formulation of virtue, then, is also figured in terms of love, but a love for the sovereign guarantor, predicated upon governance through fraternal force. How do we resist the call to revolution and governance through a violence understood only as either sanctioned or unsanctioned? And how do we seek an impotent virtue, or a virtue which resists inscribing legal subjects into the logic of sacrifice in the name of love?

This chapter unfolds in four parts. This first returns to an archetypal scene of revolution, with its invocation of power's paradoxical foundations of virtue and terror. The second part uses a 'third-wave' feminist approach to discuss masculinist constructions of sovereign subjectivity and sovereign state relations. I propose that international law imagines sovereign subjectivity (the ontological constitution of the nation-state) as being predicated upon a whole, territorialized body ruled by a single sovereign's voice and empowered with both terror and virtue to enforce its word. I argue that this leaves open the international—the space between territorial bodies—as an ambivalent space, and that law created and spoken in this space, far from being a nexus of power, is a performance of jurisdiction; the hysteric manifestation of a depopulated, deterritorialised gesture without a unified voice or power of enforcement. For feminists seeking to institute a different kind of ethics or a different mode of politics, this is a site, perhaps, of revolution.

The third part of this chapter addresses a problem of metaphysics which arises at this moment, and which lurks at the heart of feminist enterprise. In short, I argue here that *both* the masculinist subjectivity core to the idea of the sovereign state *and* feminist critique itself, are founded on the idea of a utopic body outside of a system of law guaranteed by a transcendental being. The final part of this chapter addresses a final problem facing those feminist international lawyers in search of virtue: any revolution risks erasing something else, or of being subsumed into the existing order in its entirety, as has occurred (as Charlesworth argues) with the discourse of gender-mainstreaming within the state-building programme. The answer, perhaps, to these challenges of our project, is to hold on to both resistance *and* revolution as feminist telos, but to distinguish in our minds between the institutional *structures* of international law (which we must continue to engage with and resist in order to achieve our political goals), and the *space* created by failures of masculinist international law discourse which we can fill with revolutionary readings, writings, speakings and beings.

ANXIETY AT THE GATES, OR CRISES IN INTERNATIONAL LAW

In thinking about what it means to be a feminist working on, or in, international law, and in looking at the operations of desire—manifest in speech and writing—in the place between nations, I will look to psychoanalytic theories of subjectivity. Sovereign jurisdiction is founded on the occupation and possession of territory.[5] The creation of a sovereign identity as 'speaking

---

[5] For a more detailed explanation of this ontological analysis of sovereign subjectivity see Y Otomo, 'Of Mimicry and Madness: Speculations on the State' (2008) 28 *Australian Feminist Law Journal* 53.

subject'[6] (one who speaks the law) within the community of nations is founded upon the concept of occupation and possession of a body, thus able to act as a unitary One, to speak, and to enforce its word. At the moment of realisation of separation (from the mother's body; from the community) the subject experiences a loss which is subsequently covered over: the subject initially incorporates the image of the (m)Other in order to deny the 'internal rupture and [conceive] of itself as the source of its own origin and unity',[7] and forgets this loss in mirror images of itself which reflect back a fantasy of wholeness.

Luce Irigaray explains, however, that women's bodies have been defined as the Other of masculine sexuality and men's bodies.[8] Similarly, Kristeva explains the process of this 'othering':

> [W]e see that the social and symbolic pact … brothers rebelling against the father's authority in order to establish a socius—is a transversal link that is constituted by the evacuation of the maternal: in order to establish the symbolic pact, one has to get rid of the domestic, corporal, maternal container.[9]

This consolidation of the sovereign-as-speaking-subject is predicated upon the sacrifice of its binary other, the maternal feminine. The legal theorist Anne Orford has affirmed that this 'prior unacknowledged sacrifice of the feminine'[10] enables us to locate the fraternal structure of the law, and moreover, the 'economic nature of Christian sacrifice'[11] which underlies the fraternal bond. As she describes, the 'economy of sacrifice is … founded on the circulation of risk and reward between fathers … and sons',[12] suspending the 'question of the feminine [which] haunts the institutions founded on [that] economy'.[13]

The subjectivity of the speaking sovereign is further consolidated through the operation of recognition[14] between states, which function to reunify each

---

[6] 'In order to bring the body back into theories of language, she develops a science that she calls "semanalysis", which is a combination of semiotics, taken from Charles Pierce and Ferdinand de Saussure, and psychoanalysis, taken from Sigmund Freud, Jacques Lacan, and Melanie Klein.' K Oliver (ed), *The Portable Kristeva* (New York, Columbia University Press, 2002) xvi. See also xvi: 'Kristeva attempts to bring the speaking body back into discourse by arguing both that the logic of language is already operating at the material level of bodily processes and that bodily drives make their way into language.'

[7] E Grosz, *Jacques Lacan: A Feminist Introduction* (London, Routledge, 1990) 47.

[8] Oliver, above n 6, xix.

[9] J Kristeva, *The Sense and Non-Sense of Revolt: The Powers and Limits of Psychoanalysis* (New York, Columbia University Press, 2001) 21.

[10] A Orford, 'Beyond Harmonization: Trade, Human Rights and the Economy of Sacrifice' (2005) 18(2) *Leiden Journal of International Law* 179–213.

[11] Ibid 197.

[12] Ibid 198.

[13] Idem.

[14] Recognition, according to Kojève, is only possible when enacted between *equals*, since man can only be satisfied by recognition from those whom he himself recognises. On Kojèvian recognition see, eg, A Kojève, *Outline of a Phenomenology of Right* (BP Frost ed, BP Frost and R Howse tr, Lanham, Rowman & Littlefield Publishers, Inc, 2000).

subject with their (masculine) mirror images. In short, modern international law—founded on the 'family of nations'—can be seen as a story of brothers. Given that modern international law presents itself as a secular system, there is no immediate transcendental (in psychoanalytic terms, the Father) who is able to constitute each state's subjectivity. Their relations to one another are thus officially configured as homosocial[15] (through the language of equality, recognition, etc) and shored up by systems of occupation and exchange, impelled by desire to attain a whole, white, 'clean-and proper' subjectivity.

The problem arises when those sovereign subjects must *speak* international law; make a decision; enforce their word. Since jurisdiction cannot operate without a body, voice and power to enforce, their inability to do so results in hysteria, visible in the form and language of the texts of international law. Is this, perhaps, the site of revolution? Might it be possible, using the psychoanalytic metaphor of hysteria, to respond to Orford's call to 'read for those moments when this closed circle is under threat of being breached or at least pulled out of shape by other relations?'[16]

To summarise briefly, the concept of hysteria (from the word *hystera*, meaning womb) extends back almost 3,000 years in European history.[17] Hysteria has alternately been accorded status as a (usually female) disease or illness, or as a medical *category* under which the uncontrollable elements of difference and danger—the feminine being one—have been placed. The hysteric symptom was reinscribed in the early twentieth century by Freud as 'the product of a psychical trauma which had been forgotten by the patient',[18] 'a series of perfectly rational thoughts...[that] have been transformed into the symptom by means of condensation and the formation of compromises ... and also, it may be, along the path of regression.'[19] Is there then, as Luce Irigaray suggests, 'a revolutionary potential in hysteria',[20] and if so, how can we read it into this closed circle of sovereigns? The appropriation of hysteria as a 'specifically feminine pathology that speaks to and

---

[15] See Eve Kosofsky Sedgwick's response to this term, coined by Rene Girard: *Between Men: English Literature and Male Homosocial Desire* (New York, Columbia University Press, 1985). For further discussions about the themes of masculinity and international law, see Nesiah and Kouvo, below, this collection.

[16] Orford, above n 10, 211.

[17] E Showalter in SL Gilman, H King, R Porter, GS Rousseau, E Showalter, *Hysteria Beyond Freud* (1993) ix, accessed online: www.content.cdlib.org/xtf/view?docId=ft0p3003d3&brand =eschol.

[18] S Freud, *The Interpretation of Dreams* (A Richards ed, Hayes Barton Press, 1991) (original translation by J Strachey, first published in 1953 by the Hogarth Press and the Institute of Psycho-Analysis by arrangement with George Allen & Unwin Ltd) (original publication in 1900 as *Die Traumdeutung*) 14.

[19] Ibid 756.

[20] L Irigaray, 'Any Theory of the "Subject"' in *Speculum of the Other Woman* (GG Gill tr, Ithaca, Cornell University Press, 1985) 47: 'It is because they want neither to see nor hear that movement that they so despise the hysteric.'

against patriarchy'[21] took place from the late 1960s onwards by Jacques Lacan, and by the so-called French feminists (Hélène Cixous, Luce Irigaray and Julia Kristeva). There are two main opposing feminist views on hysteria; one which proposes that '[h]ysteria is the very stuff of revolutions',[22] and the other which is 'skeptical about the ultimate power of hysteria as a form of feminine subversion'.[23] I suggest a place for hysteria which lies somewhere between the two. Rather than conflating the performance of hysteria with an affirmation of the female sex, it may be more useful to consider it a symptom which arises out of, and in reaction to, a particular gendered construction (in the form of a *masculine* nation-state).

Elaine Showalter refers to Josef Breuer's metaphor of hysterics as being 'the flowers of mankind, as sterile, no doubt, but as beautiful as double flowers'[24] and to the feminist Olive Schreiner's imagination of the cultivated flower which, 'having no more need to seed turns all its sexual organs into petals, and doubles, and doubles; it becomes entirely aesthetic.'[25] The hysteric voice, then—a mimicry or self-parody—occurs when Law no longer needs to, or is able to, reproduce itself. The subject can neither be, nor have, a corporeal guarantor required for participation in the fraternal economy of sovereign recognition. In terms of international relations and international law, hysteria arises when the speaker has no unitary voice; no power to enforce the word, nor *polis* to stand in for the clean-and-proper body. The drive to revolt against its own impossible office can only be discharged through aesthetic signification.[26] The voice of the hysteric, I argue, is a symptom which may indicate both the impossible office (in Law), and a moment where the *possibility* of the ethical encounter arises.[27] Hysteria—spasmodic separations from the dominant discourse—is a remembering of what Kristeva calls the 'loss of loss' itself.[28]

---

[21] Showalter, above n 17, 286.

[22] A Stevenson, 'The Hysterical Women's Movement' *Times Literary Supplement* (9 September 1983) 961.

[23] Showalter, above n 17, 332.

[24] J Breuer and S Freud, *Studies on Hysteria* (New York, N Luckhurst tr, Penguin Classics, 2004).

[25] O Schreiner, letter to Karl Pearson, in *The Letters of Olive Schreiner* (R Rive ed, Oxford, Oxford University Press, 1988) 86.

[26] J Kristeva in *The Sense and Non-Sense of Revolt: The Powers and Limits of Psychoanalysis* (New York, Columbia University Press, 2001) 56 explains: 'This, in sum, represents a profound integration of the Hegelian dialectic into Freudian thought. The libido detached from the object turns toward Narcissus and threatens him. What will act as a counterbalance and prevent Narcissus from being destroyed? It is a new object, which is not mommy or daddy, the breast or any other external erotic object, or the body itself, but an artificial, internal object that Narcissus is capable of producing: his own representations, speech, sounds, colors, and so forth.'

[27] This is somewhat analogous to Jacques Derrida's call for an 'unconditional sovereignty', which will be discussed in the following section.

[28] See S Beardsworth, *Julia Kristeva: Psychoanalysis and Modernity* (New York, State University of New York Press, 2004) for an excellent reading of Kristeva's oeuvre.

In the Name-of-the-Father?
But without voice to speak,
Law's empty office lies
In that place between nations;

A wild inhabitation
Where bodiless machinations
Conjure empty significations
And delay, the decision ...

Hysteria's rose lips
Transform into petals
And doubles, and doubles—
A mad recognition,
Her disorder of organs
Exceed, the decision—

BLIND SPOTS AND HOOK TURNS

So back to the questions with which we began: where are our revolutions, and what of virtue? Kristeva nuances our position between resistance and revolt when she says that 'revolt as a producer of purity in our modern world is endangered by an easy—not to say perverse—fit between law and transgression; it is spoiled by constant authorization, if not incentives, made by the law itself, to transgress the law and to be included'.[29] Kristeva undertakes an etymological analysis of 'revolt', discovering its multitude of meanings: to turn; to cover around; to envelop; to return; to exchange; to displace; to repair; to repeat; to re-read; to disgust.[30] She notes that the word was initially far removed from politics,[31] with the Latin 'volta' meaning

---

[29] Kristeva, above n 26, 25.

[30] '*Volta* also means "time" ... Another direct derivative from Latin belongs in this lineage, the adjective *volubilis*, "that which turns with ease" as in *volubilitas linguae*; the French equivalent is *volubile* (voluble). And *volumen*, sheets of paper rolled around a stick, with the spatial meaning of "wrapping" or "covering," results in "volume," which comes to mean "book" in the thirteenth century ... That the book has kinship with revolt might not be self-evident at first, but I will try to remedy this obfuscation. The linguist Alain Rey stresses the cohesion of these diverse etymological evolutions, which start with a matrix and driving idea: "to twist, roll, wrap" ... and "covering," an object that serves as a wrapping. The idea of twisting or enveloping, a topological and technical concept, is dominant ... More interesting as far as the modern meaning of the word is that "the revolt" and "revolt" which comes from Italian words that maintained the Latin meanings of "to return" and "to exchange," imply a diversion at the outset that will soon be assimilated to a rejection of authority. In sixteenth-century French, "to revolt" is a pure Italianism and signifies "to turn," "to avert" (to revolt the face elsewhere)'. ibid 2.

[31] 'The Latin verb *volvere*, which is at the origin of "revolt", was initially far removed from politics. It produced derivatives with meanings—semes—such as "curve," "entourage," "turn," "return". In Old French, it can mean "to envelop," "curvature," "vault," and even "omlet," "to roll," and "to roll oneself in"; the extensions go as far as "to loaf about" (*galvauder*), "to repair," and "vaudeville" (*vaudevire*, "refrain")'. ibid 1.

'time', then 'book' ('volume') in the thirteenth century, and then transforming in the fourteenth century to mean:

> mirrors, interlocking objects, the projection of images ... Gradually, the term comes to signify change, mutation. In 1550, and for a century afterward, it is applied to another semantic field: that of politics: thus the revolution of time leads to the revolution of State ... In the eighteenth century, 'revolution' becomes more specific and widespread, with parallels frequently drawn between planetary and political mutations.[32]

The law provides us with our only condition of possibility (to speak), while at the same time denying any office of the secular feminine. Any revolt within this structure seems impossible. However, Kristeva points out that: 'if one considers law obsolete, prohibition weak, and values empty or flimsy, a certain dialectical link between law and transgression is impossible.'[33] This means that if we can identify hysteria in the space between nations (the symptom of a bodiless Law), then this dialectical link is indeed broken, and another kind of revolt, outside the binaries of prohibition/transgression or resistance/compliance, may become possible.

To summarise, feminist critiques of psychoanalysis are helpful for revealing the fraternal structuration of states and making explicit the operation of sacrifice and violence within that structure.[34] Moreover, it has enabled us to identify a crisis that lies at its heart—an hysteric manifestation of its lack or loss, with all the pleasure and pain of its initial castration from the body of the maternal feminine, which rupture opens up the possibility of revolt. Before imagining what such revolt may look like, however, we must first note key challenges for the feminist project. If our two options for revolt against the fraternal economy are: one, to figure language as a process of pure production and pure waste, and two, to write stories or minor histories of the sacrifice of the maternal feminine (as proposed by Kristeva and Orford), both carry separate risks which cannot be ignored. I will now briefly outline those risks before turning back to the question of revolution.

The first problem, in relation to an aesthetic production by the writing body, is identified by Orford who points out that 'each attempt to read, speak or write the law differently ... imposes a new form. In this rewriting, an other disappears.'[35] Not only is this writing-over of others something

---

[32] Ibid 3.

[33] Ibid 27.

[34] The extent to which Lacanian psychoanalysis and so-called 'French feminism' can be applied outside of their context (ie a writing which imagines the nation-state as the revolutionary nation-state) to international relations and international law more generally, remains a question.

[35] See Orford above n 10, 211: 'Although in "Circumfessions" Derrida dreams of a writing that could directly express the living body without violence, for him, language is always the dead remains of a living body: "If I compare the pen to a syringe, and I always dream of a

that must be negotiated at every turn, but there is, in this negotiation, the added threat that this aesthetic production might lose its relation to that against which it revolts. In other words, we risk being no longer able to trace the operations of real political power when production shifts from parody to pastiche.[36] The second problem relates to the writing of sacrifices. The logic of sacrifice itself is always already inscribed into the aporias of unconditionality; sovereignty; possession, within which the politics of everyday negotiation with the Other become difficult to discern. There lies a risk, in acknowledging or even venerating a maternal feminine, that we transform that body into icon[37] while neither explicitly recognising that the icon of the masculine divine also participates in the construction of social gender identities, nor having a process for the transubstantiation of that maternal icon back into culture. The risk, in short, is that subjects may be forced to locate themselves within the fraternal economy, identifying either with the victim/God or its Other; the heroic masculine, or the mythic feminine.[38]

In relation to the writing of 'forgotten sacrifices', Anne Orford suggests that 'the demand to sacrifice cannot be met [when] we ... find that we cannot bring ourselves to exchange that which we love, and thus do not in fact possess it.'[39] This suggestion reveals the paradox at the core of sacrifice (ie that the object of sacrifice—what we most love—is also

---

pen that would be a syringe, a suction point rather than that very hard weapon with which one must inscribe, incise, choose, calculate, take ink before filtering the inscribable, playing the keyboard on the screen, whereas here, once the right vein has been found, no more toil, no responsibility, no risk of bad taste or violence, the blood delivers itself all alone, the inside gives itself up." (p.12). Even as Derrida imagines writing that is like a transfusion of the living body into language, he resigns himself to the violence of trying to inscribe the uninscribable. The living body is this uninscribable.' Oliver, above n 6. Kristeva, on the other hand, sees language as something which is infused with life by the bodily drives, and does not see it as something which has been cut off from the body: 'while for Kristeva bodily drives involves a type of violence, negation, or force, this process does not merely necessitate sacrifice and loss. The drives are not sacrificed to signification, rather, bodily drives are an essential semiotic element of signification.' ibid.

[36] Fredric Jameson terms 'pastiche'—a blank parody: 'Pastiche is, like parody, the imitation of a peculiar or unique, idiosyncratic style, the wearing of a linguistic mask, speech in a dead language. But it is a neutral practice of such mimicry, without any of parody's ulterior motives, amputated of the satiric impulse, devoid of laughter.' F Jameson, *Postmodernism, or, the Cultural Logic of Late Capitalism* (Durham, Duke University Press, 1991).

[37] As Kristeva notes: 'even though maternal religions exist, they are always already on a path toward splitting the symbolic being from its psychological and maternal basis.'

[38] 'The term "gender" refers to the social relations between the sexes, and the social construction of sexual roles. It stresses the relational aspects of masculinity and femininity as concepts defined in terms of each other, and it engages with other analytic categories of difference and power, such as race and class. Rather than seeking to repair the historical record by adding women's experiences and perceptions, gender theory challenges basic disciplinary paradigms and questions the fundamental assumptions of the field.' Showalter, above n 17, 288.

[39] Orford, above n 10.

that which *cannot* be sacrificed since it cannot be substituted, is therefore inexchangeable, and was therefore never possessed to be offered in the first place). Not only does this logic of sacrifice pose difficulties for feminists abjuring the concept of possession, but it is also, here and elsewhere,[40] figured in terms of *love*, which faces its own set of limitations when proposed as an ethical framework for legal subjects. By this, I mean that both the modern subject emerging out of the French Revolution and the feminist response to that 'masculine' subject are founded upon the utopic body of a secular subject (that is, a subject without God; outside of Law).

When thinking revolt with international law, it is difficult to conceive of an ethics of love which answers for *legal* subjects constituted by and through the force of law. How do we imagine an ethics for reading and writing law—even international law—when the legal subject has been forced to give up that which could not be sacrificed? When the other is *not* one which can or should be approached with love—an enemy; an occupier; a master; an institution; a state? When a relation with another legal subject has already been inscribed and decided by the law, with no room left for the possibility of love? When what is at stake is not salvation of—or by the law, but physical survival? How can we open up the legal decision to feminist readings without inscribing bodies into an aporetic logic of sacrifice and possession? How can we revolt when we know not what virtue looks like?

> Hook turns
> Strange part-revolutions
> Rolling the contours of others' bodies
>
> A terror barbaric
> Mad women in the attic
> Marking the corners of Law's cardboard walls
>
> Mute virgin/queen
> Exudes milk and tears
> Estranged —
> Is virtue found
> In Law's violent fears?
> Return, repair, re-read.

---

[40] Both Julia Kristeva *The Sense and Non-Sense of Revolt: The Powers and Limits of Psychoanalysis* (Herman, Jeanine trans, 2001 ed) [trans of: *Sens et non-sens de la révolte: Pouvoirs et limites de la psychanalyse*, 1999]; *Tales of Love* (Roudiez, Leon, trans, 1987) [trans of: *Histoires d'amour*, 1984], and Luce Irigaray, *Je, Tu, Nous: Towards a Culture of Difference* (Martin, Alison, trans, 1993 ed).

SEARCHING FOR VIRTUE

Our revolt, then, becomes possible when law (our condition of possibility; the third term) no longer functions as a guarantor. The jurisdiction of international law relies, not upon a sovereign body which it always already possessed, but upon a dialectical movement between the fragile recognition of fraternal states and its Others. The revolt of jurisdiction is inherent in the form of international law, and displacement of authority[41] can take place, not through an exchange of one power for another, but at these eventual sites of hysteria through historical materialist analyses of international law.[42]

To explain, it may be possible to nuance the relations between legal subjects by thinking them through an ethics of *hosting*:[43] the host is a person who receives guests; a lord of strangers; but also a multitude; a coloniser; an enemy; an army; a stranger. The body of Christ; the Eucharist; a body that hosts parasites. A woman; a womb; a hostage.[44] An ethics of hosting complicates the notion that a relation to the other can always be figured in terms of love, and introduces the possibility of thinking about the a priori conditional nature of legal subjects' occupations of each other's bodies, and the modes of exchange between them. An ethics of hosting would not require the subject to *love* another, because in the event of hosting, desire is always already displaced. It does not depend upon any will to hospitality, but rather, foregrounds a bare survival. While this idea of hosting is a response to my earlier engaging (even through critique) with the masculine/feminine binary, the concept of a hosting body is by no means a gender neutral one. We may, for example, remain with a maternal metaphor, but rather than writing it into the sacrificial fraternal economy, hold onto the more nuanced (parasitic, symbiotic, combative) relations between mother and

---

[41] 'Entering the social order requires assimilating its authority through a revolt by which the individual makes meaning his or her own. Revolt, then, is not a transgression against law or order but a displacement of its authority within the psychic economy of the individual'. Oliver, above n 6, 410.

[42] 'Evental' was coined by the translator of Alain Badiou's *Being and Event* (London, Continuum, 2006).

[43] (1) 'Person who receives guests' c.1290, from O.Fr. *hoste* 'guest, host' (12.c), from l. *hospitem* (nom. *hospes)* 'guest, host', 'lord of strangers' from PIE *ghostis* 'stranger' (*cf* O.C.S. *gospodi* 'lord, master' Goth. *gasts* 'guest; (2) 'Animal or plant having a parasite' c.1857; (3) 'Guest, enemy' (O.E. *gaest, giest;* (4) 'Multitude' from O.Fr. *host* 'army' (10.c), from M.L. *hostis* 'army, war-like expedition', from L. *hostis* 'enemy'; (5) 'Body of Christ, consecrated bread' c.1303, from L. *hostia* 'sacrifice'. If I may draw the parallel, the female body also receives and 'hosts' other bodies, and in which sense the idea of the hosting body may be subject to a feminist reading.

[44] Interestingly, the word 'hostage' derives from the c.1275 meaning of 'a lodger held by a landlord as security' (O.Fr. *hoste* 'guest'), or from the Latin *obsidanus*, 'condition of being held as security'. The modern use of 'hostage' in discourses of terrorism dates from the 1970s.

child when thinking about international law's regulation of such relations. Such a nuanced reading of the feminine is advocated by Kristeva:

> First, the speaking being's relationship with maternal space is precisely an 'archaic' relationship in which borders are nonexistent [non-differentiation] or unstable, a relationship of osmosis in which separation, if it is under way, is never absolutely clear. This is the realm of narcissism and the instability of borders between mother and child, in the preoedipal mode of the psyche.[45]

By rethinking the legal categories of occupation and exchange (or investment) in terms of this 'instability of borders' we can begin to write about the ongoing negotiations which make up the corporeal relation of host and its Other. For while hosting-as-event is an entirely conditional occupation and exchange of and between legal subjects, it also enables an ethics outside of the aporia of conditionality which on the one hand presumes a 'clean and proper body'[46] (in a conditional relation; relation in which conditions can be established), or an iconic body (in an unconditional relation, where entry into the economy of 'words and rewards'[47] is predicated upon the sacrifice of an Other).

At the end of the twentieth century, Jacques Derrida asks: 'Must one resist? And, first of all, psychoanalysis?'[48] International law's hysteric resistance against its own impossible office, too, must be interpreted.[49] And if we resist, our interpretations and our revolutions can act, not only as a displacement of authority, but as a *wrapping around*, a *protective covering*. Undertaking critique with sensitivity to sexual difference *qua* hosting relations is perhaps one way of thinking through the treacherous landscape of resistance and revolution.

> Drawing clay from still hallowed earth
> Thrown on potter's wheel and drawing
> Centrifugal tensions drawing
> Shapes of multiple dimensions—

---

[45] Kristeva, above n 26, 21.

[46] As described by J Kristeva, *Powers of Horror* (LS Roudiez tr, New York, Columbia University Press, 1982).

[47] Orford, above n 10.

[48] J Derrida, *Resistances of Psychoanalysis* (P Kamuf, PA Brault, and M Naas tr, Stanford, Stanford University Press, 1998) 1.

[49] 'Resistance must be interpreted; it has as much meaning as what it opposes; it is just as charged with meaning and thus just as interpretable as that which it disguises or displaces: in truth, it has *the same meaning*, but dialectically or polemically adverse, if one can say that.' ibid 13. Derrida explains: 'Every resistance supposes a tension, above all, an internal tension. Since a purely internal tension is impossible, it is a matter of an absolute inherence of the other or the outside at the heart of the internal and auto-affective tension' (at 26).

Is this what we are searching for?
A raw and tender revolution?
This, as Law's decomposition
Reveals its fate—

The vertigo of these inversions
Make our anxious hands
Redrawing virtue without sacrifice,
We trace our own debris

4

Feminist Project(s): The Spaces of International Law

ZOE PEARSON*

INTRODUCTION

I AM SITTING writing this in an apartment with a commanding view
of the cities of Ankara. I am here as a (working) 'tourist'—the benefits
of research leave in academia and the friendly relations between New
Zealand and Turkey, which allow extended tourist visits—'Yeni Zelanda,
no visa, no problem'! I say cities of Ankara, because there are (at least)
two cities on view out the window. The wealthier Çankaya, Kavaklidere
and Kızılay shopping, residential and diplomatic areas cluster down the
hill towards the heavily protected Parliament, military and police build-
ings, before, on the other side of the large Kocatepe mosque, giving way to
the discrete, older parts of Ankara; Ulus, the old town and the gegecondu
squatter housing, where Turkish friends have suggested I will not want
to go. While in these older areas there are some of the same conspicuous
signs of wealth that I can see in my immediate vicinity, in these areas the
dichotomies that exist between the different cities of Ankara are much
more marked. Passing underneath the satellite dishes on roofs I notice an
old woman bundled up against the cold and the snow carrying a heavy
sack through the streets of the old town; around the corner from the main
shopping area is a woman who threw an empty water bottle at me for
stopping to photograph the unexpected presence of chickens by the side of
the road rather than paying attention to her family selling trinkets to passing foreigners. Being a visitor to an unfamiliar country makes me acutely
aware of unintended transgressions of social, cultural and legal norms; it
also makes me alert to the diversity of the spaces of their creation. Here

* I am grateful for the generosity of the International Relations department at the Middle
East Technical University, Ankara in facilitating access to their library, which has helped the
progress of this chapter immeasurably; and to feedback from a staff seminar there at which
part of this work was presented. I am also indebted to Anna Grear, Sari Kouvo and Sharon
Pearson for their insightful, enthusiastic comments on earlier drafts.

in a country where historic violences and leadership of men are celebrated for their role in the creation of a modern democratic state, where the traditional *ezan* (call to prayer) is heard in streets otherwise devoted to conspicuous cigarette, car and clothing consumption, where East and West meet in the debate about membership of the European Union and human rights, particularly women's rights, I am also aware of the fluidity and porosity of these spaces, and their normative potential as well as their limitations.

As Hilary Charlesworth notes, the feminist critique of international law is fundamentally a normative one,[1] one that highlights the limitations of an international legal structure that excludes women and seeks to reconstruct a framework that challenges the unequal position and legal treatment of women and women's concerns. In my mind, this is a project that directs our gaze to the 'who' of international law; who is involved in creating international law; whose concerns are heard and addressed by international law? This is, of course, a simplification; feminist critiques of international law are rich, diverse, complex and multilayered. However, it highlights the consistent theme of feminist work in international law that seeks to address the inaudibility of women's voices and concerns within the structures and processes of the international legal regime.[2] In asking this 'who' question, it is perhaps implicitly a 'where' question as well.[3] Recent feminist scholarship has examined the linkages between the 'who' and the 'where' in terms of the extent to which women's concerns and voices have been included within international legal institutions and discourse.[4] Despite the strength of the critique, there are concerns that feminism has made only partial and limited gains into knowledge discourses and institutional power structures of international law,[5] and that the normative project remains trapped within the restrictive structures of international law; caught 'between resistance and compliance'.

This chapter argues that a further explicit focus for these normative projects could productively be on the 'where' of international law. It argues that it is necessary to question assumptions about the locations of the law because of the ways assumptions about the 'spaces' of international law 'normalise and obscure from critical comment "the assumed divide between law and

---

[1] H Charlesworth, above, this collection.

[2] C Chinkin, S Wright and H Charlesworth, 'Feminist Approaches to International Law: Reflections from Another Century' in D Buss and A Manji (eds), *International Law. Modern Feminist Approaches* (Oxford, Hart Publishing, 2005) 19.

[3] D Buss and A Manji, 'Introduction' in D Buss and A Manji (eds), *International Law. Modern Feminist Approaches* (Oxford, Hart Publishing, 2005) 8. Buss notes: 'Feminists began to ask, perhaps with Susan Marks' "faux naiveté", where were the women in international law, and how might international law be made to work better for women?'

[4] See, eg, S Kouvo, *Making Just Rights? Mainstreaming Women's Human Rights and a Gender Perspective* (Sweden, Iustus Publications, 2004).

[5] See, eg, reflections in Chinkin, Wright and Charlesworth, above n 2, 17–45.

social and political life that undergirds the soi-distant objectivity of law"'.[6] The critical legal geographies literature argues that space and law are mutually constitutive, drawing upon an understanding of space as resulting from complex and multidimensional social practices. This promotes reflection on fluidity, openness and interconnectedness of spaces of norm creation in international law and the engagement of feminist politics in spaces that we might describe as both inside and outside dominant structures of international law, as simultaneously 'centre' and 'periphery', as paradoxical. The chapter argues that a spatial analysis allows for reconceptualisation of the normative spaces of international law and might assist the feminist critique of international law to think beyond the restrictive structures that bind the critique within the resist/comply dichotomy.

SPACES AND CRITICAL GEOGRAPHIES

The Production of Space

The critical geographies literature, which highlights 'space' as a key concept, provides much that is useful to elucidate and understand the 'where' of international law. Space, as is now commonly understood, refers to more than fixed physical or geographic realities. It focuses on the understanding of space as both socially produced and interpreted, constantly altered and created by human action.[7] Space is produced by social, economic, political, historical and cultural processes, and is fundamentally constitutive of these processes. 'Space', Richard Ford argues, is 'the product, and not the fixed context, of social interactions, ideological conceptions, and of course, legal doctrine and public policy'.[8] Insights from the feminist geographies literature are particularly useful to highlight the dynamic nature of space and its connections with society, and in particular, gender relations.[9] Feminist geographers have highlighted how the gendered nature of space is produced

---

[6] D Buss, '*Austerlitz* and International Law: A Feminist Reading at the Boundaries' in D Buss and A Manji (eds), *International Law. Modern Feminist Approaches* (Oxford, Hart Publishing, 2005) 88, quoting N Blomley, *Law, Space and the Geographies of Power* (New York, The Guildford Press, 1994) xii.

[7] See, for a useful summary of the history of the concept of space: G Rose, N Gregson, J Foord, S Bowley, C Dwyer, S Holloway, N Laurie, A Maddrell & T Skelton, 'Introduction' in Women and Geography Study Group, *Feminist Geographies. Explorations in Diversity and Difference* (Harlow, Pearson Education, 1997) 7. Also see E Soja, 'The spatiality of social life: towards a transformative theory' in D Gregory and J Urry (eds), *Social Relations and Spatial Structures* (London, Macmillan, 1985); G Prakash, 'Introduction' in G Prakash and KM Kruse (eds), *The Spaces of the Modern City* (Princeton, Princeton University Press, 2008) 9.

[8] RT Ford, 'The Boundaries of Race: Political Geography in Legal Analysis' (1994) 107 *Harvard Law Review* 1841, 1859.

[9] L Bondi and J Davidson, 'Situating Gender' L Nelson and J Seager (eds), *A Companion to Feminist Geography* (Malden, Blackwell Publishing, 2005) 20.

by social practices that clearly delimit the roles of men and women, serving to reinforce power, privilege and oppression and resulting in the exclusion of women from certain spaces.[10] They identify the importance of asking 'where' as 'a crucial entrée into understanding the world in which we live, particularly a world marked by difference including but not limited to gender. Asking "where" forces us to map the complex relationships between bodies, identities, places, and power'.[11]

Henri Lefebvre's work is useful for its presentation of a multidimensional understanding of space and its emphasis on the production of space.[12] This multidimensional conception of space focuses on three characteristics of space as production: *spatial practices* ('the perceived'—daily routines, physical practices and realities of social life); *representations of space* ('the conceived'—conceptualised spaces, knowledge that arises out of institutionalised use and organisation of space); and *spaces of representation* ('the lived'—complex symbolisms linked to the experiences of individuals as interacting with cultural traditions, creative and clandestine practices to contest dominant social spatialisations created by the first two spaces).[13] Lefebvre's work is useful to reflect on because of the emphasis that it is all three of these spaces that make up the broad concepts of social space. However, authors such as Edward Soja give particular importance to the *spaces of representation*, from an understanding of these lived spaces as strategic locations for political projects, as 'terrain for the generation of "counterspaces", spaces of resistance to the dominant order arising precisely from their subordination, peripheral or marginalized positioning'.[14] An awareness of the produced and multidimensional nature of space and the dynamic nature of lived spaces seems to be an attractive one for feminist

---

[10] L McDowell and JP Sharp, 'Introduction' in L McDowell and JP Sharp (eds), *Space, Gender, Knowledge. Feminist Readings* (London, Arnold, 1997) 3.

[11] L Nelson and J Seager, 'Introduction' in L Nelson and J Seager (eds), *A Companion to Feminist Geography* (Malden, Blackwell Publishing, 2005) 7.

[12] H Lefebvre, *The Production of Space* (Oxford, Oxford University Press, 1991) 30–34, 36–39.

[13] Ibid 36–46. Also see C Butler, 'Critical Legal Geography and the Social Theory of Henri Lefebvre: Space, Everyday Life and the Right to the City', paper presented at Joint Annual Meeting of the Law and Society Association and the Research Committee on the Sociology of Law, Berlin, 25–28 July 2007, 8 for a helpful summary of Lefebvre's arguments. Butler notes that in this work 'space is not depicted merely as a geographical or physical location or a commodity, but as a political instrument, as part of the relations of production and property ownership and as a means of creative and aesthetic expression.' Also E Soja, *Thirdspace: Journeys to Los Angeles and Other Real-And-Imagined Places* (Cambridge, Mass, Blackwell Publishers, 1996) 65–69; S Elden, *Understanding Henri Lefebvre* (London, Continuum, 2004) 189–90; R Shields, 'Henri Lefebvre' in P Hubbard, R Kitchin and G Valentine, *Key Thinkers on Space and Place* (London, Sage Publications, 2004) 208–14.

[14] Soja, above n 13, 68.

projects that seek to explore the 'where' in relation to the normative spaces of international law.

Openness of Space

While it is impossible to do justice to the richness of this literature in this chapter, some of the insights and methodologies offered by critical feminist geographers are particularly useful to think about in relation to elucidating the lived spaces of international law. The notion of space as dynamic, open-ended and provisional, rather than fixed and bounded has developed from the recognition of the ways in which space is socially produced and changed by human activity.[15] In exploring the creation of space, particularly in the context of labour, the feminist geographies literature has emphasised the way in which binary categories so central to Western conceptual frameworks are created and maintained by (gendered) social relations. This literature makes important links to ways in which these dichotomous categories result in the (gendered) production of spaces and the resulting boundaries that define the location of people.[16] One of the undertakings of feminist geographies, then, is to explore how dichotomous ways of constructing space are misplaced, and in doing so, challenge the fixity of space produced by such binaries. By highlighting the less visible side of spatial binaries (private/public, home/work, informal/formal, for example), the gendered and hegemonic processes are made more visible instead of being seen as natural. The binaries are further exposed by illustrating that the boundaries between these binaries are much less stable than as constructed but in fact are blurred by instances of everyday resistance.[17] The political resistance to these binaries is seen as important sites for political action, as 'potential spaces', 'in which gender identities can be negotiated, resisted and changed';[18] resonating with Lefebvre's lived spaces.

One of the implications of work that uncovers the dichotomous ways of constructing space is the recognition that space is always open to contestation and redefinition by different actors, and is, as a result, necessarily

---

[15] D Massey, *For Space* (London, Sage Publications, 2005) 3. Also see N Laurie, F Smith, S Bowlby, J Foord, S Monk, S Radcliffe, J Rowlands, J Townsend, L Young and N Gregson, 'In and out of bounds and resisting boundaries: feminist geographies of space and place' in Women and Geography Study Group, *Feminist Geographies. Explorations in Diversity and Difference* (Harlow, Prentice Hall, 1997) 112.

[16] Laurie et al, above n 15, 112–14.

[17] Ibid 114–15.

[18] Ibid 140.

open, fluid, and changeable.[19] In this way, it is hoped, non-dichotomous ways of thinking can be developed to explore and understand spaces.[20] Openness, fluidity and recognition of the contested nature of spaces seem attractive features of an international legal system that seeks to confront the restrictive normative structures of international law for women. However, it is important to note the limitations of this approach. It may offer some resistance to binaries in terms of exposing the concealed 'other' and challenging hegemony as 'natural'. It may also offer some resistance in terms of blurring the boundaries and thus questioning fixity of binaries. However, in doing so, these strategies nevertheless implicitly accept the binary construction; neither highlighting the suppressed side of the binary nor suggesting the blurring of the boundary seems to undermine the concept of the binary or of the boundary per se. Thus, while understandings of the production of space as always open to contestation and redefinition are useful, it is important to be aware of the durability of binaries. Openness and fluidity of space alone do not offer us the answer to transcending the binaries of resistance and compliance.[21]

Multiplicity of Space

As well as exploring the openness and fluidity of space, the feminist geographies literature has drawn attention to the multiplicity of spaces. Doreen Massey conceives space as inevitably dynamic and this 'inherently implies the existence in the lived world of a simultaneous multiplicity of spaces: cross-cutting, intersecting, aligning with one another, or existing in relations of paradox or antagonism'.[22] Integral to the dynamism that results from recognition of the multiplicity of spaces is the identification of linkages between spaces. Considering the movement and connections between spaces underscores the generative nature of space, that is, it is the connections between physical, material, and symbolic spaces that produce and sustain oppression.[23] The multiplicity of spaces would seem to offer a way of moving beyond the tendency towards dichotomous spaces noted above, because of the movement and interaction implied between spaces. The concept of movement between multiplicitous spaces can be seen in ways in which feminist scholars have challenged the taken for

---

[19] Rose et al, above n 7, 7. Also see N Smith and C Katz, 'Grounding metaphor: towards a spatialized politics' in M Keith and S Pile (eds), *Place and the Politics of Identity* (London, Routledge, 1993).

[20] Laurie et al, above n 15, 141.

[21] This section owes a great deal to the insightful comments of Anna Grear.

[22] D Massey, *Space, Place and Gender* (Minneapolis, University of Minnesota Press, 1994) 3.

[23] Nelson and Seager, above n 11, 7.

granted scale of the global or international. Feminist geographers have presented analyses that demonstrate the mutually constitutive nature of the spaces of the local and the global, arguing for recognition that the scales of international law and politics are entangled.[24] 'The relationship between the local, the regional, the national, and the global is not a geo-metrical nesting. "Local", "regional", "national", "global" are topologi-cal matters, intra-actively produced though one another'.[25] For example, both Matthew Hannah and Jennifer Hyndman present analyses of how the different scales of the body (for example, of Afghan women, and of combatants on all sides) and of the geopolitical, of power and space are interwoven in the 'war on terror'.[26]

In exploring the themes of openness, fluidity, movement and connection in their work, feminist geographers have usefully highlighted how these characteristics of space can assist the interrogation of that which seems immutable and unchangeable.[27] By highlighting, as Kim England puts it, 'the very untidy materialities' that produce particular spaces, feminist geog-raphers also realise the importance of engaging with multiplicitous and fluid spaces. She argues that engaging 'with the lives of actually existing people can uncover the contradictions, continuities, and nuances in what might otherwise be seen as monolithic and inevitable, in turn offering potential avenues and strategies for social change'.[28] Recognising that space is open, fluid and dynamic, and elucidating lines of movement and connection is

[24] E Kofman, 'Feminist Political Geographies' in L Nelson and J Seager (eds), *A Companion to Feminist Geography* (Malden, Blackwell Publishing, 2005) 527.

[25] K Barad, 'Re(con)figuring space, time and matter' in M DeKoven (ed), *Feminist Locations. Global and Local, Theory and Practice* (New Brunswick, Rutgers University Press, 2001) 103. Also A Secor, 'Toward a feminist counter-geopolitics: gender, space and Islamist politics in Istanbul' (2001) 5 *Space and Polity* 191–211, 193 quoted in M Hannah, 'Virility and Violation' in L Nelson and J Seager (eds), *A Companion to Feminist Geography* (Malden, Blackwell Publishing, 2005) 552–53.

[26] Hannah, above n 25, 560–62. Also J Hyndman, 'Feminist Geopolitics and September 11' in L Nelson and J Seager (eds), *A Companion to Feminist Geography* (Malden, Blackwell Publishing, 2005) 573. See also Buchanan's exploration of the concept of the 'borderlands' as disrupting the separation of international and national: R Buchanan, 'Border Crossings: NAFTA, Regulatory Restructuring and the Politics of Place' in D Delaney, R Ford, N Blomley (eds), *The Legal Geographies Reader: Law, Power and Space* (Oxford, Blackwell Publishers, 2001). Also see Buss, above n 6, 101–03.

[27] P Moss and K Falconer Al-Hindi, 'An Introduction' in P Moss and K Falconer Al-Hindi (eds), *Feminisms in Geography. Rethinking Space, Place and Knowledges* (Plymouth, Rowman & Littlefield Publishers, 2008) 7. As Moss and Falconer Al-Hindi note in the introduction to their 'anti-anthology' for feminisms in geography, 'the revolutionary potential in thinking is not always manifest in the content of the message; rather it is also apparent in the disbandment of the naturalizing tendencies to think that something (anything) is unassailable, immutable, unchangeable. So, with regard to knowledge, mucking about in the processes of its production to understand the power accorded to authority seems more generative than locating sources of influence in sets of power relations.'

[28] K England, 'Caregivers, the Local-Global, and the Geographies of Responsibility' in P Moss and K Falconer Al-Hindi (eds), *Feminisms in Geography. Rethinking Space, Place and Knowledges* (Plymouth, Rowman & Littlefield Publishers, 2008) 204.

fundamental to a normative project because of the possibilities that this opens up for conversation between spaces and thus knowledge creation.[29] These notions of multiplicity illustrate the potential of reconceptualising the production of space in non-binary terms.

Paradoxical Space

Gillian Rose's work is useful to understand how these insights from the feminist geographies literature about the open and multiplicitous nature of space can assist a feminist normative project in international law that seeks to navigate the tensions of the resistance and compliance binary. Her work is motivated by a similar sort of enquiry that drives this volume; that is, she seeks to explore, in the context of geography, both how to avoid complicity in engagement with a discipline that feminist geographers have argued is thoroughly racist and gendered, while also exploring how to undertake a feminist critique of hegemonic (geographical) knowledge that challenges the exclusions and absences without presenting an essentialised version of Woman.[30] Seeing the potential of a space that does not replicate the masculine 'same/other' binary present in the creation of (geographical) knowledge, she seeks to explore how feminist theories can contribute to the development of a spatiality that acknowledges difference, a 'sense of space which refuses to be a claim to territory and thus allows for radical difference'.[31]

---

[29] G Pratt, 'Complexity and Connection' in P Moss and K Falconer Al-Hindi (eds), *Feminisms in Geography. Rethinking Space, Place and Knowledges* (Plymouth, Rowman & Littlefield Publishers, 2008) 69–72. As Pratt identifies, these characteristics of space play a central role in knowledge creation for 'a renewed feminism' in three ways: by enabling recognition of competing, situated universal norms and claims, and a commitment to translating experiences across places (based on articulation of specific experiences rather than generalisations); providing recognition that any single place is densely populated by different histories from many difference places, which opens up possibilities of diverse political critique and practice; and by encouraging the uncovering and mapping of lines of connection, so as to blur 'the purity of our geographical categories and the fixity of borders—first world/third world; global north/global south; core/periphery; developed/underdeveloped.' Knowledge creation for Pratt draws strongly upon notions of space as multidimensional and fluid, and pays explicit attention to how knowledge may be constructed in different spaces. Knowledge creation for her is about 'a process of translating across different worlds and competing, situated universal norms and claims', as opposed to 'simply accepting or rejecting universal norms and universalizing generalizations about women's experience.' It is also important to note the limitations in terms of fluidity however, because it is not necessarily experienced equally—fluidity in terms of movement across national and international borders, eg, is experienced very differently by different categories of migrants.

[30] G Rose, *Feminism and Geography. The Limits of Geographical Knowledge* (Minneapolis, University of Minnesota Press, 1993) 137.

[31] Ibid 150. Of course, while the notion of radical heterogeneity is an attractive one, it does not necessarily present a challenge to the binary either, but presents a more open, less homogeneous version of it. This raises further questions about the nature of the binary and feminist discourse. Do our theories need to attempt to transcend the binary in all its forms—or just in terms of its oppressiveness? I am grateful to Anna Grear for her insightful comments on this point.

Rose outlines the concept of 'paradoxical space', which she identifies traces of in much feminist work.[32] This space, she argues 'is multidimensional, shifting and contingent. It is also paradoxical, by which I mean that spaces that would be mutually exclusive if charted on a two-dimensional map—centre and periphery, inside and outside—are occupied simultaneously'.[33] The paradoxical space as Rose explores it, links concepts of space as multidimensional with a reminder that this complexity results from a 'never self-evident matrix of historical, social, sexual, racial and class positions which women occupy … These feminist maps are multiple and intersecting, provisional and shifting, and they require "ever more intricate skills in cartography" '.[34] The concept of paradoxical space focuses on the movement or oscillation between the same/other, insider/outside binaries, the simultaneous occupation of centre and periphery; as well as understanding that these spaces depend on 'a sense of an "elsewhere", spaces beyond the hegemonic where differences can be acknowledged'.[35] She concludes that 'the subject of feminism, then, depends on a paradoxical geography in order to acknowledge both the power of hegemonic discourses and to insist on the possibility of resistance'; or rather, 'not so much a space of resistance as an entirely different geometry through which we can think power, knowledge, space and identity in critical and, hopefully, liberatory ways'.[36]

Rose's concept of paradoxical space resonates in some ways with Lefebvre's lived space.[37] The concept of paradoxical space is an attractive one for a normative project that explores the spaces of international law. It captures the openness and fluidity of space and avoids the dangers of reifying binaries, while at the same time acknowledging their durability. It does so because of the way it envisages such dualities as constantly moving in relation to each other, and thus simultaneously occupying centre and periphery, while also recognising an 'elsewhere'. The question remains about how these concepts that emphasise resistance through fluidity, contingency and openness can be utilised in a normative project that explores the spaces of international law. The following section argues that the concepts of space as fluid, open and multidimensional might assist a feminist critique to make visible and recognise the productiveness of the 'small spaces of law and politics',[38] the 'untidy materialities' that might resonate with Rose's paradoxical spaces and Lefebvre's lived spaces but are otherwise overlooked as spaces of norm creation in a focus on the scale of

---

[32] See discussion, ibid 138–41.

[33] Ibid 140.

[34] Ibid 155.

[35] Ibid 151–55.

[36] Ibid 155, 159.

[37] In addition, Soja finds it makes useful links to his concept of 'Thirdspace'; see Soja, above n 13, 68.

[38] Buss, above n 6, 92.

the international. In doing so, the chapter explores the utility of the concept of space as a way to rethink the capture of the binaries of resistance and compliance for feminist engagements in international law.

SPACES OF INTERNATIONAL LAW

Law and Space

Critical legal geographers utilise concepts of space as socially produced, and as fluid, malleable and multidimensional to examine the relationships between space and the law, and to understand the consequences of legal spaces on society, and vice versa.[39] An underlying theme of these inquiries focuses on asking 'where is law?',[40] arguing that unacknowledged assumptions about space and its relationships with law may work to stabilise entrenched legal processes, as well as the cultural, political, historical, economic, and social processes identified by critical geographers.[41] The focus on the production of space allows for interrogation of hegemonic sites of law, an undertaking which seeks to 'contest and politicise our formerly "neutral" conceptions of space',[42] our assumptions of law as a 'thing that precedes practice',[43] and aims to challenge the invisibility of law that results from the supposed neutrality of law, law from nowhere in particular perspective. By drawing attention to the mutually constitutive nature of space and law, legal geography also serves as a reminder to critical legal scholars that law itself is produced, a set of social practices. Soja identifies two different approaches of the critical legal geographies literature, which are useful to explore in the context of international law: first, examining how different spaces affect the processes and substance of law; secondly,

---

[39] K Aoki, 'Space Invaders: Critical Geography, the "Third World" in International Law and Critical Race Theory' (2000) 45 *Villanova Law Review* 913, 917–18; R Oh, 'Comments: Law and Geography. International Law Weekend—West Conference: Proceedings and Articles' (2007) 5 *Santa Clara Journal of International Law*, 507, 510.

[40] See D Delaney, R Ford, N Blomley, 'Preface: Where Is Law?' in D Delaney, R Ford, N Blomley (eds), *The Legal Geographies Reader: Law, Power and Space* (Oxford, Blackwell Publishers, 2001) xiii. Also see R Oh, 'Remapping Equal Protection Jurisprudence: A Legal Geography of Race and Affirmative Action' (2004) *American University Law Review* 1305, 1316, who notes that critically challenging the embedded spatial constructs in a legal narrative involves examining the geographic scale or setting of the legal narrative, and the movement of people within the spaces in which the narrative takes place; that is 'where does the story take place?' and 'where are the "characters" from? Where are they now? How did they get from there to here?' See also Massey, above n 22, 150–51 in relation to 'power geometry'—noting the discrepancies between those who are able to move and are in charge of the movement or flows—and those that are not.

[41] Oh, above n 39, 511; Delaney et al, above n 40, xiii.

[42] Aoki, above n 39, 916.

[43] RT Ford, 'Law's Territory (A History of Jurisdiction)' (1999) *Michigan Law Review* 843, 856.

exploring the ways in which law and legal institutions shape and control the physical world and the organisation of space.[44]

International Law as Shaped by Space

The connections between international law and concepts of space are not entirely new. Critical projects of international law have highlighted some of the problematic aspects of international law in ways that are either explicitly or implicitly spatial. The connections between race, law and space, for example, have been revealed in the creation and utilisation of racial hierarchies between states and the geographically entangled 'civilising mission' of international law.[45] Sustained critique from feminist scholars has implicitly used concepts of spatiality to identify the gendered nature of international law. This literature has demonstrated the way in which international law fails to adequately address the concerns of women, hiding behind the spatial binary of public/private that allocates responsibility for women's rights to the space of the domestic realm rather than the international.[46] Others have focused on the deconstruction of the space of the state as the focus of the international legal system, arguing that concepts of regulation should reflect the increasing recognition that global regulatory change is dependent on the interactions of many actors in many different spaces of norm creation.[47] For example, a number of scholars have highlighted the role of transnational actors, such as non-governmental organisations (NGOs), in

---

[44] E Soja, 'Afterword: Surveying Law and Borders' (1996) 48 *Stanford Law Review* 1421, 1425–26. Also see Oh, above n 40, 1359. Oh reminds us of the power of legal narratives to shape and distort our grasp of concrete, material reality—and the necessity therefore of critiquing the deeply embedded geographic and spatial assumptions in the law.

[45] H Osofsky, 'The Geography of Climate Change Litigation Part II: Narratives of Massachusetts v EPA' (2008) 8 *Chicago Journal of International Law* 573, 603; A Anghie, *Imperialism, Sovereignty and the Making of International Law* (Cambridge, Cambridge University Press, 2005) 3; S Razack, 'When Place Becomes Race' in S Razack (ed), *Race, Space and the Law: Unmapping a White Settler Society* (Toronto, Between the Lines, 2002). See generally T Mahmud, 'Geography and International Law: Towards a Postcolonial Mapping' (2007) 5 *Santa Clara Journal of International Law* 525–61, 534–48; A Anghie, B Chimni, K Mickelson and O Okafor (eds), *The Third World and International Order* (The Hague, Martinus Nijhoff, 2003); B Rajagopal, *International Law from Below: Development, Social Movements and Third World Resistance* (Cambridge, Cambridge University Press, 2003); M Mutua, 'What is TWAIL?' (2000) 94 *American Society of International Law Proceedings* 31; Ford, above n 43; Ford, above n 8.

[46] See Buss, above n 6, 94–96 for a useful summary of the public/private debate in international feminist critique, and its connections with space.

[47] J Braithwaite and P Drahos, *Global Business Regulation* (Cambridge, Cambridge University Press, 2000) 10, 608, 612. Osofsky, eg, argues for the importance of recognising the role that climate change litigation can play in influencing both domestic and transnational climate regulation and policy. Osofsky, above n 45, 575.

shaping the spaces (and often the outcomes) of international law creation exercises.[48]

As a very broad generalisation, these critiques have highlighted the limited pedigree of the framework of international law and the absences that result from the homogenising effect of legal regulation. By drawing attention to the 'blind spots'[49] that result from its Eurocentric, masculine, state-centric lineage, these critiques are drawing attention to spaces and their relationship—or lack thereof—with international law. In Soja's terms, these inquiries are concerned with how different spaces—or absences—affect the processes, substance and the development of international law. One of their limitations however, seems to be that these inquiries are still captured within binaries—state/non-state, public/private, international/national, first/third world. Much of the analysis of NGOs for example, concentrates on their impact on the decision-making of states in terms of the development or implementation of international legal instruments. For example, the participation of NGOs in the multilateral negotiations that led to the signing of the Rome Statute of the International Criminal Court[50] and the Ottawa

[48] See generally A Boyle and C Chinkin, *The Making of International Law* (Oxford, Oxford University Press, 2007) 41–97; Z Pearson, 'Non-Governmental Organizations and the International Criminal Court: Changing Landscapes of International Law' (2006) 39 *Cornell International Law Journal* 243; AK Lindblom, *Non-Governmental Organisations in International Law* (Cambridge, Cambridge University Press, 2005) 15–22; P Sands, 'Turtles and Torturers: The Transformation of International Law' (2001) 33 *New York Journal of International Law and Politics* 527–59; P Spiro, 'Globalization, International Law and the Academy' (2000) 32 *New York University Journal of International Law and Politics* 567; H Cullen and K Morrow, 'International civil society in international law: The growth of NGO participation' (2000) 1 *Non-State Actors and International Law* 7; J Mertus, 'Considering Nonstate Actors in the New Millennium: Toward Expanded Participation in Norm Generation and Norm Application' (2000) 32 *New York University Journal of International Law and Politics* 537; M Keck and K Sikkink, *Activists Beyond Borders: Advocacy Networks in International Politics* (Ithaca, Cornell University Press, 1998). See esp L Wexler, 'The International Deployment of Shame, Second-Best Responses and Norm-Entrepreneurship: The Campaign to Ban Landmines and the Landmine Ban Treaty' (2003) 20 *Arizona Journal of International and Comparative Law* 561, 565; P Willetts, 'From "Consultative Arrangements" to "Partnership": The Changing Status of NGOs in Diplomacy at the UN' (2000) 6 *Global Governance* 191; K Nowrot, 'Legal Consequences of Globalization: The Status of Non-governmental Organizations under International Law' (1999) 6 *Indiana Journal of Global Legal Studies* 579, 589–90; J Boli and G Thomas (eds), *Constructing World Culture. International Nongovernmental Organizations since 1875* (Stanford, Stanford University Press, 1999) 42–43.

[49] D Kennedy, 'Background Noise? The Underlying Politics of Global Governance' (1999) *Harvard International Review* 52.

[50] *Rome Statute of the International Criminal Court*, adopted and opened for signature on 17 July 1998, by the United Nations Diplomatic Conference of Plenipotentiaries on the Establishment of an International Criminal Court, UN Doc A/CONF/183/9, 37 ILM (1998) 999, entered into force 1 July 2002.

Convention Banning Landmines[51] has been well documented.[52] While this spatial analysis is useful to highlight the complexity of law creation, it does not appear to capture the recognition of these spaces in their own right that the law and geography analysis seems to promise. Rather, it seems to be in danger of reinforcing only one of Lefebvre's spaces; to further highlight the conceptualised space of the state as the key international legal space that is an integral part of the institutionalised *representations of space* of international law.

This echoes the concerns raised above about the capture of the binary. Doris Buss has similar hesitations with the public/private debate in feminist critiques of international law. She argues that on the one hand, these critiques have drawn attention to the political processes of the constitution of spaces of international law—as public or private, international or national, global or local. But at the same time as attention is drawn to the spatiality of international law, the critiques also by and large reinforce the hegemonic space of international law and a commitment to that space.[53] This happens partly through a process of inclusion, by which the boundaries of what is seen to be public shift to include that which was private—such as concerns of women.[54] Buss questions whether processes of inclusion necessarily represent progress: 'What are we being included in, and under whose terms?'[55] These processes of inclusion are potentially limited because they do not necessarily challenge the fundamental 'architecture' of international law: 'the structure's own violence is left intact, and we assume, rather than interrogate, the functional capacity of such a structure'.[56] The question remains whether a

---

[51] Convention on the Prohibition of the Use, Stockpiling, Production and Transfer of Anti-Personnel Mines and on Their Destruction (the 'Ottawa Convention'), 26 ILM (1997) 1507, entered into force 1 March 1999.

[52] On the role of NGOs at the ICC negotiations, see generally Pearson, above n 48; Lindblom, above n 48; WR Pace, 'The Relationship Between the International Criminal Court the Non-Governmental Organizations' in HAM von Hebel, JG Lammers and J Schukking (eds), *Reflections on the International Criminal Court* (Cambridge, Cambridge University Press, 1999); WR Pace and J Schense, 'Coalition for the International Criminal Court at the Preparatory Commission' in RS Lee (ed), *The International Criminal Court: Elements of Crimes and Rules of Procedure and Evidence* (Transnational Publishers, 2001). In relation to the Ottawa negotiations, see MA Cameron, RJ Lawson, and BW Tomlin (eds), *To Walk Without Fear: The Global Movement to Ban Landmines* (Oxford, Oxford University Press, 1998) for a comprehensive outline of the process from the perspectives of NGO and state representatives. Also see K Anderson, 'The Ottawa Convention Banning Landmines, the Role of International Non-Governmental Organizations, and the idea of International Civil Society' (2000) 11 *European Journal of International Law* 91; K Rutherford, 'The Evolving Arms Control Agenda: Implications of the Role of NGOs in Banning Antipersonnel Landmines' (2000) 53 *World Politics* 74.

[53] Buss, above n 6, 96. Also see similar concerns in D Otto, 'Lost in translation: re-scripting the sexed subjects of international human rights law' in A Orford (ed), *International Law and Its Others* (Cambridge, Cambridge University Press, 2006) 351.

[54] Buss, above n 6.

[55] Ibid 98. Also see discussion of projects of inclusion in Nesiah, below, this collection.

[56] Ibid 99.

spatial analysis can help to transcend the binary of resistance and compliance. How might engagement with the paradoxical spaces Rose envisages, or the lived spaces of Lefebvre, assist us to uncover the 'elsewhere', multiplicitous and untidy materialities of spaces of international law?

Space as Shaped by International Law

One of the reasons for the durability of the binary that remains, despite the recognition of some aspects of the spatiality of international law, might be the assumed nature of the space of international law. The spaces of international law seem at once hyper visible ('global', 'international') and at the same time invisible, in the sense of the presumed limited connection of the international with any particular physical space, structure, ideology, or tradition.[57] Despite the fact that international space is more a product of 'imagination than it is a singular, unified space or place',[58] a product of an assumed spatial claim and scale,[59] this juxtaposition between the hyper visibility and the invisibility of the space of international law is powerful for shaping our perspectives of international law as being both universal (applicable everywhere) and neutral (a view from nowhere in particular).[60] The assumptions are reflected in beliefs of the role, the substance and processes of international law—the 'normative dimension of international law's spatial ordering'.[61] This 'detached view from above' is able to construct and effect with some authority 'hopes for [an objective and unified] world order'; the 'global' becomes 'a way of looking that eclipses all others', as well as 'a space or place' where international law happens.[62] A spatial analysis then must be interested in not only the physical spaces of international law, such as the state, but also the conceptual spaces, through which international law is associated not only with neutrality, universality, but also with power, exclusion, detachment,[63] an observation with clear resonance to feminist critiques. In this way, a spatial analysis of international law can address Soja's second focus for law and geography—the

---

[57] Z Pearson, 'Spaces of International Law' (2008) 17 *Griffith Law Review* 489, 501–03.

[58] D Delaney, 'Introduction: Globalization and Law' in N Blomley, D Delaney and R Ford (eds), *The Legal Geographies Reader* (Oxford, Blackwell Publishing, 2001) 252.

[59] Buss, above n 6, 87.

[60] A Riles, 'The view from the international plane: Perspective and scale in the architecture of colonial international law' in N Blomley, D Delaney and R Ford (eds), *The Legal Geographies Reader* (Oxford, Blackwell Publishing, 2001) 280–81. Riles has argued, 'The unique aspect of this global perspective that [has] made of the world a subject of viewing, however, [is] precisely the fact that it [is] a perspective from no point in particular'.

[61] Buss, above n 6, 88.

[62] Riles, above n 60, 280–81.

[63] See Pearson, above n 57, 498–505.

ways in which our assumptions about law and legal institutions can shape and control how space is organised and expressed in the physical world.[64]

This spatial inquiry then, argues for a closer interrogation of the spaces of the international or global. Lefebvre's understanding of the production of space assists such a project because of the multidimensional and dynamic picture it suggests of how the spaces of international law are perceived, conceived and lived. The simultaneous movement and occupation that Rose envisages between multiple spaces in paradoxical space further supports a careful examination of the spaces of global and local, recognising the enduring power of these dichotomies but suggesting ways in which this may be transcended. The critical feminist and legal geographies literature thus assists us to problematise the fixity and certainty of spaces of international law and their detachment from social, legal and political realities.[65] From this perspective the normative spaces of international law are not the fixed, one dimensional sites suggested by the all-encompassing concept of the 'global', which frequently renders the importance, complexity and dynamism of space invisible.[66] As Massey argues '"Space" is created out of the vast intricacies, the incredible complexities, of the interlocking and the non-interlocking, and the networks of [social] relations at every scale from local to global'.[67] The utility of concepts of space for this inquiry is that the focus is brought more strongly to the locations of the law within the fluid, multiple societal contexts in which law operates, and to the creation, visibility and longevity of these locations and their connection to the social, political, economic, cultural, historical and legal realities.

In particular, these insights about the multidimensional production and occupation of space are important to explore in a project that seeks to avoid becoming another 'project of inclusion', or establishing seemingly intractable discussions that establish and dwell on the global/local binaries.[68] It is not a project of inclusion because of the emphasis on multidimensionality, the understanding that spaces of international law are fundamentally and simultaneously made up of many dimensions. As much as international lawyers give weight to the conceived, the hegemonic *representations of space* of our discipline that focus on the global sites and institutions, we must also recognise the intra-actively produced nature of the local, regional and global that means the seemingly peripheral lived spaces of international law are spaces that are in fact integral to our conceptions of the spaces of international law. Critical feminist and legal geographies literatures

---

[64] Soja, above n 44, 1425–26. Also see Oh, above n 46, 1359.
[65] Aoki, above n 39, 917–18; Oh, above n 39, 510; Delaney et al, above n 40, xvi.
[66] Delaney et al, above n 40.
[67] Massey, above n 22, 264–65.
[68] See also Soja, above n 13, 119–25 for a discussion of feminist geographies, Lefebvre and Soja's concept of 'Thirdspace'.

contribute to critiques that make visible the 'blind spots' and the structuring binaries of international law and thus illustrate how the traditional sites and structures of international law are tools of hegemonic closure. They also highlight the multidimensional and paradoxical concepts of international legal space, providing opportunities to pay attention to different voices, interactions and the resulting lived spaces that have potential for transformations of international law.

Identifying the Lived Spaces of International Law

The insights and methodologies offered by critical feminist geographers may best illustrate how the spatial critique can assist the reconstructive normative project that feminist critiques of international law ultimately seek to engage in. In recognising that space is inherently dynamic, this literature argues for a conception of space that recognises its openness and fluidity. In doing so, the feminist geographies literature also argues for the importance of recognising a multiplicity and a multidimensionality of spaces, and the necessary connections that are made between spaces. In their analyses of these multiplicitous spaces, these lived spaces, feminist geographers argue for reflection on the influence of spaces on knowledge creation, to avoid replicating hegemonic masculinist binaries, and make strong links to the mutually constitutive nature of space, society and gender relations. They draw upon notions of space as open, fluid, connected and dynamic, as paradoxical, to argue for the necessity to pay attention to the contingency of norms and the importance of translating experiences and practice across spaces to allow opportunities for social change.

It is these characteristics of space that might allow for an understanding of how the lived spaces of international law contribute to the production of international law. These insights from feminist geographies seem to offer further support for feminist critiques of international law, both in terms of a deconstructive project that challenges the fixed borders of hegemonic binaries, discourses and structures of international law, and a reconstructive project that seeks to explore the lived spaces of international law and ultimately how the resistance/compliance binary may be reimagined. As well as further serving to make visible the structuring binaries of international law, a spatial analysis seeks to problematise these binaries of international law by questioning their fixity and homogeneity. It does this by identifying multiple 'small places of law and politics' where some form of normative behaviour might be at work, and exploring the role that these spaces might have in the destabilisation or on the maintenance of hegemonic legal discourse and practice. The concept of 'paradoxical space' is a particularly useful one, because it encourages reflection on the multiplicity of these different sites of international law and the connections between them that mean the spaces are paradoxical—simultaneously centre and periphery, fluid and contingent. Because of the stress that concepts of space put on making clear the connections between law, society and space, a spatial project brings the focus very clearly to the production of law that results. This echoes what Philip Allott says about the self-creating of law and of international law: 'the actual is not natural and inevitable. The actual was made by us and can be remade by us'.[69] Concepts of space therefore highlight the potential for resistance and accommodation of difference that might emerge from the fluidity of paradoxical space. The paradoxical nature of space can therefore be productive; the resistance/compliance binary can be seen in this light as full of possibility.

Managing Diversity and Difference

Concepts of space, however, do create a number of challenges for the disciplinary thinking of international law. As Keith Aoki notes, 'how to inhabit a world of multiplied, splintered, mutating, overlapping and conflicting spaces and places'[70] certainly presents conceptual and practical issues for international law. It is undoubtedly a change to see spaces in international law as fluid and evolving, as flows created out of interactions and interrelationships[71] at the everyday level, rather than falling back on the development of fixed, decontextualised and abstract categories. The concepts of space that provide us with tools to emphasise the fluidity, openness and interconnectedness of spaces of norm creation in international law resonate with some of the ways in which feminist authors have conceptualised diversity, difference and dialogue. Feminist engagement with international law then seems to represent a potential site where these challenges can be taken up.

Feminist engagements with international law are increasingly mindful of the challenges involved in managing diversity and difference. A number of feminist engagements with international law have contributed concepts and methodologies that explore how acknowledging and managing plurality in terms of spaces of international law might be possible. Several commentators highlight the usefulness of a dialogic process of interaction between different actors (or spaces) for managing and facilitating plurality in international law. Such a focus creates opportunities for the engagement and interaction of a plurality of actors and voices in different spaces, through the establishment

---

[69] P Allott, 'New International Law: First Lecture of the Academic Year 20-' in British Institute of International and Comparative Law (ed), *Theory and International Law: An Introduction* (London, British Institute of International and Comparative Law, 1991) 116.

[70] Aoki, above n 39, 956.

[71] Buss, above n 6, 100.

of inclusive structures of communication, negotiation and decision-making, where each actor is valued for their particular characteristics, acknowledging that all participants have partial perspectives.[72] This approach insists on the dialogue between these different perspectives, 'aimed at the collective generation of fuller pictures of reality', with the goal of developing strategic connection and linkages between the particularities.[73]

An approach that recognises that 'open, respectful, and participatory' dialogue between diverse actors can help to create alliances emphasises the possible connections between actors in different spaces, while recognising the importance of their differences.[74] As an example, Dianne Otto argues that dialogue in the context of human rights law must be based on a common ethical commitment among participants to address the material aspects of human dignity, particularly economic justice and equality.[75] These commonalities in terms of ethical goals can then be used to inform the struggles involved in negotiating differences and diversity.[76] Otto argues for recognition of the 'diversities, incommensurabilities, and contingencies' that could productively restructure relationships, referring to these as concepts of 'multiple consciousness' or 'multiple literacies'.[77] These concepts are useful because of the potential they suggest for establishing common ethical commitments while still recognising the value of diversity; they also emphasise the openness and fluidity that are inherent parts of such dialogues. While embracing a diversity of spaces in the international arena might seem to add unmanageable complexity, the ability for diversity to coexist with the development of multiple, fluid commonalities or solidarities shows that diversity can inform our understandings of the spaces of the international system.[78]

---

[72] C Eschle, *Global Democracy, Social Movements and Feminism* (Boulder, Westview Press, 2001) 40, 132, 207, 218; M Keck and K Sikkink, *Activists Beyond Borders: Advocacy Networks in International Politics* (Ithaca, Cornell University Press, 1998) 1–2, 12–13; D Otto, 'Rethinking the "Universality" of Human Rights Law' (1997) 29 *Columbia Human Rights Law Review* 32–33. Keck and Sikkink note that structures and spaces that are committed to dialogue can assist in recognising and addressing the disparities in bargaining power that exist between groups, which may otherwise impact on their respective abilities and opportunities to participate in the processes of dialogue in the international arena.

[73] Eschle, above n 72, 132.

[74] Ibid 146, 203. Eschle equates this approach to a feminist approach of 'transversal politics', a process that emphasises development of a common perspective through dialogue within a coalition, which avoids both the abandonment and entrenchment of differences. Essentially, Eschle's approach is about 'building democratic bridges across differences.'

[75] Otto, above n 72, 32–35.

[76] Idem.

[77] Ibid 28–29, 45–46. See also, in a similar vein, discussion of 'cosmopolitanisms' in R Buchanan and S Pahuja, 'Collaboration, Complicity and Cosmopolitanism' (2002) 71 *Nordic Journal of International Law* 297–323, 321.

[78] See further discussion of these points in A Carline and Z Pearson, 'Complexity and Queer Theory Approaches to International Law and Feminist Politics: Perspectives on Trafficking' (2007) 19 *Canadian Journal of Women and the Law* 73–118.

The openness and fluidity of concepts of space also prove useful for avoiding Buss's concerns about the dangers of projects of inclusion. Viewing spatial projects of international law as critical processes, which seek to uncover and emphasise diversity rather than to produce a definitive new 'map', assists us to avoid the capture of the binaries inherent in the limited legal imagination. The process is necessarily fluid, acknowledging the fleeting nature of the undertaking. This necessitates moving from seeing space as a bounded and certain concept to seeing space as about fluidity and flows,[79] as 'lines of connection and lines of movement',[80] 'as undergoing continual construction exactly through the agency of things encountering each other in more or less organized circulations'.[81] In a way that resonates with Rose's 'paradoxical space', Otto argues that an approach that challenges the dualisms enables us to pay attention to the 'in-between spaces', 'because they take us beyond the confines of dichotomous thinking to a deeper analysis of the multiplicitous interactions between diverse networks of public, private and hybrid forms of power'.[82] Crucially, feminist and spatial engagements seem able to explore the intricacies present in contemporary issues that impact on women's rights and everyday lives, and articulate and facilitate this diversity and difference without 'sliding into an uncritical celebration of plurality and uniqueness'[83] through an understanding of the importance of dialogues in the process of translating experiences across different worlds. This further helps to overcome a key objection to exploring the spatiality of international law; that is, that a move away from the traditional, state-centric structures towards recognising a multiplicity of spaces of normativity would result in an overly complex, chaotic and unmanageable system. Such concerns are echoed in the fears of the functional integrity of the international system inherent in the resist/comply dichotomy.

---

[79] N Thrift, 'Space: The Fundamental Stuff of Human Geography' in S Holloway, S Rice and G Valentine (eds), *Key Concepts in Geography* (London, Sage Publishing, 2003) 99–100.

[80] Buss, above n 6, 101.

[81] Thrift, above n 79, 96.

[82] D Otto, 'Handmaidens, Hierarchies, and Crossing the Public-Private Divide in the Teaching of International Law' (2000) 1 *Melbourne Journal of International Law* 35–69, 54. This notion of 'in-between spaces' resonates with Rose's 'paradoxical space' in many ways. Also see S Pahuja, 'Trading Spaces: Locating Sites for Challenge within International Trade Law' (2000) 14 *Australian Feminist Law Journal* 38–54, 40, who uses 'in-between spaces' to explore the possible areas that may open up between the separation of international trade and human rights law. Pahuja borrows this term from HK Bhabha, *The Location of Culture* (London, Routledge, 1994) 1–2, who uses 'in-between spaces' to refer to the space between constructed identities where differences may be articulated and negotiated: 'These "in-between" spaces provide the terrain for elaborating strategies of self-hood—singular or communal—that initiate new signs of identity, and innovate sites of collaboration and contestation, in the act of defining the idea of society itself.'

[83] G Pratt, 'Reflections on Poststructuralism and Feminist Empirics, Theory and Practice' (1993) 25 *Antipode* 51–63, reprinted in P Moss and K Falconer Al-Hindi (eds), *Feminisms in Geography. Rethinking Space, Place and Knowledges* (Plymouth, Rowman & Littlefield Publishers 2008) 58.

CONCLUSION

Feminist projects that utilise dynamic concepts of space to explore the multiplicitous, paradoxical lived spaces of international law, and examine ways in which the diversity that this entails can be productive, seem to offer hopeful opportunities for reconstructive normative projects of international law. It seems possible that spatial critiques that emphasise the mutually constitutive nature of law, space and society and the resulting production of normative spaces might assist us to overcome the exclusive and binary driven tendencies of international legal responses. The political resistance to such binaries that might be found in these lived spaces presents potential areas in which the hegemonies that continue to construct global gender identities can be challenged. By emphasising that space is fluid, porous and multiplicitous, and is, as a result, always open to contestation and redefinition, spatial and feminist critiques assist important reflection on the challenging issues of plurality, difference and uncertainty for law and feminist projects. These critiques stress the importance of movement, connection and dialogue between spaces and thus highlight the dynamism of possible normative spaces of international law. The concept of paradoxical space is particularly useful for exploring how spatial critiques might help move our thinking beyond the closure of the binaries of resistance and compliance into something more dynamic, to explore and understand spaces of international law. There are, of course, many questions that remain for such projects. Can the recognition of the diversity of lived spaces of international law be a foundation on which to create spaces of genuine social solidarity at the international level? Spaces in which diversity is integral, in which the paradoxical and fluid nature of space are seen as inherent and productive characteristics of the production of international law? And, as Anna Grear notes, 'might genuine diversity in community, and the security that emerges from it, to some extent render the state security discourses obsolete or at least diminished in their power?'[84]

During this process of writing, I've wandered again in the streets of Ulus. I can see why our Turkish friends on the 'other' side of Ankara have said that we will not want to visit—that is, I can see that they would be worried about how our Western gaze would rest on the 'untidiness' of it—not the nicely organised apartment blocks, nor the wide leafy streets that the modern planned city of Ankara is known for, not the glitzy shops, no Starbucks![85]

---

[84] A Grear, discussant comments, at the 'Between Resistance and Compliance? Feminist Perspectives on International Law in an Age of Terror and Anxiety', IISL, Oñati, Spain, May 2008, copy on file with author.

[85] Also see B Ekici, *Perceptions of different socio-economic status groups living in Ankara* (2004) Unpublished MS thesis, Middle Eastern Technical University, Ankara, who considers

But what I also see is the vibrancy of the lived spaces here—young boys playing with stick 'swords' or taking advantage of the appearance of two *yabancı* on a quiet Sunday morning to give us information about the area in hope of payment of '*bir lira?*', men talking in the street, *simit* sellers' cries as they walk the streets selling their bread, neighbours greeting each other with the toot of a car horn, the cat sitting on the sunny doorstep, the *ezan* from the mosque minarets and ash from fires wafting around us and settling in our hair, small girls and women selling trinkets and scarves near the old city walls, the sound of televisions, the bustle of kitchen pots, the sharp snap of a carpet shaken out a window, the sounds of everyday life.

I reflect on where international law is in these spaces, I reflect on the relevance of my discipline and work to these lived spaces, introspection partly brought on by the usual existential angst that accompanies the start of new research projects; but partly because I cannot recognise international law here. I have in mind Foucault's conception of the value of these everyday spaces: 'A whole history remains to be written of spaces—which at the same time would be a history of powers (both of these terms in the plural)—from the great strategies of the geo-politics to the little tactics of the habitat'.[86] It occurs to me that I am not looking in the right way, looking for international law *here*; that this in fact is the disciplinary insularity that privileges the space of the international that I have been trying to get beyond. Or rather, like international legal approaches often do, particularly regarding women's concerns (highlighted in this collection by Vasuki and Kouvo, in particular), my gaze has only touched upon the surface appearances, without capturing the lived complexities that are present. A spatial analysis suggests that the task is to interrogate our assumptions of the international that render these spaces peripheral to international law; a deconstructive project that challenges the fixed nature of the hegemonic binaries and spaces of international law. The task is also to recognise and understand the power of these everyday spaces in terms of their normative potential, and also in terms of their shortcomings—as this should not be seen as an uncritical celebration of the everyday, with the danger and limitations inherent in the private, particularly for women. This then, is the potential of the paradoxical nature of spaces for reconstructive projects of international law; the multiplicity of these different spaces of international law and the connections and movement between them that mean the spaces are simultaneously centre and periphery, fluid, contingent. The task then might then be to consider how,

---

the geographic and social divisions between different socio-economic groups living in Ankara.

[86] M Foucault, 'The Eye of Power' in *Power/Knowledge: Selected Interviews and Other Writings, 1972-1977* (Colin Gordon ed and Colin Gordon et al tr, New York, Pantheon Press, 1980) 146, 149.

as feminist international lawyers, we can explore and become acquainted with these multiplicitous, porous, fluid and dynamic normative spaces of international law. This might be key to understanding our own occupation of the paradoxical spaces of resistance and compliance, and assist our search for an 'elsewhere'.

Part Two

Feminist Perspectives on National and International Security

Three Feminist Critiques of Varying Feminist Capitulations to Crisis-Hegemony

Reflections on Otto, Mertus and Grahn-Farley

ANNA GREAR

THE SEEMINGLY INTRACTABLE pull between the Scylla of 'resistance' and the Charybdis of 'compliance' and the agonistic dilemmas presented by the complexity and difficulty of positioning feminism in relation to them both is well-traced in these chapters by Dianne Otto, Julie Mertus and Maria Grahn-Farley. While a range of themes emerges from reflection on these nuanced and thoughtful chapters, at the heart of each, in different ways, the colonisation of certain emancipatory feminist projects and agendas by the crisis-driven post 9/11 international legal discourse emerges as a central concern, along with a set of related sub-themes: the traction (and inequality) of hegemonic and counter-hegemonic thought-worlds and actions; the pernicious effects of decontextualisation (either the transcendence or the 'emptying out' of context (including, worryingly, lived experience of violation)); the fragile potency of ground-level viewpoint, action and perspective; the false totality of the security-hegemon; its liquid propagandism, and related concerns circling around co-opted feminist responses.

These themes emerge from three rather different reflections. In brief, for Otto, the dangers presented to feminism by the post-9/11 'language of crisis' forms the heart of a critical reading of the colonisation and auto-colonisation of feminism in the context of a hegemonic and all-consuming juridification of life driven by a discourse of 'emergency'. Reflection upon that post-9/11 discursive hegemony, in Mertus's chapter, takes the form of a consideration of the dominance of the post-9/11 security agenda and its ideological co-option of feminist and human rights non-governmental organisation (NGO) agendas, while Grahn-Farley addresses a particularly revealing and problematic convergence between hegemonic security-driven agendas and a decontextualised 'feminist' notion of agency as constructed by Halley, representing a troubling convergence between 'agency theory' (per Halley) and Bush-era type 'justifications' for torture.

Otto's chapter addresses the normative expansion of 'crisis governance' implicated in the authorisation of a hegemonic legal order and reflecting a juridical expansionism that has marginalised space for political contestation. Both the exploitation of feminist ideas by those promoting a permanent state of crisis and the concomitant invocation of the language of crisis by feminists, for Otto, heightens the need for feminists to engage in political resistance to the limitations of crisis thinking and to confront a new politics of the every day—a politics now supported by 'a crisis-driven sanctification of aggressive masculinity and domesticated womanhood'. One of the greatest dangers identified by Otto (and by Grahn-Farley's critique of Halley) is the emptying out of context—the sense in which broader analyses situating international problems within the wider context of structural inequality and injustice are partially or wholly excluded by crisis discourse.

For Otto, then, it is vital to resist international law's colonisation of politics (life itself) and to contest the logic of crisis-thought (as well as to prevent the appropriation of opportunity by the dominant actors within crisis governance). A particular problem identified by Otto is the highly selective harnessing of feminist ideas to crisis-management agendas. For her this suggests the importance of maintaining a clear distinction between feminist ideas and the vocabulary of crisis governance. To this end, Otto argues that we should focus on the power of local, while maintaining a continuing commitment to feminist critique of the mainstream crisis-driven agenda. We need to move, as Otto puts it, towards 'un-crisis' thinking, and for her, creative solutions to international problems require ongoing feminist engagement with the sites of international law, but also a commitment to the idea that life and politics overflow the boundaries of legal change: 'Un-crisis thinking requires supporting the activism of women outside the mainstream institutions of law and politics as well as carving out spaces on the inside'.

However, various instances of institutional and non-institutional internalisation of the security agenda seem simultaneously to emphasise both the importance and the potential fragility of Otto's point. 'Un-crisis' thinking depends, in the final analysis upon genuine resistance to the ideology of panic, upon resistance to the internalisation of insecurity. This may be difficult to achieve, as implied by the chapters by Mertus and Grahn-Farley respectively.

For Mertus, women's rights and feminist advocacy NGOs face reductive patterns of 'framing' in which the 'security' agenda simply excises much of importance and in which the NGO landscape is littered with new sets of impediments to progress in the form of enhanced scrutiny, burdensome restrictions and intrusive regulation. The colonisation, discursively and bureaucratically, of NGO advocacy emerges with troubling clarity from her analysis—lending 'on the ground' credibility to Otto's analysis of crisis-hegemony but suggesting the sense in which 'un-crisis' thinking faces a range of highly complex and obdurate impediments.

Reprising the 1990s' role of NGOs as critical advocates pressing their international political agenda upon states and in the process implicitly emphasising the dispersal of sites of power, Mertus notes that the event of 9/11 produced a political landscape dominated by 'security matters'. Advocacy NGOs found themselves confronted by 'an obstacle course to meaningful participation by non-state actors' with 'new rules of the road', 'blind spots' and 'speed bumps'. Outlining some of these, Mertus suggests that hegemonic power is gained precisely by the possession of a privileged position within the existing rules and institutions of international law, and is served up, even under the Obama administration, as American hegemony, 'albeit with a twist'. The new Obama-style 'partnership model' of hegemony, moreover, renders sources of hegemonic power even more elusive. Steering a path between resistance and compliance requires taking these complexities into account, recalling that at the NGO level, crisis-hegemony has meant that various security-oriented NGOs have taken the centre ground while other NGOs have reconstituted themselves within the security frame. In this process, feminist insistence upon complexity and multiple truths is abandoned while the challenges facing feminist and women's rights NGOs remain as perplexing and intransigent as ever—an insight thoroughly confirmed by Grahn-Farley's chapter.

For Grahn-Farley, the crisis-colonisation dynamic reaches into the depths of the academy, threatening academic freedom and reducing 'agency' to a 'negotiation between resistance and compliance' best exemplified by Halley's production of a theoretical agency for women and children to 'consent to rape' and her critique of the criminalisation of war rape.[1]

Halley's thesis employs a colonisation of material fact (and of the embodied suffering of those testifying on their own behalf in a war-crime trial) through the construction of a radically decontextualised reading of an international legal case[2] in the service of producing a theory of decontextualised agency. This amounts to a strategy reflecting a troubling coalition between

---

[1] J Halley, P Koiswaran, H Shamir, C Thomas, 'From the International to the Local in Feminist Legal Responses to Rape, Prostitution/Sex Work, and Sex Trafficking: Four Studies in Contemporary Governance Feminism' (2006) 29 *Harvard Journal of Law and Gender* 335.

[2] *Kunarac et al* (IT-96-23 & 23/1) Foča, ICTY-TPIY.

a variant of thinking presenting itself as 'feminist' and the neo-Conservative 'Bush doctrine'. The brutal reinvention of rape in this theoretical recon-struction represents a complete reversal of traditional readings of sexual violation. As Grahn-Farley puts it, '[i]n Halley's view, the criminalization of rape as torture took something away from the Bosnian women kept in the control of Serbian soldiers, namely, their ability to choose to have sex with their male guards'. This reversal of meanings is achieved, arguably, precisely by the emptying out of lived context and a radical decontextualisation: unlike the general approach of agency and power-related theories (which contextualise agency in relation to local power) Halley employs agency as a decontextualised organising principle.

Noting that the tension between resistance and compliance deepens in times of terror and anxiety because the consequences of arguments are aug-mented by the pressures, Grahn-Farley argues that we too easily overlook the influence of terror and anxiety on the 'neutral' interpreter. We forget that feminist interpretation itself may struggle in the space between resistance and compliance. Halley's reduction of agency to a technique through which the individual can accept oppression by institutions produces a 'politics of inevitability' which, rather than reflecting the one being interpreted, reveals the position of the interpreter. Halley's theory produces the paradox of an anti-feminist 'liquid feminism', a feminism constituted by a methodological shift towards acts, no matter how contingent upon oppression, as constitut-ing a form of self expression in the construction of an agency denuded of structural context. This, Grahn-Farley argues, directly and problematically mirrors the shift towards decontextualised state expressions of terror and anxiety.

Taken together these chapters expose the production of a nested series of decontextualisations, closures, co-options and reconstitutions that ill-serve emancipatory feminist agendas. What, then, can we propose in response? The chapters suggest, either implicitly or explicitly, the central importance of recapturing an emphasis upon context, and perhaps of interrogating what 'context' means and is to include. Additionally, a related but distinguishable critical theme also presents itself—typical of feminism's traditional strate-gies—in the form of a focus on the material, the concrete, the day-to-day lived-realities of embodied, context-located lives and an endorsement of the critical potency of grass-roots, bottom-up trajectories of engagement. This focus on local context, local emplacement, local energies is, however, accompanied by a vivid sense of the need for continuing critical feminist focus upon the structural inequalities of the life-world, and ongoing, if ambivalent, engagement with the notionally 'global' sites of production of international legal norms and discourse.

5

Remapping Crisis through a Feminist Lens

DIANNE OTTO*

INTRODUCTION

THE LANGUAGE OF 'crisis' has become ubiquitous in international law and politics. Rising to a crescendo with the 9/11 crisis of international terror, 'emergencies' now dominate global intercourse. Official crises are no longer confined to military and monetary emergencies—although these are not in short supply—but have been declared with respect to a widening range of everyday matters including food,[1] water,[2] development,[3] climate change,[4] HIV-AIDS[5] and peacekeeping sex.[6] Globally, it

---

* With thanks, as always, to Joan Nestle for her creative thinking and unwavering encouragement, and to the many people who responded so generously at the lectures and seminars where I presented this paper in various forms.

[1] 'The World Bank tackles food emergency', *BBC News*, 14 April 2008; Secretary General's High Level Task Force on the Global Food Security Crisis, established 28 April 2008; Human Rights Council, 7th Special Session on 'The negative impact on the realization of the right to food of the worsening of the world food crisis, caused inter alia by the soaring food prices', Geneva, 22 May 2008, the first Human Rights Council Special Session to focus on a thematic issue; High-Level Conference on World Food Security: The Challenges of Climate Change and Bioenergy, Rome 3–5 June 2008.

[2] 'Global water crisis looming, UN says', *The West Australian*, 19 March 2008; 'Water: a crisis of governance says second UN World Water Development Report', UN-Water Newsroom, 9 March 2006, referring to *Water: A Shared Responsibility, The United Nations World Water Development Report 2* (New York, UNESCO & Berghahn Books, 2006).

[3] 'To put it bluntly, we face a development emergency', UN Secretary-General Ban Ki Moon, addressing the first day of General Debate at the 63rd Session of the United Nations General Assembly, 23 September 2008.

[4] 'Impact of Climate Change on International Peace and Security', Security Council Open Debate, 17 April 2007.

[5] *Declaration of Commitment on HIV/AIDS, 'Global Crisis—Global Action'*, UN General Assembly, A/RES/S-26/2, 2 August 2001; 'HIV/AIDS and international peacekeeping operations', UN Security Council, S/RES/1308 (17 July 2000).

[6] 'Crisis in the Congo: Sex Charges Roil UN', *Fox News*, 3 March 2005; *Human Trafficking and United Nations Peacekeeping* (DPKO Policy Paper, March 2004) 1: 'For Peacekeeping (UN and other) there is a crisis of perception in relation to trafficking and the linked issue of sexual exploitation and abuse'.

seems we are more or less permanently suspended in states of crisis which, in turn, are rapidly reshaping our conceptions of international peace and security.[7] The sense of cataclysm has generated a mantra of speedy diagnosis and robust response, crafted by technocratic and military experts. Reflecting this shift in power, away from inclusive law and policy-making to experts in crisis management, the Security Council is now the epicentre of international action.[8] The new dominance of the Security Council ensures that crisis is 'securitised';[9] diminishing the importance of the United Nation's (UN) other main contributions to peace—sustainable development and the realisation of human rights.[10] In this chapter, I critically examine the challenges that the ascendancy of 'crisis' governance produce for feminist legal theory and activism in the context of international law.

The understanding that today's international crises, whether real or imagined, are best addressed by military solutions pushes aside the pacifist methods of conflict resolution that have long been promoted by women's movements for peace. As Julie Mertus discusses in this collection, the new emphasis on military security has put pressure on feminist peace groups to reinvent themselves in order to remain 'relevant' to funding bodies and policy-makers.[11] Mertus uses the example of 'Women Waging Peace' renaming itself as the 'Initiative for Inclusive Security'. In order to stay relevant, the more compliant aspiration of advocating for the participation of women in the existing paradigm was adopted to mask the group's long-standing pacifist agenda. The feminist vision of peace is thus reduced by crisis to a hope for militarised security.

One way to read the metamorphosis of Women Waging Peace is that feminism is pushed 'off the map' in a crisis, as was 'gleefully' suggested to feminist author Susan Faludi by a journalist seeking her reaction to the 9/11 attacks.[12] His forecast was that a crisis necessitates the return of 'manly men'

---

[7] The similarities between this 'reshaping' and the earlier imperial order of international law are striking. See further A Anghie, 'On critique and the other' in A Orford (ed), *International Law and its Others* (Cambridge, Cambridge University Press, 2006) 389.

[8] This shift was anticipated by the Security Council as early as 1992, when the President of the Security Council, following its 3,046th meeting, held at the level of Heads of State and Government, made a Statement on behalf of members which asserted that 'non-military sources of instability in the economic, social, humanitarian and ecological fields have become threats to international peace and security'. Note by the President of the Security Council, S/23500, 31 January 1992.

[9] SV Scott, 'Securitizing climate change: international legal implications and obstacles' (2008) 21 *Cambridge Review of International Affairs* 603.

[10] Report of the Secretary-General, *In Larger Freedom: Towards Development, Security and Human Rights for All*, A/59/2005, 21 March 2005, para 12. See further, para 17: 'Accordingly, we will not enjoy development without security, we will not enjoy security without development, and we will not enjoy either without respect for human rights'. Endorsed by 2005 World Summit, High Level Plenary Meeting of the General Assembly, 14-16 September 2005, A/59/HLPM/CRP.1/Rev.2.

[11] See Mertus, below, this collection.

[12] D Aitkenhead, 'Home and the Hero', in conversation with Susan Faludi discussing her new book, *The Terror Dream: Fear and Fantasy in Post-9/11 America*, *The Australian Books Supplement*, 12 April 2008.

and 'domesticated women'. Indeed, following 9/11, Faludi soon found that the American media was saturated with reports of women's 'mass retreat' into domesticity and the ascendancy of a 'new John Wayne masculinity'.[13] The journalist's view echoed that of neo-conservative Francis Fukuyama, who suggested several years earlier that the increased 'femin[ist]ization' of politics in the West may prove to be a liability, as states in Africa, the Middle East and South Asia continue to be led by young men whose 'biological' predisposition for aggression remains unconstrained by feminism.[14] In a similar vein, Christian fundamentalists Jerry Falwell and Pat Robertson jumped at the opportunity presented by 9/11 to warn that it was punishment from God for the immorality and secularism of many Americans, notably doctors who performed abortions, as well as feminists, gays and lesbians.[15] While these examples are located in the West, it is my contention that crises everywhere are a particularly dangerous time for feminism, and indeed for all progressive ways of thinking. That this contention sounds so obvious, illustrates the problem that we all too readily fall into the trap of thinking that nuanced political and legal thinking must be sacrificed at times of crisis. Increased danger for feminist ideas may necessitate different feminist strategies, but my argument is that we need to ensure that liberatory ideas are not diluted in the process. In this spirit, it is to be hoped that the radical vision of Women Waging Peace has found a way to stay alive, despite its new mantle of inclusive security.

The revitalisation of gender hierarchy in the American popular imagination following the crisis of 9/11 has its parallel in governmental reactions, which treat crises as moments that typically demand more 'muscular' laws, extensive reliance on executive power, and the downgrading of impediments to robust action posed by the 'soft' laws of human rights and due process, which are threatened, like feminism, with being pushed 'off the map'. The urgency implicit in the rhetoric of crisis has facilitated an 'explosion of [often executive] law',[16] like the Security Council's requirement that all UN member states adopt a far-reaching and detailed set of anti-terrorism measures under its supervision.[17] In the wake of 9/11, as

---

[13] S Faludi, *The Terror Dream: Fear and Fantasy in Post-9/11 America* (Melbourne, Scribe, 2008) 4. See Kouvo, below, this collection.

[14] F Fukuyama, 'Women and the Evolution of World Politics' (1998) 77 *Foreign Affairs* 24, 36–39. Contra responses from B Ehrenreich, K Pollitt, RB Ferguson and JS Jaquette, 'Fukuyama's Follies: So What If Women Ruled the World?' (1999) 78 *Foreign Affairs* 118–29.

[15] 'Jerry Falwell and Pat Robertson say immorality and anti-Christian groups should share in the blame for the Terrorist Attacks on American—Truth!', www.truthorfiction.com/rumors/f/falwell-robertson-wtc.htm (visited 29 May 2009). Under pressure from the administration, Falwell apologised two days later in a CNN interview, www.archives.cnn.com/2001/US/09/14/Falwell.apology/ (visited 29 May 2010).

[16] G Noll, 'Force, Partisanship, Dislocation: An Essay on International Law in the State of the Exceptional' in J Petman and J Klabbers (eds), *Nordic Cosmopolitanism: Essays in International Law for Martti Koskenniemi* (Leiden, Martinus Nijhoff, 2003) 207.

[17] Security Council Resolution 1373, UN Doc S/RES/1373 (28 September 2001).

in the wake of other crises, the 'balance' between human rights and state security has been 'substantially recalibrated' in favour of security concerns,[18] and many established international legal norms have been strained to breaking point, such as the absolute prohibition of the use of torture and the ban on pre-emptive self-defence.[19]

The turn to crisis governance intensifies the already complicated challenges that feminists face in engaging with international law.[20] Calculating how it might be possible to carve out a space for critique in an environment that is so strongly marked by hostility to feminism becomes even more urgent. Indeed, what space is left for any critical or progressive politics at a time of emergency? Does the invocation of an emergency itself 'enforce compliance' by silencing dissenting voices and displacing law's emancipatory potential (assuming it exists)? Or is it possible at the moment of crisis to 'seize the legal ground without simultaneously being imprisoned within it?'[21]

I develop my thoughts in four parts, beginning with an examination of the spreading normativity of crisis governance. I argue that crises have become an everyday technique of global governance, authorising the operation of a more hegemonic legal order and reducing (though not eliminating) the space for political contestation and critique. In the second and third parts I examine two ways that feminist ideas and crisis thinking interact: first, when feminist ideas are used in the service of crisis governance, like their deployment to legitimate the military interventions in Afghanistan and Iraq, and second, when feminists invoke the language of crisis to serve feminist ends, as in efforts to have violence against women addressed urgently. I examine whether these interactions between the vocabularies of feminism and crisis governance raise new opportunities for feminist engagement with international law and, if so, whether this must be at the cost of critical perspectives and the longer term emancipatory goals of feminism. I argue that when crisis thinking dominates the map of possibilities, feminists seeking to engage with law need also to engage politically, actively contesting the constraints of crisis thinking and remaining aware of the unpredictability of law and the contingency of its certainties.

---

[18] O Gross and F Ni Aolain, *Law in Times of Crisis: Emergency Powers in Theory and Practice* (Cambridge, Cambridge University Press, 2006) 399.

[19] Ibid 380–84.

[20] D Otto, 'Lost in translation: re-scripting the sexed subject of international human rights law' in A Orford (ed), *International Law and its Others* (Cambridge, Cambridge University Press, 2006) 318.

[21] M Craven, S Marks, G Simpson and R Wilde, 'We Are Teachers of International Law' (2004) 17 *Leiden Journal of International Law* 363, 366.

THE EVERYDAY-NESS OF CRISIS

Italian philosopher, Giorgio Agamben, offers one way of understanding the proliferation of crisis talk, the international legal responses that it makes possible, and the difficulties that feminist scholars and activists face in offering a critique. He suggests that crises are not the exceptional events they are claimed to be, but are instead ordinary; that by the middle of the twentieth century, the 'state of exception' had become the 'dominant paradigm of [modern] government'.[22] In his view, the fiction of the emergency creates a new space for law's production and reproduction, enabling law to extend its empire, to further colonise 'life itself' by taking possession of the sphere of human action that we know as 'politics'. Agamben's concern with the blurring of the exception and the norm is similar to David Kennedy's discussion of the continuities that have emerged between the politics and practices of war and peace.[23] Both scholars lament the increasing dominance of law over politics which, as Kennedy says, creates 'only the most marginal opportunities for engaged political contestation'[24] and, in Agamben's view, produces only 'bare life' at its extremities.[25] By bare life, Agamben means life that is not recognised as such by law. His examples include those incarcerated in the Nazi concentration camps and, more recently, those detained at Guantanamo Bay, where bare life has reached its 'maximum indeterminacy'.[26] I must add to his list the 60-year crisis of the Palestinian people, whose 'Nakba' (catastrophe) grew directly from the earlier crisis of the holocaust.[27] Agamben's implication is that all of our lives are gradually being so reduced through the governmental technique of the emergency.

In Agamben's analysis, the adoption of more muscular legal measures in response to an emergency is unlikely to be a short term and limited derogation from ordinary law as is usually claimed, but instead, the emergency is constitutive of ordinary law; the exception produces what becomes the everyday. Rather than acting as a constraint on executive power and action in the face of a crisis, law offers a means of authorising what would otherwise be an excessive use or abuse of power. He argues that at the very moment that it is crucial for law to place limits on the state, it becomes extraordinarily permissive. Agamben's thesis has been born out in the wake of 9/11, as existing law has proved incapable of restraining the new resort

---

[22] G Agamben, *State of Exception* (K Attrell tr, Chicago, University of Chicago Press, 2005) 2.

[23] D Kennedy, *Of War and Law* (Princeton, Princeton University Press, 2006) 5.

[24] Ibid 25.

[25] Agamben, above n 22, 87–88. See further, G Agamben, *Homo Sacer: Sovereign Power and Bare Life* (D Heller-Roazen tr, Stanford, Stanford University Press, 1998).

[26] Agamben, above n 22, 4.

[27] Reuters, 'Lieberman's party proposes ban on Arab Nakba', 14 May 2009 www.haaretz.com/hasen/objects/pages/PrintArticleEn.jhtml?itemNo=1085588 (visited 29 May 2010).

to pre-emptive military force, as in the case of Iraq, and unable to counter the new indifference to the requirements of human rights and due process, evident in many of the demands of the Security Council in the name of combating international terrorism.[28] In fact, many neo-conservative legal scholars have welcomed the legal developments that cause Agamben and Kennedy (and me) to despair, defending them as necessitated by today's world of crisis.[29]

Seeing the moment of crisis as an opportunity to achieve otherwise impossible legal 'reform' has spread to everyday matters of governance. The 2006 UN World Water Development Report took the view that 'a perceived or real crisis due to floods and droughts' may be necessary 'to create conditions under which it is politically possible to undertake [water] reform'.[30] President Obama's chief of staff, Rahm Emanuel, has reportedly said 'never allow a crisis to go to waste' so often that it has become the administration's 'semi-official mantra'.[31] The Howard Government in Australia harnessed the crisis of sexual abuse of Aboriginal children to push through harsh legislative measures which reduced many of the rights of Aboriginal people in the Northern Territory[32] and, in complete disregard of its international human rights obligations, exempted this legislation from the operation of the Racial Discrimination Act 1975 (Cth).[33] In the guise of responding to an emergency, proponents of crisis governance remap the legal and political landscape, laying the groundwork for the operation of (or return to) a more hegemonic legal order, which is less constrained by political deliberation and less open to contestation and critique.

---

[28] See, eg, Security Council Resolution 1390, UN Doc S/RES/1390 (28 January 2002) and Security Council Resolution 1453, UN Doc S/RES/1453 (24 December 2002) which mandated the freezing of funds of various non-state actors including Osama bin Laden and others believed to be members of the Al-Qaeda network or the Taliban, without any provision for a fair hearing or effective judicial review. However, it seems that at least in the European Community, the founding principles include protection of fundamental human rights, which cannot be abrogated by international legal obligations under the UN Charter. See joined cases C-402/05 P and C-415/05 P, *Kadi and Al Barakaat International Foundation v Council and Commission*, judgment of 3 September 2008.

[29] MJ Glennon, 'The Fog of Law: Self-Defense, Inherence, and Incoherence in Article 51 of the United Nations Charter' (2001–02) 25 *Harvard Journal of International Law & Public Policy* 539; J Yoo, 'International Law and the War in Iraq' (2003) 97 *American Journal of International Law* 563, 575; R Wedgwood, 'The Fall of Saddam Hussein: Security Council Mandates and Preemptive Self-Defence' (2003) 97 *American Journal of International Law* 576, 585; RF Blomquist, 'The Presidential Oath, the American National Interest, and a Call for Presiprudence' (2004–05) 73 *University of Missouri-Kansas City Law Review* 1.

[30] *Water: A Shared Responsibility*, above n 2, 60.

[31] A Davies, '100 days in FDR's shadow', *The Age Insight*, Melbourne, Saturday 25 April 2009, 3.

[32] Northern Territory National Emergency Response Act 2007 (Cth).

[33] Ibid s 132.

American author, Naomi Klein, has a similar thesis about the technique of crisis, or 'disaster' as she prefers, in the economic sphere.[34] She argues that the Milton Friedman School of economics, incubated during the 1950s at Chicago University, fostered the spread of America's 'free market' policies through the exploitation of deliberately inflicted economic 'shock therapy', producing disaster-shocked, and therefore compliant, populations. She locates the Chicago School's hatching of the methods of 'disaster capitalism', which are now considered 'normal' by many economists,[35] in the 'laboratory' of Latin America, beginning with Pinochet's coup in Chile in 1973.[36] The methods of disaster capitalism have since been embraced by international economic institutions, which have often imposed drastic economic liberalisation measures and 'shock therapy' stabilisation programmes as a condition of their loans.

Klein discusses the methods of disaster capitalism used more recently in Iraq, where the crisis created by the US led international intervention ensured that Iraqis were preoccupied with daily emergencies while new laws were passed that transformed Iraq's economy, enabling American corporations to buy up publicly owned enterprises at bargain basement prices and creating a fully privatised new market for American products.[37] In South-East Asia, the disaster of a tsunami made it possible for entire coastlines of beautiful beaches, where many fishing communities had previously lived, to be 'cleared' and allocated to developers for 'reconstruction' as tourist resorts.[38] Klein's thesis is that crises are inflicted, or harnessed, as a kind of shock treatment, and the resulting disorientation is exploited by free market economists to undertake a radical reshaping of the economic system in the name of 'freedom', which includes the privatisation of state assets and services, economic liberalisation and a radically downsized public sector. As in Agamben's analysis, measures taken in response to the purported exceptional circumstances are normalised, reducing 'life itself' by intensifying its subjection to the free market.

International law has also relied on crises for its development, as many from within the discipline have observed.[39] Hilary Charlesworth argues that, as a result, crises have dominated the imagination of international lawyers, fostering short term, quick-fix and 'truncated' ways of thinking that

---

[34] N Klein, *The Shock Doctrine: The Rise of Disaster Capitalism* (Melbourne, Penguin/Allen Lane, 2007).

[35] There is some tentative evidence that this may be changing in the face of the global crisis of 'extreme capitalism' that emerged during the second half of 2008.

[36] Klein, above n 34, 75–87.

[37] Ibid 345–46.

[38] Ibid 387–88.

[39] H Charlesworth, 'International Law: A Discipline of Crisis' (2002) 65 *Modern Law Review* 377, referring to, eg, M Riesman and A Willard (eds), *International Incidents: the law that counts in world politics* (Princeton, Princeton University Press, 1988) 15.

simplify the 'facts', dismiss analytical and critical perspectives, and silence the larger picture of everyday structural inequalities and injustices.[40] These characteristics of crisis-fuelled legal thinking are readily observable in the examples of crisis governance I have mentioned. The simplification of facts that renders complex histories and multiple causes irrelevant is demonstrated by the Australian Government's crisis legislation that enabled its far-reaching intervention into Aboriginal communities.[41] The denigration of analytical thinking in a crisis as dangerous—even seditious—was captured by George W Bush's infamous pronouncement after 9/11 that 'you're either with us or against us'[42] and, in many places including Australia, is evident in the anti-terror legislation mandated by the Security Council, whereby a range of censorship and sedition offences have been enacted.[43] The erasure of the larger picture of underlying structural discrimination and disadvantage can be seen in the techniques of disaster capitalism and the popular resurgence of hierarchical gender and racial stereotypes which are treated as if they were 'natural' by crisis-driven thinking, a phenomenon that Maria Grahn-Farley discusses in this collection and describes as 'the politics of inevitability'.[44]

It follows, then, that international law, as the product of crisis, is well-suited to normalising the state of exception as the paradigmatic form of modern government. As events have played out in the extended post 9/11 emergency, there is considerable evidence to confirm Agamben's thesis that laws adopted or reshaped to serve the emergency become the norm.[45] In the process, a new politics of the everyday is emerging for feminist contestation. Supported by a crisis-driven sanctification of aggressive masculinity and domesticated womanhood, the new everyday does threaten feminist thinking, along with other analyses that would situate current international legal and political problems in a broader topography of economic and social inequality and injustice. My question is whether, if founded on crisis, international law is always already committed to serve as the 'handmaiden'

---

[40] Ibid 382–86.

[41] See generally, J Altman and M Hinkson (eds), *Coercive Reconciliation: Stabilise, Normalise, Exit Aboriginal Australia* (Melbourne, Arena Publications, 2007).

[42] 'You are either with us or against us', CNN Washington, 6 November 2001 www.archives.cnn.com/2001/US/11/06/gen.attack.on.terror/ (visited 29 May 2010).

[43] Criminal Code Act 1995 (Cth), ss 80.2(1)–(8). See further D Otto and J-C Tham, 'Deconstructing the logic of responding to one threat with another: The perils of countering terrorism by eroding human rights' in Australian Human Rights Working Group, *Australian Human Rights Critique: A Selection of Essays* (Melbourne 2006) 22.

[44] See Grahn-Farley, below, this collection.

[45] K Macdonald, 'Coming Out of the Shadows', Crown Prosecution Service inaugural lecture, London, 20 October 2008, 12: 'it is in the nature of State power that decisions taken in the next few months [to increase State power in efforts to counter terrorism] ... are likely to be irreversible. They will be with us forever. And they in turn will be built upon', www.cps.gov.uk/news/articles/coming_out_of_the_shadows/index.html (visited 29 May 2010).

of crisis governance and disaster capitalism,[46] or whether the possibility of an emancipatory agenda is also present. As Aboriginal scholar and activist Marcia Langton has argued with respect to the Northern Territory intervention,[47] a crisis also creates opportunities that did not exist before. While opportunities are always risky, there seems no reason to assume that they cannot be turned to progressive ends.[48]

The challenge is to re-read the maps of short term, quick fix, top-down, market-friendly and, often, military interventions, which are the mainstay of crisis governance, in order to 'see' the opportunities for feminist activism. We also need to understand how these opportunities might be exploited without legitimating crisis thinking and silencing feminist legal critique. These are not easy tasks. In the face of crisis-driven legal developments that seem considerably more oppressive than the problematic old law, I have often found it tempting to defend the existing law as a better alternative.[49] But as China Mieville argues, this risks 'legitimising ... the very structure of international law that critical theory has so devastatingly undermined'.[50] Does this mean that feminists are trapped, along with other critical international lawyers, in the 'imperial [and gendered] actuality of law'?[51] Or is it possible to challenge the orthodoxies of crisis law-making from within the discipline? Several starting points are suggested by the preceding discussion: we need to find ways to resist international law's colonisation of politics (life itself), to contest the logic of crisis thinking, and to prevent the forfeit of opportunities created by crisis to the masters of crisis governance.

WHEN FEMINISM IS DEPLOYED IN THE SERVICE OF CRISIS

One way that feminism and crisis thinking may come to interact is when feminist ideas are co-opted to serve crisis governance. While feminism is threatened by crisis, it is not wiped completely off the map, despite the predictions of journalists and hopes of conservative pundits. Instead, the selective deployment of feminist issues to justify or legitimate the new laws

---

[46] P Alston, 'The Myopia of the Handmaidens: International Lawyers and Globalization' (1997) 3 *European Journal of International Law* 435. See further S Scott, 'International Lawyers: Handmaidens, Chefs, or Birth Attendants? A Response to Philip Alston' (1998) 4 *European Journal of International Law* 750.

[47] M Langton, 'Trapped in the Aboriginal reality show' (2008) *Griffith Review: Reimagining Australia* 145.

[48] C Gordon, 'Government Rationality: An Introduction' in G Burchell, C Gordon and P Miller (eds), *The Foucault Effect: Studies in Governmentality* (Chicago, University of Chicago Press, 1991) 46–47.

[49] See also Craven et al, above n 21, 363–74.

[50] C Mieville, *Between Equal Rights: A Marxist Theory of International Law* (London, Pluto Press, 2005) 299.

[51] Ibid 300.

and techniques of crisis management keeps feminism, like the former colonies of Europe, still on the map, but seriously compromised, complicating the possibility of grasping opportunities and maintaining critique. A familiar example is the Bush administration's belated engagement with the 'humanitarian crisis' of women in Afghanistan,[52] in order to justify the US military intervention and shore up waning domestic support for the continuing occupation. In the preceding years, many feminists had used the rhetoric of crisis to argue that the brutal treatment of Afghan women during the Taliban regime should be taken up as an issue of international peace and security.[53] Indeed, they were successful insofar as both the General Assembly and the Security Council adopted resolutions that condemned the Taliban's 'discrimination' against women and girls,[54] and several Special Rapporteurs of the UN Commission on Human Rights provided chilling accounts of women's mistreatment.[55] However, it was a deeply compromising moment when US First Lady Laura Bush, six weeks after the American invasion, described the 'fight against terrorism' as 'also a fight for the rights and dignity of women', in a national radio address.[56] While many feminists applauded her statement, shoring up the military and Islamophobic agendas of the administration was not the purpose to which feminist efforts to improve the situation of women in Afghanistan had been directed. Clearly feminist ideas are able to serve diverse purposes including those of crisis governance, as in this case, by helping to legitimate the extension of the ideological and military dominance of the US and its allies. The question is whether, once utilised as a technique of crisis, these ideas are permanently divested of their feminist politics or whether they can be (re)claimed, like the African-American civil rights movement claimed liberal rights discourse as their own, using it to further their struggle against racial discrimination in the US.[57]

---

[52] D Kandiyoti, 'The Politics of Gender and Reconstruction in Afghanistan', UNRID Occasional Paper 4, New York, UNRISD, February 2005, 1, describes women's situation in Afghanistan as a 'humanitarian crisis'. See, Kouvo, below, this collection.

[53] Eg, US-based NGO Feminist Majority's campaign against 'gender apartheid' in Afghanistan, which commenced in the late 1990s. For discussion, see C Hirschkind and S Mahmood, 'Feminism, the Taliban, and Politics of Counter-Insurgency' (2002) 75 *Anthropological Quarterly* 339.

[54] General Assembly Resolution 52/145 (12 December 1997); General Assembly Resolution 53/65 (25 February 1998); Security Council Resolution 1193, UN Doc S/RES/1193 (28 August 1998); Security Council Resolution 1214, UN Doc S/RES/1214 (8 December 1998).

[55] Report by K Hossain, Special Rapporteur on the Situation of Human Rights in Afghanistan, UN Doc E/CN.4/1999/40 (24 March 1999); Report by Radhika Coomaraswamy, Special Rapporteur on Violence Against Women, its Causes and Consequences, *Mission to Pakistan and Afghanistan*, UN Doc E/CN.4/2000/68/Add.4 (13 March 2000).

[56] L Bush, 'Radio Address to the Nation', 17 November 2001.

[57] PJ Williams, *The Alchemy of Race and Rights* (Cambridge, Harvard University Press, 1991) 163.

There have, of course, been feminist efforts to utilise the opportunities that a crisis can present. One example is the promotion of gender-mainstreaming in Iraq by the Women's International League for Peace and Freedom (WILPF), following the US and UK-led invasion in March 2003, despite its determined opposition to the intervention. The WILPF, in coalition with other NGOs, pressed the Security Council to ensure that gender mainstreaming took place in Iraq's reconstruction.[58] While the Security Council did not authorise this invasion, it later adopted a resolution which 'permitted' the ongoing occupation and gave the UN a role in providing humanitarian assistance.[59] As a result of lobbying by feminists in New York, this resolution recalled the Security Council's earlier Resolution 1325 on Women, Peace and Security[60] in its preamble, in the context of encouraging the establishment of a 'representative' Iraqi government. Resolution 1325 had been adopted in 2000, as the end result of a concerted feminist campaign to have the Security Council take seriously the contributions that women can make to peace, in addition to addressing the many ways that women are harmed in armed conflict and its aftermath.[61]

The invocation of Resolution 1325 in the Security Council's resolution on Iraq implicated WILPF in the legitimation of the Iraqi occupation, compromising WILPF's long-standing anti-militarism in much the same way as the decision by Women Waging Peace to change its name. Further, as Sheri Gibbings points out, the advocacy of the NGOs also assumed that Iraqi women, who had suffered for many years under the Security Council's sanctions regime, would welcome the Council's endorsement of their participation in reconstruction.[62] On the surface, at least, the feminist strategy to promote gender mainstreaming in Iraq's reconstruction was infected by the selective fact-telling and counter-analytical thinking of crisis governance. Yet I find it hard to justify why WILPF should have passed up the chance to make Resolution 1325 available to Iraqi women to leverage their participation in post-conflict Iraqi politics, if they wished to use it. Rather, the issue is how best to facilitate Iraqi women's taking up of these opportunities in a way that does not compromise them. My view is that the potential of the strategy is crucially linked to feminist advocates remaining critical of the intervention, and the legal developments it is said to have crystallised, by actively contesting the implication that this strategy can be equated with

---

[58] S Gibbings, *Governing Women, Governing Security: Governmentality, Gender Mainstreaming and Women's Activism at the UN* (2004) Unpublished thesis, Graduate Programme in Social Anthropology, Toronto, York University, 84–85.

[59] Security Council Resolution 1483, UN Doc S/RES/1483 (22 May 2003).

[60] Security Council Resolution 1325, 'Women, Peace and Security', UN Doc S/RES/1325 (31 October 2000).

[61] D Otto, 'A Sign of "Weakness"? Disrupting Gender Certainties in the Implementation of Security Council Resolution 1325' (2006) 13 *Michigan Journal of Gender and Law* 113.

[62] Gibbings, above n 59, 87–88.

feminist endorsement of the invasion and occupation, or feminist support for the earlier sanctions regime. That is, short term expediencies will not translate into longer term change without the benefit of critical analysis, which necessitates maintaining a clear distinction between feminism and crisis governance.

It is clear that the architects of contemporary crisis governance have realised the traction of at least some feminist issues in helping to legitimate the techniques of emergency. When Paula Dobriansky, US Under Secretary of State for Global Affairs, addressed Iraqi women participating in a day of workshops in July 2003, she conveyed a 'personal message' from President Bush commending them on their commitment to creating a free and inclusive Iraq.[63] A similar appeal to women as supporters of 'freedom' was repeated later in Afghanistan, when a statement from the US State Department heralded women as the 'new democracy leaders'.[64] These new representations of women in a crisis, as formal actors with decision-making power, have an uncanny resonance with the concept of 'inclusive security' which has replaced the idea of Women Waging Peace, although they stand in some tension with the domesticating images of women that usually accompany crisis, which I referred to earlier. The idea that women have a important political contribution to make to conflict resolution and post-conflict reconstruction prompted the feminist campaign that led the Security Council to adopt Resolution 1325.[65] As someone who supported this campaign, which aimed to shift the emphasis from women's vulnerability to their agency, I have been astounded at the ease with which women's participation has come to serve as the Trojan horse of crisis governance.

Can the selective mapping of feminist ideas, such as the importance of women's political participation, onto the new geographies of crisis management and law-making really create new opportunities for feminist change? The experiences of women in Afghanistan and Iraq, since the military interventions,[66] suggest that they may not and that the sponsor of feminist ideas matters a great deal. Despite some formal recognition of

---

[63] Ibid 91. The workshop, initiated by the US, entitled 'The Voice of Women in Iraq' was held in Baghdad on 9 July 2003. Gibbings cites the Permanent Mission of the United States to the United Nations, 'Statement by Ambassador John D Negroponte, United States Representative to the United Nations, Remarks to the United Nations Security Council, New York, 29 October 2003'.

[64] J Brinkley and C Gall, 'Afghans Delay Vote a 3rd Time: Assembly Elections Moved to September', *The International Herald Tribune*, 18 March 2005, 5.

[65] Otto, above n 62; H Charlesworth, 'Are Women More Peaceful?' (2008) 16 *Feminist Legal Studies* 347. See also Charlesworth, above, this collection.

[66] I am not suggesting that feminist ideas were absent in Afghanistan or Iraq, but I am tracing the formal and conscious deployment of feminist ideas by the US and its allies, and the UN, to support the urgency and the legitimacy of these interventions.

women's equality and rights in both new constitutions,[67] in many parts of both countries women's position may even have worsened. Two years after the launch of President Bush's fight for women's rights in Afghanistan, a UNIFEM study confirmed that Afghan women were feeling 'neither secure nor safe'.[68] In 2003, Human Rights Watch reported that violence against women in Afghanistan seemed to be increasing, perpetrated not only by family members, but also by local police and militias.[69] In March 2004, the *New York Times* reported that increasing numbers of young women were committing suicide to escape forced marriages and domestic violence.[70] And in September 2008, a resurgent Taliban launched a wave of deadly attacks on women across the country, apparently targeting those who have assumed public roles.[71] The 'new democracy leaders' appear to have been abandoned by their sponsors.

In Iraq, soon after Dobriansky's praise for women's leadership in the cause of freedom, Noeleen Heyzer, the executive director of UNIFEM, was warning that women were 'worse off' than before the US invasion.[72] In September 2006, following a month-long investigation, *The Observer* described Iraqi women as the 'hidden victims' of the conflict which had erupted in the wake of the US occupation.[73] The investigation found that women had increasingly become the targets of rape, abduction and murder simply because they work, they wear the 'wrong' clothing, they participate in public life, they have the 'wrong' religious affiliation, or because of the 'wider permissive brutalization of women's lives'.[74] The much feted American 'surge' in troop numbers in early 2008, which relied heavily on recruiting and empowering the local militias of sheiks and tribal leaders, was declared a success in military terms, but led to additional restrictions being placed on women in the name of 'Islam' and a further rise in violence

---

[67] Constitution of Afghanistan (2004), art 22, declares that 'the citizens of Afghanistan—whether man or woman—have equal rights and duties before the law'; Constitution of Iraq (2005), art 14, states that 'Iraqis are equal before the law without discrimination based on gender, race, ethnicity, origin, color, religion, creed, belief or opinion, or economic and social status'.

[68] E Rehn and EJ Sirleaf, *Women, War and Peace: The Independent Experts' Assessment on the Impact of Armed Conflict on Women and Women's Role in Peace-Building* (G Jacobs ed, New York, UN Development Fund for Women, 2002) 2.

[69] Human Rights Watch, 'Killing You is a Very Easy Thing for Us': Human Rights Abuses in Southeast Afghanistan, July 2003, 24–30.

[70] C Gall, 'For more Afghan women, immolation is escape', *New York Times*, 8 March 2004.

[71] JF Burns, 'Taliban assassinates high-profile woman police officer', *International Herald Tribune*, 28 September 2008.

[72] S Pleming, 'Iraqi women no better off, UN official says', Common Dreams News Centre, 24 September 2003, www.commondreams.org/cgi-bin/print.cgi?file=/headlines03/0924-03.htm (visited 29 May 2009).

[73] P Beaumont, 'Hidden victims of a brutal conflict: Iraq's women', *The Observer*, 8 October 2006.

[74] Ibid.

directed at women in the family and in public spaces.[75] As in Afghanistan, the co-option of feminist ideas by crisis governance in Iraq has not opened opportunities for feminist political engagement or led to positive change in women's everyday lives. In fact, as soon as their fleeting instrumental value was exhausted, they were discarded.

One reason that the feminist ideas, which arrived with the international interventions, failed to lead to substantive change for women is that there was little effort to engage with Iraqi and Afghan women, other than those in the diaspora. Yet in both countries, there was an extended history of women's resistance to oppressive policies and practises. Many women, like those involved with the Revolutionary Association of the Women of Afghanistan (RAWA),[76] had risked their lives, in their efforts to promote women's equality. As Sari Kouvo argues in this collection, the failure to engage with local women's groups in Afghanistan compounded the lack of understanding of the complexities that different cultures, religions, levels of poverty and education bring to discrimination experienced by Afghan women, which helped to ensure that the rhetoric of women's participation and gender mainstreaming had no effects beyond symbolically legitimating the occupation.[77] In both countries local feminists continue to face threats to their lives and social ostracism, despite the lip-service of the occupiers, their own governments, the UN, and international feminist NGOs.

While it is not surprising to find that feminism as a tool of crisis governance, rather than as a grass roots political movement, does not lead to concrete improvement in the status of women, the question remains whether feminist ideas, even when they are conveyed by the architects of crisis governance, might yet provide footholds for feminist change. Intuitively, it seems preferable to have a place on the map of possibilities, rather than to disappear altogether in the selective fact-telling and historical simplifications of the politics of inevitability. But, as the examples of Afghanistan and Iraq show, it is not easy for local feminists to translate instrumental endorsement of feminist ideas into opportunities that can serve their local struggles for emancipation; to breathe 'new life' into the promotion of women's political participation and gender mainstreaming in order to claim them as their own, as African Americans did with civil rights.

If the *quid pro quo* for the US administration's professed commitment to the promotion of women's rights in Afghanistan and Iraq was the silencing of feminist critics of its larger agenda, then this ensured that any emancipatory

---

[75] S Spring and L Kaplow, 'Sacrificed to the surge: Tribal fighters have cut down Iraq's violence. But they're subjecting women to often-medieval mores', *Newsweek*, 14 April 2008.

[76] Revolutionary Association of the Women of Afghanistan (RAWA) www.rawa.org/index.php (visited 29 May 2010).

[77] See Kouvo, below, this collection.

potential was 'effectively captured by the right',[78] well before those feminist ideas were able to link with and become useful to Afghan and Iraqi women. However, the capture of ideas can never be complete because of their continual reconstitution in language and practices. In order to exploit these discursive and practical opportunities, it is important that feminists maintain a distinction between feminist ideas and the vocabulary of crisis governance. One way to do this is to build strong links with local feminists and support the advancement of the issues they identify as important, against the grain of the international blue-print of crisis governmentality. Another way to remain at arms length from hegemonic power is to ensure that feminist critique of the larger agenda continues to be heard, in coalition with other critical voices, outside the institutions of government, in the political domain. This will enable more 'pragmatic' assessments of the opportunities for using international law to challenge gendered actualities,[79] and help to avoid the silencing of critique as a condition precedent. It is necessary to re-situate the short term crisis capture of feminist ideas in the broader geographies of complex histories and multiple struggles against empire and domination.

WHEN FEMINISTS UTILISE THE LANGUAGE OF CRISIS

Another way that feminist ideas and crisis thinking interact is when feminists engage in 'crisis talk' themselves in the hope of eliciting serious responses to some of the pressing problems that women face. Indeed, a great deal of feminist legal scholarship and activism has been concerned with recasting everyday sexual violence as a crisis that must be addressed as a priority.[80] In this way, adopting the language of crisis can be a strategy of desperation aimed at drawing attention to the everyday brutalities suffered by far too many women, hoping to propel them onto the official maps of international law and politics. The call by feminists, long before 9/11, for forceful intervention in Afghanistan to protect women from the cruelty of the Taliban, was one such attempt which (thankfully) failed.[81]

Feminist utilisation of the language of crisis has enjoyed some success in extracting international commitments to eliminate sexual abuse during armed conflict and sexual exploitation in post-conflict peace-keeping.

---

[78] K Engle, 'Liberal Internationalism, Feminism, and the Suppression of Critique: Contemporary Approaches to Global Order in the United States' (2005) 46 *Harvard International Law Journal* 427, 439.

[79] D Kennedy, 'The International Human Rights Movement: Part of the Problem?' (2002) 15 *Harvard Human Rights Journal* 101.

[80] C Bunch, 'Women's Rights as Human Rights: Toward a Re-vision of Human Rights' (1990) 12 *Human Rights Quarterly* 486–98.

[81] See above n 54.

However, in both cases, consistent with Agamben's analysis, the invocation of crisis has precipitated an 'explosion of law'. These explosions have dramatically increased the number of sexual crimes explicitly recognised by international criminal law,[82] and resulted in a prohibition of sex that extends to (almost) all forms of consensual sexual conduct in peace support operations.[83] These 'successes' can be explained by feminist reliance on 'sexual negativity', which treats human sexuality as a dangerous force that needs to be tightly controlled by legal and cultural norms,[84] a view that resonates strongly with conservative views about sexuality. The resulting laws and codes of conduct build on a long history of 'sexual panics' providing the pretext for states to extend their power to regulate erotic behaviour,[85] which is a cautionary reminder of the role that sexuality has played in the genealogy of crisis governance. Like other emergency laws, these developments may be symbolically reassuring in the short term, but they suffer from vague and over-inclusive definitions which catch many forms of consensual sex in the net of criminalisation and prohibition.[86] They compromise human rights protections associated with privacy and sexual self-determination, recalibrating the balance between human rights and state power in favour of a more repressive state. Like the vague and over-inclusive definitions of 'terrorism' employed in the cause of counter-terrorism, these new laws and policies create a dangerously vast space in which a wide range of official interventions can be legitimated in the name of feminism.

Another example of feminist invocation of crisis is Catherine MacKinnon's suggestion that the international response to the crisis of 9/11 presents a model for possible emulation by feminists in their efforts to have men's

---

[82] K Askin, 'Reflection on Some of the Most Significant Achievements of the ICTY' (2003) 37 *New England Law Review* 903; V Oosterveld, 'Sexual Slavery and the International Criminal Court: Advancing International Law' (2004) 25 *Michigan Journal of International Law* 605.

[83] Secretary-General's Bulletin, *Special measures for protection from sexual exploitation and abuse*, ST/SGB/2003/13, 9 October 2003. See further, D Otto, 'Making sense of zero tolerance policies in peacekeeping sexual economies' in V Munro and CF Stychin (eds), *Sexuality and the Law: Feminist Engagements* (Oxford/Cambridge, Routledge-Cavendish, 2007) 259–82.

[84] G Rubin, 'Thinking Sex: Notes for a Radical theory of the Politics of Sexuality' in CS Vance (ed), *Pleasure and Danger: Exploring Female Sexuality* (Boston, Routledge & Kegan Paul, 1984) 267, 278. Rubin uses the term 'sexual negativity' to describe the prevalence of the idea that sex is a 'dangerous, destructive, negative force', unless performed pursuant to a narrow set of socially approved 'excuses' like 'marriage, reproduction, and love'.

[85] KM Franke, 'Sexual Tensions of Post-Empire' (2004) *Columbia Law School, Public Law and Legal Theory Working Paper Group*, paper number 04-62.

[86] J Halley, 'Rape in Berlin: Reconsidering the Criminalization of Rape in the International Law of Armed Conflict' (2008) 9 *Melbourne Journal of International Law* 78; D Otto, 'The Sexual Tensions of UN Peace Support Operations: A plea for "sexual positivity"' (2007) XVIII *Finnish Yearbook of International Law* 33.

violence against women outlawed as a 'war' on women.[87] MacKinnon draws parallels between international terrorism and the war on women to make her point—she argues that they both involve premeditated violence (which can be seen in the war on women in gang rapes, stalking and sex trafficking for example), which is perpetrated by non-state actors (men), against 'innocent' civilians (women), for ideological or political reasons (sexual violence being the practice of the politics of misogyny), and they both result in large victim numbers.[88] Yet, 'what will it take', MacKinnon asks, 'for violence against women ... to receive a response in the structure and practise of international law anything approximate to the level of focus and determination inspired by the September 11th attacks?'[89]

While MacKinnon's comparison has some intuitive attractiveness, it is important to work against the emotional response that the idea of a 'war on women' engenders precisely because it contains a kernel of truth, because her proposal relies on the problematic thinking that is characteristic of crisis governance. First, she reads 'the facts' of the war on women through a narrow and totalising prism, as a conflict fought by 'men' against 'women', which leaves no room for contextualisation in history, culture, past feminist campaigns, or present specific realities. Secondly, analytical thinking is foreclosed by MacKinnon's version of 'us' and 'them'—as if all men are perpetrators and all women are their victims, which relies on misleading sexual stereotypes and seems to leave no room for pleasurable sex between women and men. We also know that gendered violence is commonly accepted as a normal everyday occurrence, which will not be eradicated by armed intervention or by criminalising its most sensational forms. Thirdly, MacKinnon's singular focus on the gendered nature of violence against women ignores intersecting systems of inequality, like those of culture, religion and levels of poverty and education, as in Afghanistan, leaving these aspects of gendered violence to 'the politics of inevitability'. Her analysis treats women's struggle for liberation as if it was disconnected from other struggles against disadvantage and oppression.

The truncated lens of MacKinnon's crisis analogy of a 'war' on women suggests military solutions, yet we know that armed interventions, and even Security Council sanctions, inevitably make the lives of the majority of women significantly worse, as has been demonstrated again in Afghanistan and Iraq. Although MacKinnon attempts to distance herself from this problem by claiming that she is not necessarily arguing that the war on terror

---

[87] CA MacKinnon, 'Women's September 11th: Rethinking the International Law of Conflict' (2006) 47 *Harvard International Law Journal* 1, 3. MacKinnon goes on to argue that violence against women is also analogous to a crime against humanity and even genocide 13–14.

[88] Ibid 11–12.

[89] Ibid 19.

is the 'right model' for opposing violence against women,[90] she does not offer an alternative. Employing the language of crisis, in efforts to have a problem taken more seriously, securitises the issue, prioritising militarism over progressive social change and law over politics, and making it possible for law to extend its empire deeper into the everyday lives of women and men, reducing the space for 'life itself'.

Even at my most optimistic, I find it hard to see how feminist invocation of crisis could further the goals of feminism. The discourse of crisis requires the kind of thinking that is antithetical to an emancipatory agenda. Women's inequality, like most issues of international peace and security, is a structural problem that is not amenable to a quick-fix. As feminists, we need to resist the seductions of the language of crisis by refusing to sacrifice nuanced political and legal thinking. Feminist counter-crisis thinking is called for, which embraces rich and complex facts, promotes critical analysis, resists the politics of inevitability, and refuses the false promises of 'inclusive security' and its instrumental embrace of women's rights.

TOWARDS RE-MAPPING EMERGENCIES

To contest the maps and techniques of crisis governance, it is necessary to resist the impoverished thinking that is legitimated by crisis, and question the inevitability of the 'rules' that emerge from the crucible of urgency, by reviving international politics. What moments of official crisis often do is fleetingly expose the vastness of the systemic discrimination, poverty and despair that is maintained and normalised by the international order. The crisis of 9/11, for example, brought dramatic visibility to the widespread dissatisfaction with the dominance of American financial and political power, and revealed the vast space this has created for dissatisfaction to convert into deadly hatred and fundamentalisms. This created an important opportunity for feminists to resist the polarising politics of 'us' and 'them'. As Faludi observed, there was a moment for moral leadership, which would 'challenge Americans to think constructively about [their] place in the world, to redefine civic commitment and public responsibility'.[91] This brief moment of emancipatory opportunity soon passed as talk of exceptionality and crisis quickly camouflaged the continuities of the laws and practices which have served the (super)power of America and its allies at the expense of many inside as well as outside the West. What is at stake at such a moment is that the inequalities which are briefly exposed will remain visible and come to be identified for what they are—the product of the 'normal' operation of international law and politics. Maintaining the visibility of systemic inequalities

---

[90] Ibid 28.
[91] Faludi, above n 13, 3.

would not allow the problem to be cast as a crisis, but locate it instead in the imperial and gendered everyday actualities of the structures and practices of international law and politics.

Once the initial moment of visibility has passed, and emergency thinking has come to dominate public opinion and legal response, what then could feminists hope to achieve from within the discipline of international law? I have some sympathy for Mieville's view that looking to the existing law as a means of progressive change undermines feminist criticism of the law as fundamentally gendered—especially at times of crisis. However, unlike Mieville, I do not think that international law's capture or co-option of otherwise revolutionary ideas is ever total. Like Mieville's fantasy city of Un Lun Dun, which is the flip-side of the city of London we are familiar with, where many of London's unwanted people (like bus conductors), lost umbrellas, libraries, broken and discarded objects, and its smog, end up hidden from view,[92] international law also has parallel universes, where other ways of thinking about the law and its possibilities are possible. One unlikely place that I experience this shadow world is in the corridors and bars of the annual meeting of the American Society of International Law, where feminists, and others who engage critically with international law, seek each other out.

Feminist tenacity, now spanning decades, has led to international law's repeated formal commitment to realising the equality of women, which gives the law an 'irresolution' that enables it to be 'both appropriated to imperial ends and used as a force for liberation', as Sundhya Pahuja argues with reference to the 'postcoloniality' in international law.[93] Following Pahuja's argument, the vacillation in international law between the inevitability of women's secondary status and their emancipation through the discourse of equality and non-discrimination, creates a dynamic (or parallel universe) which might be called its 'post-patriarchalism'. This is not to suggest that law may not be 'part of the problem', or to claim that law is the optimum location from which to pursue a feminist agenda for change. It is also not to underestimate the difficulties of promoting emancipatory readings and applications of the texts of international law. But it is to say that the markings that have been left by feminist engagement with international law remain, including the markings of Resolution 1325 in Iraq, the increased representation of women in Afghanistan's legislature and the redefinition of international crimes to specifically include sexual violence. These traces of earlier feminist efforts provide bearings from which further strategies for change can be mapped—whether it is in the corridors of international law conferences or behind the walls of women's homes in Kabul.

---

[92] C Mieville, *Un Lun Dun*, 2nd edn (London, Pan Macmillan, 2008).
[93] S Pahuja, 'The Postcoloniality of International Law' (2005) 46 *Harvard International Law Journal* 459, 460.

Drawing further on Mieville's story of Un Lun Dun, what we need is 'un-crisis' thinking—the flip side of crisis logic—if we are to find creative solutions to international problems using international law. Like the 'un gun' (which, needless to say, does not use typical ammunition) that Mieville creates to fight the 'evil' Smog, which creeps into the brains of UnLunDuners and has addictive and malicious powers (a little like crisis thinking), un-crisis thinking frees the imagination from the strictures of crisis. It liberates the kind of thinking that is necessary to ensure that we are not seduced by the institutional embrace of some feminist ideas or that we devalue the feminist bearings already mapped onto the law. The traces of earlier feminist struggles provide vantage points from which it is possible to imagine, and struggle towards, new and better worlds.

Feminist normative projects are significantly enhanced by an awareness of the politics of the law and the shortcomings of the institutions they seek to engage for the benefit of women, without which there is a high risk of treating international law as if it were 'saviour and humanitarian'.[94] In the context of Afghanistan, a more critically informed perspective may have led feminists to expose the cynicism of the US administration's engagement with women's rights, rather than applauding it. If feminism is limited to the singular lens of 'carrying a brief for women',[95] it is very vulnerable to co-option by crisis governance, whether the brief is to increase women's participation in decision-making or to criminalise rape as a war crime. The new quotas for women in the Afghanistan legislature, for example, do not alone challenge the gendered practices associated with religion and culture, so it remains impossible for legislators to pursue an agenda that would secure the safety and political participation of all Afghan women.[96] In the context of the anti-Islamic fervour that helped to drive the military occupations of Afghanistan and Iraq, there was an opportunity for feminists to challenge (rather than reinforce) orientalist mythologies about veiled women needing rescue by the West from the barbaric traditions of Islam.[97] Similarly, in responding to inter-ethnic war-time sexual violence in the Balkans, the lack of an intersectional analysis meant that feminists generally failed to challenge the biological determinism of the assumption that the ethnicity of a child is determined by the biological father, as Karen Engle

---

[94] A Orford, *Reading Humanitarian Intervention: Human Rights and the Use of Force in International Law* (Cambridge, Cambridge University Press, 2003) 188.

[95] J Halley, *Split Decisions: How and Why to Take a Break from Feminism* (Princeton, Princeton University Press, 2006); D Otto, 'The Gastronomics of TWAIL's Feminist Flavourings: some lunch-time offerings' (2007) 9 *International Community Law Review* 345. See also Charlesworth, above, this collection.

[96] See, Kouvo, below, this collection.

[97] Ratna Kapur, 'Unveiling Women's Rights in the War on Terrorism' (2002) 9 *Duke Journal of Gender, Law and Policy* 211.

has argued.[98] Feminists need to be considerably more sceptical about the embrace of feminist ideas by crisis, searching for ways in which those ideas can be reclaimed for feminist purposes, while at the same time emphasising the continuing complicity of law in women's inequality and the long term structural nature of the struggle for change.

It is also important to remember that legal change, by itself, is never enough. Essential to exploiting the possibilities of international law's post-patriarchal dynamic is the relationship between politics (life) and law. As Klein concludes, the shock of disaster does wear off—crises are temporary, whether real or imagined. She finds hope in the emerging peoples movements of Latin America who, following the shock therapy of disaster capitalism, are roundly rejecting the idea of the unfettered free market and its false promise of trickle down prosperity, building, instead, visions and practices of democratic socialism from the grass roots up.[99] Political engagement will keep feminist attention focused on the deeply entrenched structures of inequality and help to refuse the politics of inevitability. A focus on structural inequalities will also expose the dangers of inordinate reliance on the Security Council and crisis law reform to promote feminist change; a reliance that has been fostered by crisis governance. Un-crisis thinking requires supporting the activism of women outside the mainstream institutions of law and politics as well as carving out spaces on the inside. The institutionalisation of feminist ideas will always extract a price of compromise and dilution, even more so in a crisis; but the damage to long term feminist goals can be mitigated by outside movements of women, in coalition with others, demanding that emergencies be remapped through a feminist lens. Politics, in all its richness and life-sustaining complexity, must be part of every feminist strategy in law.

---

[98] Engle, above n 80.
[99] Klein, above n 35, 443–66. See also Thomas, below, this collection.

6

Road Blocks, Blind Spots, Speed Bumps: A Feminist Look at the Post-9/11 Landscape for NGOs

JULIE A MERTUS

INTRODUCTION

ARE THE 1990s really that far away? In the early and mid-1990s, non-governmental organisations (NGOs) in all their wonderful, colourful, confusing diversity appeared to be well suited for the role of international norm provocateur—or, if you prefer, norm entrepreneur. Emerging from the doldrums of the static 1980s, often with considerable domestic advocacy experience in hand, NGO advocates were ready and willing to remind states of their international political agenda. Although differing from NGO to NGO, these efforts inherently involved a demand for greater dispersion of power—away from the state and down to them. Feminists and women's rights advocates[1] were among the most eager—and dare I say, capable—participants. The well-educated women, fluent in United Nations (UN) English and dressed in diplomatic attire (and largely from North America and Continental Europe), were the first to benefit from the NGO explosion, but it would be a mistake to underestimate the importance of this period for other women who found ways to use it for their own empowerment. Women activists from all corners of the world emerged into a big tent of NGO activism that appeared able to accommodate a wide range of issues and advocacy tactics, that is, from angry street theatre reminders of the impact of violence against women to polite, succinctly worded proposals for UN declarations asserting human rights and demanding state action for ameliorating human wrongs.

---

[1] I use the terms 'feminist advocate' and 'women's rights advocates' separately to emphasise that not all women's rights advocates are feminists.

The rapid succession of world human rights meetings—in Nairobi,[2] Vienna,[3] Cairo[4] and Beijing[5]—showcased NGO organising talent and brought the NGO challenge to state power to the fore. If new norms of international law were to emerge from these meetings, it clearly would not be without heavy NGO influence. To take but one illustration, the provisions in the government document emerging from the 1993 UN Conference on Human Rights (the Vienna Declaration and Platform for Action)[6] calling for more attention to the issue of violence against women did not suddenly emerge from the minds of diplomats and magically flow from their pens. Rather, the unprecedented attention devoted to violence against women was the product of years of dedicated NGO advocacy at the domestic level, creative networking at international stages, wide-ranging leadership training institutes, revealing investigative reports, and ongoing educational campaigns.[7]

The 1990s were heady times for women's rights advocates from the 'North' in particular, who attracted the attention of donors and networked successfully with women of the 'South'.[8] Together, they declared a global campaign directed at improving the status of women everywhere, based on the simple slogan 'Women's rights are human rights'.[9] With each well-publicised success, from the mere act of 'getting women on the agenda' at the UN Human Rights Conference in Vienna[10] to the post-Vienna creation of a highly visible Special Rapporteur on Violence Against Women,[11] they grew con-

---

[2] Report of the World Conference to Review and Appraise the Achievements of the United Nations Decade for Women: Equality, Development and Peace, World Conference, 15–26 July 1985, Nairobi, The Nairobi Forward-Looking Strategies for the Advancement of Women, 10, UN Doc A/CONF.116/28/Rev.1 (1986), www.un.org/womenwatch/confer/nfls/Nairobi1985report.txt (viewed 29 May 2010).

[3] World Conference on Human Rights, *Vienna Declaration and Programme of Action*, 25 June 1993, para 38, UN Doc A/CONF. 157/23, www.unhchr.ch/huridocda/huridoca.nsf/7dec5261b3c5d5dac12565cc0037502c?OpenNavigator (viewed 29 May 2010).

[4] International Conference on Population and Development, 5–13 September 1994, Cairo, *Programme of Action of the International Conference on Population and Development*, 4.24, UN Doc A/CONF.171/13 (18 October 1994), www.iisd.ca/cairo.html (viewed 29 May 2010).

[5] Beijing Declaration and Platform for Action 15, 17, 30, UN Doc A/CONF.177/20, (17 October 1995), www.un.org/womenwatch/daw/beijing/platform/declar.htm (viewed 29 May 2010).

[6] Vienna Declaration and Programme of Action, above n 3, para 38.

[7] See J Mertus and P Goldberg, 'A Perspective on Women and International Human Rights after the Vienna Declaration' (1994) 26 *New York University Journal of International Law and Politics* 201, www.law-lib.utoronto.ca/Diana/fulltext/mert.htm (viewed 29 May 2010).

[8] Center for Women's Global Leadership documents on file with author. For a discussion about how the international campaign for women's rights plays out in a national context, see discussion on Afghanistan in Kouvo, below, this collection; and in addition, in relation to the broader, state-building project of international law, see Charlesworth, above, this collection.

[9] Buttons, stickers, fliers and other artifacts on file with author.

[10] Vienna Declaration and Programme of Action, above n 3, Part I, para 18.

[11] UN Human Rights Council, Report of the Special Rapporteur on Violence against Women, Its Causes and Consequences, Yakin Ertürk: indicators on violence against women and State response, 29 January 2008, A/HRC/7/6, www.unhcr.org/refworld/docid/47cd6c442.htm (viewed 29 May 2010).

fident about their expanding role in standard setting and implementation of international norms.[12] Certainly, states would remain the most important element in the Westphalian system, but women human rights advocacy NGOs would grow in prominence, wisely charting a path between resistance to and assimilation in international structures. As donor dollars reached all-time highs, advocates appeared to be limited only by their own imaginations.

The events of September 11th, 2001 had a direct and immediate impact on advocacy NGOs as the world's attention turned almost exclusively to countering terrorism. Overnight, the world became carved into two universes: of enemy terrorists and allied counter-terrorists.[13] Suddenly, advocacy NGOs concerned with issues not framed as 'security matters' appeared archaic and irrelevant. The tense socio-political landscape created an obstacle course to meaningful participation by non-state actors, governed by new rules of the road that prevent many advocates from even starting their journey and that challenge advocates with blind spots (where issues are overlooked) and speed bumps (where NGO progress is slowed down). Though the experience of international human rights NGOs differs in some respects from that of American-based NGOs, they too face many of the same challenges in the post-9/11 world. In addition, many NGOs swept up in the push for security have recently found renewed confidence to push back against the trade-off of rights for security. Only by persisting in confronting these obstacles can non-state actors continue to impact the identification, interpretation and application of international human rights norms. This chapter outlines each obstacle in turn, with a specific interest in the work of feminists and women's rights advocates based in the United States (US).

RULES OF THE ROAD

The main 'rule of the road' governing modern international law is the equality of states. The UN Charter in Article 2(1) proclaims that it is 'based on the principle of the sovereign equality of all its Members'. Before 9/11, a discernable gap existed between this rhetoric and the reality. States were equal, but some states were more equal than others. Since 9/11, the equality of states remains the declared rule of the road, but the principle actually

---

[12] The 1993 World Conference on Human Rights is said to have set a precedent in mainstreaming by including women's rights in the main body of its final documents. See K Tomasevski, 'Women's Rights' in J Symonides (ed), *Human Rights: Concepts and Standards* (Aldershot, Dartmouth Ashgate, 2000) 249, 250.

[13] For an interesting discussion of this phenomena, see W Brown, *Regulating Aversion: Tolerance and Identity in the Age of Identity and Empire* (Princeton, Princeton University Press, 2006).

guiding behaviour has shifted closer and closer to what has been termed 'hegemonic international law' (HIL),[14] that is international law made and enforced in the interests of the most powerful states, often at the expense of all other states.

Hegemons are easiest to critique when they act as unabashed playground bullies, flexing their military muscle and dangling economic prizes, as incentives for other states to follow rules that the hegemon would never itself observe.[15] And, indeed, advocacy NGOs have a strong record of monitoring and reporting on this kind of conduct. However, successful hegemons are rarely self-proclaimed law-breakers.[16] Rather, they defiantly insist that their behaviour is well within the boundaries of law. This tactic works, as Chris Borgen reminds us, because 'hegemony is not only about physical power, it is about the control of ideas, of norms. It is not just about domination ... but it is about *legitimate* domination'.[17] Once operating in the realm of the legitimate, states become less susceptible to criticism.[18] Hegemonic states thus can be defined in positive terms as being supported by 'universal norms, institutions, and mechanisms which lay down general rules of behaviour for states and for those forces of civil society that act across national boundaries'.[19] To the extent that global HIL exists, it springs not just from any bad state behaviour, but rather 'from the privileged position accorded to the hegemon under the existing rules and institutions of international law'.[20]

The negative implications of hegemonic HIL are nonetheless substantial. Hegemonic states operate unilaterally, in their own self-interest, frustrating the equal application of international norms and thwarting many potential forms of dispute settlement.[21] As Jose Alvarez explains:

> HIL jettisons or severely undervalues the formal and de facto equality of states, replacing pacts between equals grounded in reciprocity, with patron-client relationships in which clients pledge loyalty to the hegemon in exchange for security or economic sustenance. The hegemon promotes, by word and deed, new rules of

---

[14] DF Vagts, 'Hegemonic International Law' (2001) 95 *American Journal of International Law* 843.

[15] GJ Ikenberry and CA Kupchan, 'Socialization and Hegemonic Power' (1990) 44 *International Organization* 283, 285.

[16] But see JR Bolton, 'Is There Really "Law" in International Affairs?' (2000) 10 *Transnational Law and Contemporary Problems* 48 (suggesting that we 'should be unashamed, unapologetic, uncompromising American constitutional hegemonists').

[17] CJ Borgen, 'Whose Public? Whose Order? Imperium, Region and Normative Friction' (2007) 32 *Yale Journal of International Law* 337 .

[18] Vagts, above n 14.

[19] Ikenberry and Kupchan, above n 15, 288.

[20] J Alvarez, 'Hegemonic International Law Revisited' (2003) 97 *American Journal of International Law* 873.

[21] See, eg, JA Mertus, *Bait and Switch: Human Rights and US Foreign Policy*, 2nd edn (New York, Routledge, 2008).

law, both treaty based and customary. It is generally averse to limiting its scope of action via treaty; avoids being constrained by those treaties to which it has adhered; and disregards, when inconvenient, customary international law, confident that its breach will be hailed as a new rule. Substantively, HIL is characterized by indeterminate rules—whose vagueness benefits primarily (if not solely) the hegemon—recurrent projections of military force, and interventions in the internal affairs of other nations.[22]

Hegemons use their power to manipulate and control to their own advantage the decisional processes of the international legal system, including, for example, the UN Security Council.[23] The failure of states to insist on a transparent and legitimate process for HIL development thus narrows the space for NGO influence.

Despite its decidedly more NGO-friendly attitude and its claimed embrace of transparency, the Obama administration has continued to rely on American hegemony, albeit with a twist. As George Packer observes, 'Obama fits [the] mold of classic realism: wary of moral posturing, he analyzes the world country by country, calibrating America's interests accordingly, without trying to impose a single abstract doctrine everywhere.'[24] Rather than using trickery and moral superiority as the foundation of America's right to dominate, Obama relies instead on pragmatic, cautious stewardship: follow us (US) and through 'partnership' we will all benefit. Because the sources of the hegemon's strength are even more non-transparent and difficult to critique under this partnership model, advocacy NGOs have an even more difficult time monitoring the rules of the road.

BLIND SPOTS

The second way in which human rights NGOs have declined in influence in normative development post-9/11 pertains to the ongoing struggle over 'framing'. This refers to the attempt of government policymakers and advocacy NGOs (of all political persuasions) to create 'patterns of understanding' that influence the way problems are understood and addressed.[25] Frames call attention to an issue and refract it through a particular lens that suggests certain understandings and outcomes.[26]

---

[22] Alvarez, above n 20.

[23] HJ Richardson III, 'US Hegemony, Race, and Oil in Deciding United Nations Security Council Resolution 1444 on Iraq' (2003) 17 *Temple International and Comparative Law Journal* 27.

[24] George Packer, 'Rights and Wrongs' *The New Yorker*, 17 May 2010.

[25] MR Lissack, 'The Redefinition of Memes: Ascribing Meaning to an Empty Cliché' (2004) *Journal of Memetics—Evolutionary Models of Information Transmission*, www.cfpm.org/jom-emit/2004/vol8/lissack_mr.html (viewed 29 May 2010).

[26] K Sikkink, 'A Typology Of Relations Between Social Movements And International Institution' (2003) 97 *American Society of International Law Proceedings* 301.

Frames reinforce and emphasise some ideas while ignoring others. NGOs attempt to 'frame' normative ideas in a way that resonates with existing norms and with the interests of the target audience. Certain words are chosen in the framing process because of their cultural significance or their memorable and emotionally charged nature.[27] In the US, the inclusion or exclusion of the words championed by the Bush administration to explain counter-terrorism strategies—favourites such as 'freedom' and 'liberty'— and the exclusion of the use of 'human rights' carries significant influence in the process of frame-building.[28] The resulting frames become tools to mobilise support for a particular response and to persuade a target audience of the appropriateness of a proposed normative response.

The work of NGOs on framing issues thus serves to give causes a name and activists an identity. [29] Through effective framing, human rights activists, for example, create the image of 'human wrongs' and 'human rights' in the public's awareness and, subsequently, the identification of some governments as 'human rights promoters' and others as 'human rights violators', while demarcating individuals as victims and violators. Accordingly, over time, reference to human rights deepens and widens, becoming nearly automatic under many circumstances.[30] All aspects of decision-making are affected by this framing process: the problem-definition,[31] the formulation of options, the moral evaluation, and/or treatment recommendations.[32]

Framing has always been highly contested and deeply political, offering multiple and often conflicting ethical choices, appealing to competing collective identities and shifting alliances. Post 9/11, the struggle of groups and individuals to dominate human rights framings has become particularly intense. The Bush administration successfully defined 9/11 as a 'war' of good versus evil, innocent target versus culpable target. While all wars are scary, the 9/11 war is particularly terrifying as it pits honour and goodness against a crafty and illusive enemy, in an epic struggle that will claim the lives of many innocent non-combatants and, most likely, never be won.

To perpetuate the belief that Americans need a strong leader to save them from an apocalypse, President Bush used pessimistic language intended to fan panic and disable people from feeling they could solve their problems. Immediately after the 9/11 attacks, President Bush told the nation that 'Americans should not expect one battle, but a lengthy

[27] Ibid.

[28] P Norris et al (eds), *Framing Terrorism* (New York, Routledge, 2003).

[29] JT Checkel, 'International Institutions and Socialization in Europe: Introduction and Framework' (2005) 59 *International Organization* 801–26.

[30] MD Young and M Schafer, 'Is There Method in Our Madness? Ways of Assessing Cognition in International Relations' (1998) 42 *Mershon International Studies Review* 63–96, 64.

[31] JF Voss, 'On the Representation of Problems: An Information-Processing Approach to Foreign Policy Decision Making' in DA Sylvan and JF Voss (eds), *Problem Representation in Foreign Policy Decision Making* (Cambridge, Cambridge University Press, 1988).

[32] RN Entman, 'Framing: Toward Clarification of a Fractured Paradigm' (1993) 43 *Journal of Communication* 51–58, 52.

campaign, unlike any other we have ever seen ... . I ask you to live your lives, and hug your children. I know many citizens have fears tonight ... . Be calm and resolute, even in the face of a continuing threat'.[33] Other fear producing statements on terrorism have included such statements as: 'Some ask how urgent this danger [in Iraq] is to America and the world. The danger is already significant, and it only grows worse with time ... Iraq could decide on any given day to provide a biological or chemical weapon to a terrorist group'.[34]

Post 9/11, when the spotlight fell on the few women's advocacy NGOs, it was the groups that were already oriented toward security that took centre stage. These included those with substantial projects dedicated to Security Council Resolution 1325 (mandating inclusion of women in peace processes),[35] as well as those who just happened to already have 'security' in their mandate.[36] To catch up, many NGOs quickly attempted to reconstitute themselves, adjusting their identities, interests and expectations in line with the more urgent matters of a post-9/11 times. Their untidy re-configuring left feminist insistence on complexity and multiple truths behind,[37] a luxury for safer days.

Instead of challenging the security sector, some NGOs sought to join the security sector. The mission statement of the Initiative for Inclusive Security (formerly Women Waging Peace) now reads:

> The Initiative for Inclusive Security advocates for women as members and overseers of the security sector. Through research, advocacy, and training, Inclusive Security prepares women to assume greater roles and responsibilities in security institutions worldwide.[38]

The goals of the programme all assume the desirability of joining the security sector. The goals are stated in concrete terms as follows:

1. Increase the number and influence of women throughout the security sector.
2. Gather best practices and recommendations on outreach, recruitment, and training.

---

[33] GW Bush, 'President George W. Bush addressing a Joint Session of the US Congress, 20 September 2001'. www.usinfo.state.gov/journals/itgic/0902/ijge/ijge0902.htm (viewed 29 May 2010).

[34] GW Bush, 'Remarks at the Cincinnati Museum Center, 7 October 2002'. www.whitehouse.gov/news/releases/2002/10/20021007-8.html (viewed 29 May 2010).

[35] PeaceWomen website at www.peacewomen.org/1325inaction/index.html (viewed 29 May 2010).

[36] The main Women in International Security website is: www.wiis.georgetown.edu/ (viewed 29 May 2010).

[37] See H Charlesworth, 'Feminist Methods in International Law' (1999) 93 *American Journal of International Law* 379.

[38] The Initiative for Inclusive Security: www.huntalternatives.org/pages/7689_security_sector.cfm. Hunt Alternatives Fund (viewed 29 May 2010).

3. Train police, military officials, and civilians to increase women's inclusion in security.
4. Assist women in government and civil society to collaborate with security sector actors.[39]

This over-reliance on security has created blind spots for NGOs, which have not magically disappeared in the Obama administration.[40] These blind spots are not limited to US NGOs either. Resolution 1373 pressures international NGOs to divert time and resources toward ensuring the continued respect for human rights in the presence of anti-terrorism measures. In the immediate aftermath of the September 11th attacks, a group of more than 150 NGOs from each continent but Antarctica released 'A Joint Civil Society Statement on the Tragedy in the US,' in which they urged the US and its allies to exercise caution, asserting that 'a safer world for all can only be achieved by the extension of human rights and the rule of law'.[41] Another coalition of women's NGOs sent a letter to the General Assembly expressing concern over Resolution 1373 and the possibility for state abuse.[42] Though many of these international groups have not felt the need to join the security sector, they have, nonetheless, found, almost overnight, a number of human rights fires related to counter-terrorism demanding their efforts' attention. The NGOs that stay close to their original mandate and strategies risk being dismissed as out-of-touch and irrelevant. But those NGOs that comply with pressure to focus more on security face the possibility of losing their own unique identity, based on their own proven strategies, for their own self-identified constituencies.

To be sure, security is an important topic, but by focusing so heavily on security, NGOs risk missing other issues. Many of the NGO activities of the 1990s have gone by the wayside: networking and coalition-building rarely occurs outside a security topic; leadership programmes have become rare; feminist efforts to dismantle the public/private split are submerged and efforts to devote state attention to 'private sphere' issues such as domestic violence receive scant attention; and everything that could possibly be cast in terms of security receives that appellation: HIV/AIDS, refugee flows,

---

[39] Ibid.

[40] See, eg, Human Rights Watch, 'Counterterrorism and Human Rights: A Report Card on President Obama's First Year, 14 January 2010, www.hrw.org/en/news/2010/01/14/us-obama-s-first-year-record-counterterrorism-reform-mixed (viewed 29 May 2010).

[41] 'A Joint Civil Society Statement on the Tragedy in the United States'. Amnesty International. 21 September 2001. www.amnesty.org.ru/library/Index/ENGACT300212001?open&cof=ENG-2AM (viewed 29 May 2010).

[42] 'Open Letter from NGOs to the General Assembly Regarding Terrorism Debate'. Women Living Under Muslim Laws. 1–2 October 2008. www.wluml.org/english/actionsfulltxt.shtml?cmd%5B156%5D=i-156-3186 (viewed 24 March 2009).

poverty, early childhood education, etc. Close scrutiny of Ford Foundation Annual Reports, for example, provide evidence of this trend.[43]

For human rights advocates from the South, this trend appeared as compliance with the bulldozer—you're-with-us-or-against-us—approach of the Bush administration and its allies to 'counter-terrorism'. The polarising politics made North/South collaboration exceedingly difficult. While some established networks of NGOs crumbled, others teetered awkwardly between strategies for resistance and the pressure for compliance, drastically limiting their ability to influence policy.[44]

SPEED BUMPS

All non-profits in the US today face great obstacles in navigating the US regulatory bureaucracy. As one comprehensive study on philanthropy post 9/11 concluded, 'despite a complete lack of hard evidence that nonprofits are the source of any systematic or widespread violations of law or connections with terrorism, the entire sector has been saddled with major restrictions'.[45] Human rights organisations are no exception. They, like all nonprofit organisations, face enhanced scrutiny, more burdensome restrictions and more intrusive regulations. These new measures act both as 'speed bumps' to slow down their effective human rights campaigns and, at least in some cases, as 'road blocks' that restrict certain actions altogether.

The kinds of obstacles facing human rights NGOs in the US today can be classified in five categories:

1. Prohibitions: 'Thou shall not';
2. Restrictions: 'You can do it, but do it this way (or else)';
3. Conditionality: 'You can do it, but only if you exclude/include, refuse/accept, according to our rules';
4. Selective enforcement: 'We have authority to act but won't necessarily tell you the rules for selection and application' (a tactic that could be useful in launching politically motivated audits, investigations and designations);
5. Targeted threats: 'We have the power and will not hesitate to use it against you if we don't like you or what you're doing'.[46]

---

[43] Trend in subject matter of NGOs drawn from temporal comparisons of mandates, programmes and other funded projects, conducted by author in April–May 2008.

[44] WG Martin, 'Beyond Bush: The Future of Popular Movements & US Africa Policy' (New York, Routledge, 2004) 31 *Review of African Political Economy* 593.

[45] N Billica, 'Philanthropy and Post-9/11 Policy Five Years Out: Assessing the International Impacts of Counterterrorism Measures' 1 December 2006, www.ombwatch.org/npa/Philanthropy-Post_9-11.pdf (viewed 29 May 2010).

[46] Ibid.

Less than two weeks after the attacks on 11 September 2001, President Bush issued Executive Order 13224, 'Blocking Property and Prohibiting Transactions with Persons Who Commit, Threaten to Commit, or Support Terrorism'.[47] This Executive Order sought to disrupt the financial support network for terrorists and terrorist organisations by authorising the US government to designate and block the assets of foreign individuals and entities that commit, or pose a significant risk of committing, acts of terrorism. To this end, one of the main purposes of the Executive Order was the creation of a listing of designated 'foreign individuals and entities that commit, or pose a significant risk of committing, acts of terrorism'.[48] Executive Order 13224 also gave states the authority to freeze assets of organisations associated with terrorist activities—even when the organisations did not have knowledge of the link.

Less than a month after Executive Order 13224 made its appearance, the US Congress did its part to protect US organisations and individuals from the terrorist threat. With very little discussion, it enacted the so-called 'USA PATRIOT Act'. Among other measures, this law amended existing counterterrorism laws to expand federal government powers to investigate flows of money, mandate information sharing, and require reporting by financial institutions of suspicious activities.[49] The grant of sweeping surveillance powers to government was made permanent in the USA Patriot Improvement and Reauthorization Act 14.[50]

Of all the departments of the US government, the US Treasury Department has played an increasingly important role in post 9/11 regulations. Significantly, the 'banned list' is maintained by the Office of Foreign Assets Control (OFAC) of the US Department of the Treasury.[51] The OFAC is charged with administering and enforcing economic and trade sanctions based on US foreign policy and national security goals against targeted

[47] See Executive Order 13224, www.lawandfreedom.com/site/constitutional/execorders/EO13224.pdf (viewed 29 May 2010).

[48] Executive Order 13224 is the source of the most widely used list of 'Specially Designated Nationals' (SDN) maintained and updated by the Treasury Department's Office of Foreign Assets Control (OFAC), and available at: www.ustreas.gov/offices/enforcement/ofac/sdn/t11sdn.pdf (viewed 29 May 2010).

[49] USA PATRIOT Act of 2001, Public Law 107-56 (115 Stat. 272), the 'Uniting for Strengthening America by Providing Appropriate Tools Required to Intercept and Obstruct Terrorism' Act, signed into law on 26 October 2001. See www.news.findlaw.com/cnn/docs/terrorism/hr3162.pdf (viewed 29 May 2010).

[50] Public Law 109-177 (120 Stat. 192), enacted 9 March 2006. The original and revised enactments are commonly referred to as simply 'the PATRIOT Act'. To date, the US Treasury has designated 48 charitable organisations as supporters of terrorism. Of these, five are US-based organisations. For the current list of designated charities, see the Treasury's list: www.ustreas.gov/offices/enforcement/key-issues/protecting/charities_execorder_13224-p.shtml#pdf (viewed 29 May 2010).

[51] Office of Foreign Assets Control Specially Designated Nationals and Blocked Persons, 27 September 2007, www.treas.gov/offices/enforcement/ofac/sdn/t11sdn.pdf (viewed 29 May. 2010).

foreign countries, terrorists, international narcotics traffickers, and those engaged in activities related to the proliferation of weapons of mass destruction.[52] Although the rhetoric against terrorism is strong, and the potential ambit of the office is great, it has since 1994 collected just $9,425 in fines for terrorism financing violations—a small amount as compared to the more than $8 million in fines since 1994, mostly from people who sent money to, did business with or travelled to Cuba without permission.[53]

The Treasury Department has also made its mark on the post-9/11 regulatory format with its 'Anti-Terrorist Financing Guidelines: Voluntary Best Practices for US-Based Charities.[54] The stated goal of the Guidelines was 'to assist charities that attempt in good faith to protect themselves from terrorist abuse'.[55] Although the Anti-Terrorist Guidelines are billed as 'voluntary guidelines', a strong argument could be made that, because other federal agencies have adopted the recommendations, the Guidelines have lost their 'voluntary nature'.[56] This was only one of several criticisms of the Guidelines. On 5 December 2005, the Treasury released revised draft Guidelines for public comment and requested comments on revisions.[57]

The revised Guidelines, like their predecessor, attracted considerable criticism.[58] As one major coalition of US-based NGOs concluded its review of the new text:

> The revised Guidelines include provisions that may create the impression that charitable organisations are closely tied to the US government. This threatens the safety of humanitarian workers who may be targeted as a result of their perceived lack of independence from the government.[59]

Compliance forced charitable organisations to run a gauntlet of information collection and reporting procedures that have served as 'speed bumps', slowing NGO progress in their advocacy efforts.

---

[52] See US Treasury, 'Office of Forerign Assets Control', www.treasury.gov/offices/enforcement/ofac (viewed 29 May 2010).

[53] J Solomon, 'More Agents Track Castro than Bin Laden', Associated Press, 29 April 2004, www.commondreams.org/headlines04/0429-12.htm (viewed 29 May 2010).

[54] See US Treasury, 'Protecting Charitable Organizations', www.treas.gov/offices/enforcement/key-issues/protecting/charities-intro.shtml (viewed 29 May.2010).

[55] Ibid.

[56] One case in point is the incorporation of the Guidelines into the memorandum accompanying the regulations for the 2006 Combined Federal Campaign (CFC), issued by the Office of Personnel Management (OPM). See Response to Comments Submitted on the US Department of the Treasury Anti-Terrorist Financing Guidelines: Voluntary Best Practices for US-Based Charities, www.Treas.Gov/Offices/Enforcement/Key-Issues/Protecting/Docs/Response.Pdf (viewed 29 May.2010).

[57] See US Department Of The Treasury Anti-Terrorist Financing Guidelines: Voluntary Best Practices For US-Based Charities, www.Treas.gov/offices/enforcement/key-issues/protecting/docs/guidelines_charities.pdf (viewed 29 May.2010).

[58] See Independent Sector: A Vital Voice for Us All, www.independentsector.org/programs/gr/TreasuryComments.pdf (viewed 29 May.2010).

[59] Ibid.

CONCLUSION

If a UN World Conference on Women were to be held next year, what would it look like? Would it, like earlier UN World Conferences, still maintain a strict division between the official meeting of government delegates—the 'GO' meeting (for 'government organisations')—and the gathering of NGOs? At the 1993 World Conference for Human Rights in Vienna, the NGOs were literally in the basement while the GOs carried on in the remainder of the conference building. Are women's rights advocates so assimilated into the GO structures that the NGO forum is no longer needed, at least not for those who have been successfully able to adapt to a post-9/11 security-crazed world? At the 1995 World Conference for Women's Human Rights in China, police could be seen on street corners with large blankets in their arms. They had been told that the lesbians were going to march naked, and they were prepared to cover them. What will police be carrying at the next meeting, who and what will they want to hide? Has the threat of radical naked lesbians been replaced by equally absurd misunderstandings about evil women in headscarves?

At the 1994 International Conference on Population and Development in Cairo, a tiny delegate, the Vatican (Holy See), exercised tremendous influence over the course of negotiations by spreading fear that the word 'gender' refers to a radical agenda of gender diversity. Will a delegate to a new conference use similar tactics? Who will attempt to play the spoiler now? And who will be the scapegoats? Even as many of the challenges for feminist and women's rights NGOs have remained constant, the post-9/11 climate presents many new road blocks, blind spots and speed bumps. Where some commentators view the entry of women's rights into security discourse as a positive sign (as if human rights has arrived!); others fear the co-option of human rights by the security agenda to justify interventions. Navigating a path between resistance and compliance will require attention to these concerns.

7

The Politics of Inevitability: An Examination of Janet Halley's Critique of the Criminalisation of Rape as Torture

MARIA GRAHN-FARLEY*

> With respect to violence against women or rape, classifying an act as 'torture' carries a considerable additional stigma for the State and reinforces legal implications, which include the strong obligation to criminalize acts of torture, to bring perpetrators to justice and to provide reparation to victims.
>
> Professor Manfred Nowak,
> Judge of the Human Rights Chamber of Bosnia-Herzegovina.[1]

INTRODUCTION

I WAS ASKED to reflect on feminist perspectives in an era of terror and anxiety, and on our relationship to resistance and compliance. At the centre of the United States' (US) terror and anxiety lies the torture debate.[2] Torture, in its essence, is the fighting of terror and anxiety with

* I thank Sari Kouvo and Zoe Pearson for the invitation to participate in this wonderful project hosted by the International Institute for the Sociology of Law, Oñati, Spain. I thank my co-panellists: Vanessa Munro, Hilary Charlesworth, and Yoriko Otomo. I also thank Brooke Ackerly and the Global Feminisms Collaborative at Vanderbilt University for their generous comments on my presentation of an earlier draft. I am grateful for the encouragement and support of Julie Mertus and Dianne Otto. Special thanks to Donna Young, Nancy Ota, Kathy Katz, Peter Halewood, and Alicia Ouellette. Finally, a great thanks to Anthony Paul Farley for all his support.

[1] UN Special Rapporteur on Torture Professor Manfred Nowak, Comment made on International Women's Day 2008, at IRCT—International Rehabilitation Council for Torture Victims Women & Torture Statement.

[2] The UN Special Rapporteur reporting on human rights violations and the security states: 'The Special Rapporteur remains deeply troubled that the United States has created a comprehensive system of extraordinary renditions, prolonged and secret detention, and practices that violate the prohibition against torture and other forms of ill-treatment.' Promotion

terror and anxiety. Post-9/11, torture by 'inflicting severe pain and suffering'[3] is the terror and anxiety imagined to prevent the terror and anxiety of yet another 9/11.[4] This idea of fighting fire with fire was central to the Bush administration and its followers.[5] Most significant are the infamous 'torture memos' providing legalistic justifications for torture.[6]

and Protection of all Human Rights, Civil, Political, Economic Social and Cultural Rights, Including the Right to Development. A/HRC/10/3, 4 February 2009, 2, para 51. The Special Rapporteur also points out that the US security system would have been possible without the cooperation from multiple countries: 'While this system was devised and put in place by the United States, it was only possible through collaboration from many other States. There exist consistent, credible reports suggesting that at least until May 2007 a number of States facilitated extraordinary renditions in various ways. States such as Bosnia and Herzegovina, Canada, Croatia, Georgia, Indonesia, Kenya, the former Yugoslav Republic of Macedonia, Pakistan and the United Kingdom of Great Britain and Northern Ireland have provided intelligence or have conducted the initial seizure of an individual before he was transferred to (mostly unacknowledged) detention centers in Afghanistan, Egypt, Ethiopia, Jordan, Pakistan, Morocco, Saudi Arabia, Yemen, Syria, Thailand, Uzbekistan, or to one of the CIA covert detention centres, often referred to as "black sites". In many cases, the receiving States reportedly engaged in torture and other forms of ill-treatment of these detainees.' Promotion and Protection of all Human Rights, Civil, Political, Economic, Social and Cultural Rights, Including the Right to Development. A/HRC/10/3, 4 February 2009, 2, para 52.

[3] Contrary to international humanitarian and human rights law in general where waterboarding would fall into the category of torture and be prohibited under both human rights law and humanitarian law, the Bybee Torture Memo provided a justification of torture. This was based on the notion that interrogation strategies such as waterboarding did not 'inflict severe pain and suffering' and therefore did not constitute torture because, as Bybee wrote, '"severe" conveys that the pain or suffering must be of such a high level of intensity that the pain is difficult for the subject to endure'. The Bybee Torture Memo, Memorandum for Albert R Gonzales, Counsel to the President. Section B, 5.

[4] 'Any act by which severe pain or suffering, whether physical or mental, is intentionally inflicted on a person.' Article 1 of the Convention against Torture and Other Cruel, Inhuman or Degrading Treatment or Punishment. G.A. Res. 39/46 (1984), entry into force 26 June 1987.

[5] The Bush administration vetoed the Anti-Torture Bill HR 2082. The 'torture memos' are a compilation of several memorandums by the Justice Department justifying torture: The Yoo Delahunty Memorandum of 9 January 2002; The Rumsfeld Order 19 January 2002; The Bybee Memorandum of 22 January 2002; The Alberto Gonzales Memo 25 January 2002; The Bush Order 7 February 2002; The Yoo/Delahunty Memo 9 January 2002. One of the lawyers authoring the torture memos, John Yoo, and Jack Goldsmith, assistant attorney general in the Justice Department's Office of Legal Counsel from 2003 to 2004, ended up at our most prestigious law schools, University of California Berkeley Law Boalt Hall and Harvard Law School. Professor Alan M Dershowitz, Felix Frankfurter Professor of Law at Harvard Law School expressed his support for torture in a CNN interview. See discussion below at n 55.

[6] The 'torture memos' are a compilation of several memorandums by the Justice Department justifying torture, ibid. The Obama administration released four memos on 16 April 2009. See Memo of Patrick F Philbin and John C Yoo, Office of Legal Counsel, Department of Justice, to William J Haynes II, General Counsel, Department of Defense, 'Possible Habeas Jurisdiction over Aliens Held in Guantanamo Bay, Cuba', 28 December 2001; Memo of John C Yoo and Robert J Delahunty, Office of Legal Counsel, Department of Justice, to William J Haynes II, General Counsel, Department of Defense, 'Application of Treaties and Laws to al Qaeda and Taliban Detainees', 9 January 2002. (Also here: Yoo's Memo on Avoiding the Geneva Convention Restrictions); Memo of Alberto R Gonzales, Counsel to the President, to President George W Bush, 'Decision Re Application of the Geneva Convention on Prisoners of War to

Not before Janet Halley, the Royal Professor of Law at Harvard Law School, has this type of reasoning—the idea of fighting terror and anxiety with terror and anxiety—had its support from the political left. Halley argues that the International Criminal Tribunal for the former Yugoslavia's (ICTY)[7] conviction of Kunarac of torture for his rapes of Bosnian women and children might lead to more rapes. In Halley's own words: 'If humanitarian law ratifies the idea that rape intrinsically causes intense suffering, it may lend legitimacy to the intense suffering that it causes. ... We could get more rapes'.[8]

The criminalising of rape as torture under international criminal law is a women's rights and a human rights issue. For the international human rights community, as expressed by Professor Manfred Nowak, the UN Special Rapporteur on Torture, making the parties to a war accountable for violence and rape specifically directed towards women is a central task of international law, and an important step towards justice.[9]

In this chapter I will discuss and critique the 'feminist' countertrend expressed by Janet Halley. Halley does not see the criminalisation of rape as torture in former Yugoslavia as advancing a feminist and women's agenda. In Halley's view, the criminalisation of rape as torture took something away from the Bosnian women kept in the control of Serbian soldiers, namely, their ability to choose to have sex with their male guards. The conflict between feminists who emphasise agency versus power can be seen in the exchange between MacKinnon and Angela Harris. Where MacKinnon applies a structural view on the relationship between women and men, Harris sees possibilities of agency as women of colour move

---

the Conflict with al Qaeda and the Taliban', 25 January 2002. (Also here: Gonzales's Memo to Bush); Memo of William H Taft IV, The Legal Adviser, Department of State, to Alberto R Gonzales, Counsel to the President, 'Comments on Your Paper on the Geneva Convention', 2 February 2002. (Also here: Taft's Memo on the Dangers of Rejecting the Geneva Conventions); Memo of Jay S Bybee, Office of Legal Counsel, Department of Justice, to Alberto R Gonzales, Counsel to the President, 'Standards of Conduct for Interrogation under 18 U.S.C. §§ 2340-2340A', 1 August 2002. (Also here: Bybee's Justice Department Memo on Torture, Letter by Bybee on Torture to White House Counsel); Memo from Secretary of Defense Donald H Rumsfeld to General James T Hill, 'Counter-Resistance Techniques in the War on Terrorism', 2 April 2003. (Also here: Rumsfeld's Memo on Interrogation Techniques.)

[7] International Tribunal for the Prosecution of Persons Responsible for Serious Violations of International Humanitarian Law Committed in the Territory of the Former Yugoslavia since 1991. For further discussion about the ICTY, see Nesiah, below, this collection.

[8] J Halley, P Kotiswaran, H Shamir, C Thomas, 'From the International to the Local in Feminist Legal Responses to Rape, Prostitution/Sex Work, and Sex Trafficking: Four Studies in Contemporary Governance Feminism' (2006) 29 *Harvard Journal of Law & Gender* 335, 383. For further discussion on Halley's work, see Munro; and Charlesworth, above, this collection.

[9] UN Special Rapporteur on Torture Professor Manfred Nowak, Comment made on International Women's Day 2008, at IRCT—International Rehabilitation Council for Torture Victims Women & Torture Statement.

between different binaries.[10] Outside of the legal field, agency- and power-related theories have found a balancing point where agency is placed within the context of the local power. Power is no longer examined as an abstract notion of structural power, but from a contextualised local understanding of how power and agency interact in that specific place.[11] This understanding of local power context is, I argue, what is missing from Janet Halley's critique of the criminalisation of rape as torture. Arguing that the criminalisation of rape as torture takes agency away from women, Halley neglects the always-important fact of power; she does not consider the power that the specific rapist has over the specific woman in that specific moment. In the torture debate, where Halley places agency as the organising principle, Nowak places power. If one includes the specific situation of the Bosnian women raped by the Serbian soldiers while in their captivity, then Halley is wrong, and these rapes should be seen as torture. Ms Yakin Erturk, the Special Rapporteur on Violence against Women, has suggested the term 'disempowerment' for such circumstances 'because it goes beyond the victim and relates also to the question of who is causing the suffering'.[12]

Feminist scholars Hilary Charlesworth, Judith Gardam, Catharine A MacKinnon and Karen Engle have all been critical of international humanitarian law's focus on rape without context. Charlesworth and Gardam argue that a narrow focus on gender violence makes the role of women in war time into moments of exception. The transformation into moments of exception prevents a holistic critique of the male-centeredness of international humanitarian law. Male-centeredness means that the only place for women is the place of the exception.[13] MacKinnon sees the appellate chamber decision in the *Kunarac* case as a combination: seeing rape as being about individual power *and* seeing rape as being about structural (ethnic) inequalities.[14] In this context, MacKinnon argues that the question of consent becomes almost moot due to power inequalities between the parties.[15] Karen Engle expands the feminist agenda in humanitarian law to go beyond rape. Engle points to the fact that both the collective and individual views on rape in war time represent women as passive victims and,

---

[10] This can most clearly be described in Angela P Harris' critique of Catharine MacKinnon, see, 'Race and Essentialism in Feminist Legal Theory' (1990) *Stanford Law Review* 581.

[11] See generally, A Subramanian, *Shorelines: Space and Rights in South India* (Stanford, Stanford University Press, 2009).

[12] Comment made at the Child Rights Information Network: 12 March 2008, an NGO briefing session on strengthening the protection of women from torture.

[13] J Gardam and H Charlesworth, 'Protection of Women in Armed Conflict' (2000) 22 *Human Rights Quarterly* 150.

[14] CA MacKinnon, 'Defining Rape Internationally: A Comment on Akayesu' (2005–06) 44 *Columbia Journal Of Transnational Law* 951.

[15] Ibid.

in large part, disregard any possibility of agency.[16] Engle argues that the effects of the ICTY ruling in *Kunarac* served to intensify ethnic difference, to minimise women's sexual, political and military agency and, finally, to replace the focus on gender with a focus on sex.[17] The feminist strategies vary but Charlesworth, Gardam, MacKinnon and Engle all share two points: a critique of international humanitarian law as too focused on sex instead of gender and an emphasis on the need for increased contextualisation in addressing the role of women in armed conflict. Halley is different. Halley argues for an increased focus on sex by de-contextualising the sexual violence from any larger understanding of armed conflicts.

HALLEY'S FEMINIST RE-EXAMINATION

This is how Halley describes her project:

> I am interested in the outcomes [of feminist victories] because they are part of the legal instrumentality of rape in humanitarian law now and because they may well have different effects in the world than anticipated, I think, by the feminists who promoted them.[18]

Halley has located rape in humanitarian law, specifically the torture conviction of Dragoljub Kunarac, a Serbian soldier,[19] as a site where an investigation is due.[20] When Halley applies her feminist examination upon this real case her theory becomes problematic, especially her critique of the torture prohibition. Kunarac, a Serbian soldier, was convicted for torture based on his rape of DB, a 19-year-old Bosnian civilian woman.[21] Halley's critique of the torture conviction in the *Kunarac* case disregards the testimonies of the 20 women and girls who were victims of rape in the *Kunarac* case. Halley takes the position of Kunarac—the defendant—that the rape was consensual.[22] This is how Halley describes the Kunarac conviction:

> Kunarac was convicted, on one of his many counts, of raping D.B., whom he had removed from Partizan Sports Hall and taken to a civilian residence, over his objection that she initiated sexual contact with him.[23]

---

[16] K Engle, 'Feminism and Its (Dis)Contents: Criminalizing Wartime Rape in Bosnia and Herzegovina' (2005) 99 *American Journal of International Law* 803.

[17] Ibid 807.

[18] Halley et al, above n 8, 378.

[19] 'The accused Dragoljub Kunarac stipulated that he was the leader of a permanent reconnaissance group of about 15 [Serbian and Montenegro] men.' Kunarac et al. (IT-96-23 & 23/1) Foča, ICTY-TPIY, para 49.

[20] Halley et al, above n 8, 379–80.

[21] *Kunarac et al*, above n 19.

[22] Idem.

[23] Halley et al, above n 8, 380.

Halley does not inform the reader that the only person concluding that the rape was consensual was Kunarac himself. Halley does not inform the reader that the court concluded that the rape was not consensual:

> The Trial Chamber rejects the evidence of the accused Dragoljub Kunarac that he was not aware of the fact that D.B. only initiated sexual intercourse with him for reasons of fear for her life. The Trial Chamber regards it as highly improbable that the accused Kunarac could realistically have been 'confused' by the behavior of D.B., ... The Trial Chamber is satisfied that D.B. did not freely consent to any sexual intercourse with Kunarac. She was in captivity and in fear for her life after the threats uttered by 'Gaga'.[24]

Halley does not inform the reader that the rape victim testified that the rape was not consensual. Here is the rape victim, DB's, testimony about the same incident:

> She was taken to a corner room on the left side of the house, Jure followed her into the room, undressed her and raped her vaginally. Then 'Gaga' entered the room and raped her, too. Finally, a boy of 15 or 16 years of age came in and raped her as well. After these events, 'Gaga' told her to have a shower because his commander was coming, and he threatened to kill her if she did not satisfy the commander's desires. He repeated this when the accused Dragoljub Kunarac walked in. D.B. took off the trousers of the accused, kissed him all over the body, and then had vaginal intercourse with the accused. D.B. said she felt terribly humiliated because she had to take an active part in the events, which she did out of fear because of 'Gaga's' threats earlier on; she had the impression that the accused knew that she was not acting of her own free will, but admitted after a question by Defense counsel that she was not sure if there would have been intercourse, had it not been for her taking some kind of initiative.[25]

On its face, Halley's project might seem to fit with other post-modern and post-colonial feminist critiques of the feminist project and its underlying normative structures, but things are more complicated than they seem. Post-modern and post-colonial feminist critiques typically direct the reader's attention to the exclusion of women who do not fit general feminist norms.[26] The feminist project has been critiqued for being heterosexist, Eurocentric, white-centric, and class-based, to name just a few. There is a significant difference between these post-modern and post-colonial critiques and what Halley provides. All the previous critiques are based upon describing and talking on behalf of women who are otherwise invis-

---

[24] *Kunarac et al*, above n 19, para 646.

[25] Ibid paras 218–19.

[26] See, eg, Critical Race Feminists such as AP Harris, 'Race and essentialism in Feminist Legal Theory' (1989–90) 42 *Stanford Law Review* 581; postcolonial and postmodern feminists such as R Kapur, 'Postcolonial Erotic Disruptions: Legal Narratives of Culture, Sex, and Nation in India' (2000–01) 10 *Columbia Journal of Gender and Law* 333; and postmodernists such as Dianne Otto, 'Rethinking the Universality of Human Rights Law' (1997–98) 29 *Columbia Human Rights Law Review* 1.

ible and unheard within the feminist project. The focus is on showing how the feminist project will be challenged and questioned by listening to the voices and learning about the lives of the women who do not fit within the general feminist frame, for example, the sex worker, the lesbian, the woman of colour, the colonised. Halley's project has nothing to do with these invisible women and their excluded voices. Halley's project does not identify another silenced voice. Halley's project relies on the voice of Kunarac, the man convicted of torture for raping Bosnian women in the ICTY trials. And, at the same time that Halley bases her entire feminist critique upon the testimony of Kunarac, the man who committed the rapes, she completely disregards the testimonies of all 20 women and girls in the case about the rapes they suffered while in Serbian custody. Halley is not able to find one single testimonial provided by the women or children in the *Kunarac* case that supports her critique of the torture prohibition in the *Kunarac* case. The only person she can locate as having been excluded by the feminist project in the *Kunarac* case is Kunarac himself, the convicted rapist and torturer.

THE EMPTYING OUT OF FACTS

What happened in the *Kunarac* case? Did the Muslim women and children who had been systematically raped by Serb soldiers argue that the overwhelming power of the international feminist experts on sexual violence deprived them of their agency, of their right to consent? In Halley's own words: 'We are seeing here a fascinating infiltration of specifically *feminist* activism into *generalist* forms of power-wielding'.[27] Did the women and girls in the *Kunarac* case claim that they had been violated by the international feminist claim that rape is a war crime, and not by the soldiers who raped them? Of course not. Here are the material facts Halley had to erase to make her agency theory appear to work on a real case.

First, reading Halley's article it is impossible to know that many of the raped women she writes about were in fact children, one as young as 12 years old. Here is a list of some of the witnesses testifying in the case (the identity of the witnesses are being protected by codes): FWS-87 (15½-year-old girl); AS (19-year-old woman); DB (19-year-old woman); FWS-50 (16-year-old girl); FWS-191 (17-year-old girl); FWS-186 (16½-year-old girl); FWS-190 (16-year-old girl); FWS-132 (15-year-old girl); FWS-175 (16-year-old girl); and A.B (12-year-old girl).[28]

Second, none of the women or children testifying in the case testified that she had wanted to be raped or have sex. All of the women and children testified

---

[27] Halley et al, above n 8, 343.
[28] I have followed the definition of the UN Convention on the Rights of the Child 1990, that every person under the age of 18 years is a child.

that they did not want to be raped and that they felt under such threat that they were afraid that if they did not seem willing to have intercourse they would be killed. The only people arguing that the intercourse was performed with consent were the three soldiers on trial for the rape of these women and children. Halley describes DB as the initiator of the sexual encounter with the accused. Halley presents this 'fact' as proof that the rape conviction was a result of international feminist overreaching. This is Halley's description of the event: 'she initiated sexual contact with him'.[29] Halley does not mention the fact that DB testified that she was raped three times by subordinated soldiers of the accused just minutes before the accused entered the room. Halley does not mention the fact that DB testified that she was then threatened with death by a subordinate soldier of the accused if she failed to satisfy the accused.

Third, the privacy of the rape locations is the basis of Halley's worry regarding over-prosecution and foundational to her argument that prosecution for war crimes committed in civilian areas constitutes an overreach of international humanitarian law. The rape of DB took place in the apartment located at Ulica Osmana Dikica no 16. What Halley calls a private apartment was in fact permanently used by the Serb forces to house their soldiers.

Fourth, Halley argues: '*none* of the rapes charged in Kunarac happened in the large detention centers: *all* of them involved victims taken from such places to apartments and homes in the region and raped there.' This is what the testimony in the same case actually states:

> Witnesses described how, as soon as they arrived at Foca High School, women and girls were either taken out of the school, or into the classrooms where they were raped. They would sometimes be raped together. Each one of them would be assigned to a soldier and raped by him. ... and many other women recounted being raped at least once or on several occasions during their time at Foca High school. The girls and women were generally taken for a few hours and returned, sometimes overnight, and some of them were taken away every day. After about 10–15 days, most of the women were transferred to Partizan Sports Hall.[30]

Women and children in Foca were kept and raped repeatedly by Serbian soldiers. The women and children that were systematically raped by Serbian soldiers are the ones that Halley argues have been oppressed, not by the soldiers who raped them, but by the international feminists.[31] Halley argues that international feminists committed an overreach because they presumed that the women and children of the Foca cases did not consent to being raped. This is how Halley describes her concerns: 'feminism will score a victory if it indeed makes non-consent inferable from the coercive circumstances of armed conflict.'[32] Halley continues: 'first, note that the rule

---

[29] Halley et al, above n 8, 380.
[30] *Kunarac et al*, above n 19, para 36.
[31] Halley et al, above n 8, 381.
[32] Idem.

would allow conviction of men who could prove consent.'[33] This is how Halley describes the possible effects of the *Kunarac* case upon women and men: 'structural feminism almost by definition does not care about this possibility, but many other feminisms, especially individualist and sex-positive feminism, care very much. Men-guilty ones, sure, but innocent ones too— are likely to object [to the *Kunarac* ruling]. Indeed, women who want to sleep with men involved in armed conflict.'[34] Recall that each and every one of the witnesses testified that she did not want to have sex but was forced or threatened to make her do so by the Serbian soldiers holding her captive.

Fifth, one of the requisites for the acts or omissions is that the torture has to be directed with a purpose: 'The act or omission must aim at obtaining information or a confession, or at punishing, intimidating or coercing the victim or a third person, or at discriminating, on any ground, against the victim or a third person.'[35] The ICTY established that the rape was directed towards these women because they were Muslims. The ICTY based this conclusion on statements made by Kunarac to the Muslim women he raped that they 'would give birth to Serb babies'[36] and 'enjoy being fucked by a Serb.'[37] Halley fails to include these statements of the court and instead writes 'the coercive circumstances relied on by the Trial Court on this count were found entirely on the fact of Muslim girls and women detained in Partizan and elsewhere in the Foca region.'[38]

AGENCY: THE INTERPRETATION ON
BEHALF OF THE NON-HEARD

Theoretical agency, or the role of interpretation, is located in the tension between resistance and compliance. The act of interpretation carries with it the tension between resistance and compliance. An interpreter would not be needed if it were possible to hear what is being said. Spivak argues that the subaltern cannot speak because no one wants to hear what is being said. This leaves the interpreter having to balance between a representation of what is being said and saying it in a way that can be heard. As feminists, we are asked to place ourselves on the spectrum between resistance and compliance in our interpretation on behalf of silenced women. In addition to being interpreters, feminists themselves exist within the spectrum between resistance

[33] Idem.
[34] Idem.
[35] The court (ICTY) identifies the crime of torture to be as follows: 'The act or omission must aim at obtaining information or a confession, or at punishing, intimidating or coercing the victim or a third person, or at discriminating, on any ground, against the victim or a third person.' Appellate Chamber, para 147.
[36] *Kunarac et al*, above n 19, para 654.
[37] Idem.
[38] Halley et al, above n 8, 380.

and compliance. Simone de Beauvoir situated this question within the family, describing the struggle between women's own interests as a class and their interests as women within families as a struggle against sons, brothers, fathers, and husbands.[39] When the relationship between resistance and compliance is addressed, emphasis is most often placed on the location of the one who is being interpreted—the woman who has been silenced or is speaking in a way that cannot be heard—with little emphasis on the feminist interpreter's location, even though both the woman being interpreted and the woman interpreting as a feminist might be located between resistance and compliance.

The tension between resistance and compliance is heightened in times of general terror and anxiety, as in American academic institutions during the Bush era, because the consequences of arguments are heightened. It is easy to forget the influence of terror and anxiety on the interpreter because she is seen as 'neutral' and is also, by definition, in a privileged position vis-à-vis the one being interpreted.[40] It is easy to forget that feminist claims, even from the position of the interpreter, might struggle in the place between resistance and compliance.

HALLEY'S TORTURE CRITIQUE

Halley's critique, one she identifies as 'left', mirrors the argument from the right on torture. Mirroring, in its literal sense, when left becomes right and right becomes left. The Bush administration promoted torture through 'enhanced interrogation measures'.[41] Halley criticises the criminalisation of torture. The difference between the positions of the right and Halley's 'left' position on torture is as follows: the Bush administration justified its position based on national security while Halley justifies her position through the right to self-expression.[42] Halley and the Bush administration both question the basic understanding of what torture is by redefining it, especially the requisite of

---

[39] S de Beauvoir, *The Second Sex* (1949) (translation by HM Parshley) (New York, Vintage Books, 1989) xxv.

[40] Here I am drawing on the work by G Spivak, 'Can the Subaltern Speak?' in C Nelson and L Grossberg (eds), *Marxism and the Interpretation of Culture* (Chicago, University of Illinois Press, 1988) 271–313.

[41] The limitation upon enhanced interrogation techniques according to the administration is described in the so-called 'torture memos': 'it must inflict pain that is difficult to endure. Physical pain amounting to torture must be equivalent in intensity to the pain accompanying serious and physical injury, such as organ failure, impairment of bodily function or death. For purely mental pain of suffering to amount to torture under Section 2340, it must result in significant psychological harm of significant duration, e.g., lasting for months or even years. ... threats of immanent deaths.' Memorandum for Alberto R Gonzales, Counsel to the President, 2 August 2002.

[42] 'Feminism has helped to construct a legal domain in which consent is crucial to personhood.' Halley et al, above n 8, 382. Halley refers to international humanitarian law's regulations of rape as war crime as 'a large amount of social content relating to sexuality'. Halley et al, above n 8,342.

'intense pain and suffering'.[43] For the Bush administration, 'severe pain ... must rise to the level of death, organ failure, or the permanent impairment of significant body functions—in order to constitute torture'.[44] For Halley, systematic rape cannot be presumed to constitute severe pain and suffering. Halley writes: 'This is a huge victory for some feminists—a full-bore legitimating of the idea that rape always causes intense suffering,' Halley continues: 'The historical fact of intense suffering becomes legally "true" now through an act of bureaucratic management'.[45] Halley goes on: 'This rule means that women need not testify to their intense suffering. It is possible to have trials, and convictions, without this testimony'.[46]

In human rights, international humanitarian law, and US legislation, the subjective requisite for torture is placed upon the torturer, not on the victim of torture.[47] It is not possible to *consent* to torture because the very purpose of torture is to break down the separation between the will of the torturer and the will of the tortured.[48] The purpose of torture is to make the will of the torturer the will of the tortured.[49] If we follow Halley's argument all the way through, torture would be impossible to criminalise because the purpose of torture is to break the torture victim down so that the victim consents to the torture.[50]

Halley is critical of the ICTY's criminalising of rape as torture because she is concerned that under the torture prohibition the Bosnian civilian women and children raped by Serbian soldiers would not be able to consent

---

[43] Halley is critical of the courts' position 'of the idea that rape always causes intense suffering'. In addition Halley fears that this position will silence women and even 'increase the value of rape as a weapon of war'. ibid 383.

[44] Memorandum for Alberto R. Gonzales Counsel to the President, 1 August 2002. US Department of Justice Office of Legal Counsel, 6, Section C.

[45] Halley et al, above n 8, 383.

[46] Idem.

[47] The court (ICTY) identifies the crime of torture to be as follows: 'The act or omission must be *intentional*', Appellate Chamber, para 147. Article 1 of the Convention against Torture and Other Cruel, Inhuman or Degrading Treatment or Punishment. G.A. Res. 39/46 (1984), entry into force 26 June 1987: 'Any act by which severe pain or suffering, whether physical or mental, is *intentionally* inflicted on a person'. Article 2 of the Inter-American Convention To Prevent And Punish Torture, Cartagena de India, Columbia 9 December 1985. Entered into force 28 February 1987: 'Torture shall be understood to be any act *intentionally* performed whereby physical or mental pain or suffering is inflicted on a person'. § 2441. US Military Code on War Crimes defines torture as a war crimes under (d) Common Article 3 Violations, (A) Torture: 'The act of a person who commits, or conspires or attempts to commit, an act specifically *intended* to inflict severe physical or mental pain or suffering' (my emphasis).

[48] I spoke to people who fled to Sweden after have been tortured in their home countries and they told me that the thing that makes rehabilitation difficult is that at one point during the torture, they did welcome it and merged with the will of their torturer.

[49] JP Sartre, 'Situation of the Writer in 1947' (1949) in *'What is Literature?' and Other Essays'* (Cambridge MA, Harvard University Press, 1988) 141, 179. As cited in AP Farley, 'The Black Body as Fetish Object' (1997) 76 *Oregon Law Review* 509.

[50] This is why the subjective requisite is placed upon the torturer and not the victim. If consent were able to undo the criminal act of torture, torture as a crime would be an impossibility.

to sex. Halley expresses her concern as following: 'Feminism has helped to construct a legal domain in which consent is crucial to personhood and in which (some) women are legally incapable of it'.[51] According to Halley, this might lead to over-prosecution of soldiers in cases where the women and children might have consented.[52] The theoretical ability to consent to this type of rape is, to Halley, a key feminist right.[53] Halley equates the recognition of women as having a sexuality with the recognition of a capacity to consent to be raped.[54] Halley replaces the feminist position that rape is about power, with her new position that rape is about sexuality.[55] The sexuality argument is a far stretch when applied to the *Kunarac* case because of the absence of any reality to the idea that any of the rapes were seen by the rape victims as an expression of sexuality or of the power to consent.[56] Halley provides the left argument in support of the Bush administration's reclassification and interpretation of torture by decontextualising the meaning of 'intense pain and suffering', and she does this by arguing that 'the centrality and urgency of the idea that rape causes intense suffering may be eroded, not fortified by its installation in a per se rule'.[57]

THE POLITICS OF INEVITABILITY:
LIQUID FEMINISM DURING THE BUSH ERA

Feminists have not yet taken sufficient account of the effects of post-9/11 terror and anxiety on feminist work, particularly the work of interpreting other women. What follows is just such an accounting, and it gives special focus on the latest turn in agency theory, herein described as 'the politics of inevitability'. The 'politics of inevitability', as will be demonstrated, is more a reflection of the location of the interpreter than it is a reflection of the one being interpreted. The politics of inevitability accepts the oppression

---

[51] Halley et al, above n 8, 382.

[52] '[N]ote that the rule would allow conviction of men who could prove consent. It invites overenforcement.' Halley et al, above n 8, 381.

[53] Ibid 382.

[54] 'Feminism has helped to construct a legal domain in which consent is crucial to personhood and in which (some) women are legally incapable of it.' ibid 382.

[55] Ibid 382. I distinguish Halley's line of argument from strands of pro-sex scholarship in the sense that there are actual facts showing that the combating of, eg, sexual services has been rejected by the women providing sexual services as being harmful to them, and I fully support the notion that women working within the industry of sex services should have a right to organise themselves and not be targets of moralisation by other women. See especially Kapur, above n 18. The difference with Halley's argument is that there are no real cases where women argue that they have been harmed by the criminalisation of the rapes in the ICTY.

[56] Moreover Halley is concerned that women might not even have to testify about the rapes for the soldiers to be convicted. Halley, idem. The situation in the *Kunarac* case upon which Halley bases her argument is based on real testimonies by the women who were raped. Halley's concern that women would not even have to testify is not shown in the case that she studies.

[57] Ibid 383.

of the individual by the institution as inevitable.[58] Instead of using agency theory to describe resistance to the institution or the subjugation, agency theory is seen as a way for the individual to make peace with her lot by willingly accepting the oppressive effects of the institution. Halley's agency is constructed through her own inscription of choice as a theory without any connection to the acts and choices actually made by the women she interprets. Halley deploys her agency theory to cancel the actual choices made by the actual women and children she interprets, the choice to testify that they were forced to have sex. Thus, in the *Kunarac* case, where none of the rape victims argued that they wanted to be raped, and instead all testified that they did not want to be raped, Halley deploys her agency theory to argue that the criminalisation of those rapes deprived the victims of agency, specifically, of the choice to consent.

Agency theory, as it passes through the politics of inevitability, becomes a new form of sexism and anti-feminism. This agency theory, this new sexism and anti-feminism, this liquid feminism of Halley's, is a reflection of the terror and anxiety that feminists within the US have experienced within their academic and political institutions. That terror and anxiety affects feminist scholarship and feminist appreciation of the possibilities and limitations of agency in between resistance and compliance that other women might possess in other oppressive institutions and situations, more threatening and devastating than US academia. In the US it is the left that has taken it upon itself to interpret agency. The left in the US, including feminists, experienced the era of terror and anxiety through the Bush administration's legalisation of torture,[59] the PATRIOT Act,[60] and the war against facts.[61]

The people connected with the legalisation of torture ended up with academic positions at Harvard Law School and the University of California at

---

[58] For a definition of 'institution' see above. 'The term 'institution,' as in 'institutional subjugation', is used herein to refer to socially-constructed power inequalities'.

[59] See discussion above at n 4.

[60] The Act originated as H.R.2975 (the PATRIOT Act) in the House and S.1510 in the Senate (the USA Act). S.1510 passed the Senate on 11 October 2001, 147 *Cong. Rec.* S10604 (daily ed.). The House Judiciary Committee sent out an amended version of H.R. 2975 on the same day, H.R. Rep No 107–236. The House passed H.R. 2975 the following day after substituting the text of H.R. 3108, 147 *Cong. Rec.* H6775-776 (daily ed. 12 October 2001). The House version incorporated most of the money laundering provisions found in an earlier House bill, H.R. 3004, many of which had counterparts in S.1510 as approved by the Senate. The House subsequently passed a clean bill, H.R. 3162 (under suspension of the rules), which resolved the differences between H.R. 2975 and S.1510, 147 *Cong. Rec.* H7224 (daily ed. 24 October 2001). The Senate agreed to the changes, 147 *Cong. Rec.* S10969 (daily ed. 24 October 2001), and H.R. 3162 was sent to the President who signed it on 26 October 2001.

[61] 'President Bush yesterday defended his assertions that there was a relationship between Saddam Hussein's Iraq and Osama bin Laden's al Qaeda, putting him at odds with this week's finding of the bipartisan Sept. 11 commission', Dana Milbank, *Washington Post*, Friday, 18 June 2004, A09.

Berkeley.[62] A fierce debate within the US academia concerns the question of whether torture is really torture.[63] Academic institutions fell under attack during the Bush administration. In addition, academic faculties emerged as places where one might witness one's colleagues openly advocate torture.[64] The two most famous academic advocates of torture are John Yoo,[65] now at Boalt Hall at the University of California at Berkeley, and Alan M Dershowitz[66] of Harvard Law School. Jack Goldsmith, Assistant Attorney General heading the Justice Department's Office of Legal Counsel, was appointed to a professorship at Harvard Law School in 2004.[67] Goldsmith authored the memo explaining the legality of 'relocat[ing] 'protected persons' (whether illegal aliens or not) from Iraq to another country to facilitate interrogations'.[68] The Goldsmith appointment to Harvard Law School was highly controversial and was met with resistance by some members of the Harvard Faculty.[69] Goldsmith later wrote a book critical of the Bush administration wherein he explained that he resigned from his position within the administration because of his disagreement regarding its broad interpretation of executive power.[70] The debate over the role of terror and anxiety was at the centre of the Harvard Law School, the faculty of Dershowitz, Goldsmith and Halley.

US academic freedom came under a general attack. One of the most publicised cases was the firing of tenured professor Ward Churchill. On 2 April 2009 a jury found that the University of Colorado unlawfully fired

[62] Goldsmith and Yoo's appointments to Harvard Law School and Boalt Hall, Berkeley respectively.

[63] Professor Alan M Dershowitz. He is the Felix Frankfurter Professor of Law at Harvard Law School and said in an interview with CNN Access, 'My basic point, though, is we should never under any circumstances allow low-level people to administer torture. If torture is going to be administered as a last resort in the ticking-bomb case, to save enormous numbers of lives, it ought to be done openly, with accountability, with approval by the president of the United States or by a Supreme Court justice. I don't think we're in that situation in this case.' CNNACCESS, Dershowitz: Torture could be Justified, Tuesday, 4 March 2003. See www.edition. cnn.com/2003/LAW/03/03/cnna.Dershowitz/ (visited 12 March 2009).

[64] Ibid.

[65] Professor John Yoo worked between 2001 and 2003 in the United States Justice Department's Office of Legal Counsel as an Assisting Attorney General in his function as legal advisor to President Bush and all the executive branch agencies. It was in this capacity he wrote the infamous torture memos.

[66] Dershowitz, see above n 63.

[67] Goldsmith—a Henry L Shattuck Professor of Law of Harvard Law School—served under Attorney General John Ashcroft and Deputy Attorney General James Comey as a United States Assistant Attorney General for the Office of Legal Counsel in the Department of Justice between October 2003 and July 2004, before he joined the faculty of Harvard Law School.

[68] Memorandum for Alberto R Gonzales, Counsel to the President, Draft 3/19/04.

[69] 'I believe that the Faculty was seriously at fault for not inquiring more deeply, prior to making this appointment, into any role Jack Goldsmith may have played in providing legal advice facilitating and justifying torture,' Elizabeth Bartholet, *Boston Globe*, 9 December 2004, interviewed by Marcella Bombardieri.

[70] JL Goldsmith, *The Terror Presidency: Law and Judgement Inside the Bush Administration* (New York, W.W. Norton & Company, 2007).

Ward Churchill for expressing his political beliefs, but the court granted immunity to the university, a decision that is being appealed.[71] During the presidential campaign, the Republican Party even went after a professor of Middle Eastern Studies at Columbia University as yet another terror suspect.[72] An overt technique deployed by the Bush administration was to decontextualise their target's message. For example, they would express and proclaim patriotism while at the same time cutting funding for health care and other benefits intended for military veterans returning home from Iraq.[73] Liquid feminism's methodological shift away from the contextualisation of agency toward the interpretation of acts, however oppressive those acts might be, as forms of self-expression, mirrors the national political shift away from context and towards decontextualised expressions of terror and anxiety.

CRITICAL THEORY OF AGENCY

Theories of agency seek to explain and describe what resistance sounds like after speech has been made impossible. Interpretation or construction is required to answer that question of agency. That is why the location of the interpreter is so important. Spivak describes the relationship between the interpreter and interpreted as a situation in which the subaltern cannot speak.[74] The subaltern cannot speak because the subaltern cannot be heard.[75] When the interpreter speaks on behalf of others, she also takes the space of the other, and she fills that space up with her own imagination of what silenced speech sounds like.[76] It is precisely for this reason that Halley's critique of the criminalisation of the Serbian soldiers' rapes of Bosnian women and children is especially problematic. Halley's agency is problematic because agency or 'the-filling-of-the-space-of-the-silenced' has, until now, been operating around the presumption that the interpretation in the place of silence should be directed against the institutions of oppression that cause the silencing, not on behalf of those institutions.

---

[71] See www.dailycamera.com/news/2009/apr/02/ward-churchill-trial-blog-jury-university-colorado/ (visited 12 February 2009).

[72] The fact that Barack Obama had run into Rashid Khalid, the Edward Said Professor of Arab Studies at Columbia University, at a dinner was used by the McCain/Palin Campaign as a means to raise suspicions about Obama's patriotism. See J Rainey, *Los Angeles Times*, 30 October 2008.

[73] The most publicised scandal was the terrible conditions at the Veterans' Hospital Walter Reed but there were several other examples as well. See A Hull and D Priest, 'It Is Just Not Walter Reed', *Washington Post*, 5 March 2007, A01.

[74] Spivak, above n 30, 271–313.

[75] Idem.

[76] SV Hartman, *Scenes of Subjection: Terror, Slavery, and Self-Making in Nineteenth-Century America* (New York, Oxford University Press, 1997).

This means, for example, that the underlying presumption in agency theory is that when agency is interpreted within the institution of slavery, agency will give an interpretation against slavery. Or, when agency is interpreted within the institution of colonialism, agency will give an interpretation against colonialism. Or, when agency is interpreted within the institution of male domination, agency will give an interpretation against male domination and will not, like Halley, give an interpretation against the women being raped and in favour of the men raping them. When the 'agency' argument is made, for whom is it made? In addition, who makes the argument when the argument is made? The premise of agency is, in this sense, a 'fiction', The premise of agency is that the structural constraints are pervasive and oppressive enough to make it necessary to 'interpret' or to 'construct' resistance.

Critical agency has been described in scholarship on slavery. Vincent Brown writes about the British Caribbean slave trade: 'Slaveholders faced a persistent threat of dispossession through slaves' suicide'.[77] Another form of agency can be seen in the refusal of medical treatment by slaves on Caribbean Plantations.[78] Saidiya V Hartman's discussion of the slave ship provides another example of agency being exercised even after all resources have been withheld. The slave ship is a space of total withholding. What happens when the oppressive structure has been able to erase the very person doing the act and all that is left in the historical archives is the act itself? An act of a woman captured by slave traders survived even the institution of slavery itself. Hartman writes with reference to such an act in a chapter entitled, 'The Supposed Murder of a Negro Girl':

> Here is a life impossible to reconstruct, not even her name survived. I suppose I could have called her Phibba or Theresa or Sally or Belinda. ... The girl declined to dance naked with the captain on the deck. The girls [had a] low spirit and refused to eat. ... Slaves from Old Calabar had a reputation for destroying themselves.[79]

Critical theories of agency are a response to Orlando Patterson's social death argument.[80] The social death argument presents slavery as an oppressive institution that obliterated social life itself. So complete was the obliteration that the slaves, who were legally forms of property, were also socially transformed into objects, and thus socially dead, per the social death theory. Critical theories of agency have been used to show that even when structures transform people into objects—including objects of property, as

---

[77] V Brown, *The Reaper's Garden: Death and Power in the World of Atlantic Slavery* (Cambridge MA, Harvard University Press, 2008) 132.

[78] Idem.

[79] SV Hartman, *Lose Your Mother: A Journey Along the Atlantic Slave Route* (New York, Farrar, Straus and Giroux, 2007) 137, 144.

[80] Idem.

with the example of slavery—agency remains at the centre and opposed to objectification. Critical theory has been useful in showing the resilience of humanity by directing us toward individuals and groups whose silenced voices remain inaudible to the structuralist ear.

I associate the general feminist project with the work of feminists such as Hilary Charlesworth and Sari Kouvo who show the standard for women and the standard for men as a way of de-naturalising male privilege and the male-as-the-norm.[81] Post-colonial and post-modern scholarship has been critical of the general feminist position, not because they do not think that there is male domination but because there are multiple forms of domination and not all are captured by looking at male/female relations. Angela Harris, for example, challenged white feminists to see the way that the structure, male-oppression-of-women, hid the racial oppression of women of colour by both men and white women. Harris's challenge shows the utility of critical agency as an internal critique of structural approaches.[82] Agency theory can split identity-based groups apart by appealing to smaller identity-based groups within larger groupings. Agency theory can also bring separate groups together. Agency provides an internal critique of different identity-based movements even as it provides a bridge between such movements. One of the strengths of agency theory is that it makes solidarity a choice, and not an essence. By making it a choice it also becomes a politics and open to all regardless of identity. Dianne Otto describes the possibilities of cross-identity based solidarities through their differences. Otto writes:

> It is not about seeking and maintaining unity at all costs against monolithic understandings of domination. Instead, it is about bringing transparency to shifting and mutating relations of power, organising around commonalities based on opposition to specific practices of domination, and re-understanding the categories of identity politics as the effects of hierarchies of power or privilege as well as potentially empowering.[83]

Agency theory is a way for women from all strands of life to join together with the gay and lesbian movement and with the civil rights movement and with other movements; it is through the agency argument that each separate movement joins the others; it is through agency that movements come together as anti-subordination approaches. This is the role agency has played in critical theory; it has been a vehicle through which different

---

[81] H Charlesworth, C Chinkin, S Wright, 'Feminist Approaches to International Law' (1991) 85 *American Journal of International Law* 613. See also works by Sari Kouvo on how to make visible naturalised gender hierarchies: S Kouvo, *Making Just Rights? Mainstreaming Gender and Women's Human Rights* (Sweden, Iustus Publications, 2004).

[82] AP Harris, 'Race and Essentialism in Feminist Legal Theory' (1990) 42 *Stanford Law Review* 581.

[83] D Otto, 'Sexualities and Solidarities: Some Thoughts on Coalitional Strategies in the Context of International Law' (1999) 8 *Australasian Gay & Lesbian Law Journal* 27.

identity-based movements have been able to join in a common project. Agency theory can both split as well as unite groups. In either case, division or unification, agency is used to make visible the structural exclusion of identities. The theory of agency will always make it possible to both split and unite already existing 'structural' formations based on identities. Judith Butler's 'The Psychic Life of Power' provides another useful example of agency theory.[84] Butler's Hegelian Master/Slave narrative shows a relation to power that has no fixed structure. Butler's interpretation of Hegel's Master/Slave allows for a constant exchange between the slave and the master, one moment the master is the slave and the next moment the slave may be the master and so on, the roles are not fixed, what is fixed is the dichotomy, the hierarchy is consistent.

AGENCY WITHOUT SUBSTANCE

Halley's agency is nothing like the above forms of agency. Halley's agency is neither agency against its structure, nor agency within its dichotomy, in other words it is an agency where power is external to the subjugation. This is exemplified by the fact that Halley, when addressing the rapes of Bosnian women by Serbian soldiers, sees the power of international feminists as the problem. Halley's agency does not look at individual agency within an overwhelmingly oppressive institutional structure, such as slavery. Halley does not struggle with questions such as 'What is agency made out of?' as Hartman and Brown do. For Hartman and Brown, agency is the example of the resilience that persists even when the oppression has voided all the material possibilities of its being. Halley's agency, unlike Butler's, does not struggle with a complex psychic relationship to a power of which it is both a product and producer.

What is Halley's agency then? Halley is critical of the international humanitarian law that labels the Serb soldiers' rapes of Muslim civilian women and children as torture. International feminists advocated the criminalisation of the rapes and Halley, opposing this criminalisation in the name of agency, argues for a re-examination of international feminism.[85]

There are, to be sure, valid reasons to examine the feminist focus on rape during war and the promotion of women as victims at the expense of more nuanced images of women in times of war.[86] There is a difference, however,

---

[84] J Butler, *The Psychic Life of Power: Theories of Subjection* (Stanford, Stanford University Press, 1997).

[85] Halley et al, above n 8, 341.

[86] K Engle, 'Feminism and Its (Dis)contents: Criminalising Wartime Rape in Bosnia and Herzegovina' (2005) 99 *American Journal of International Law* 778.

between broadening the discourse by providing a more nuanced image and actually arguing, as Halley argues, that the rulings by the ICTY might prevent women from expressing themselves.[87] As expressed by Halley, 'This rule means that women need not testify to their intense suffering'.[88] Halley is concerned by what she experiences an expansion of the torture prohibition by the ICTY.[89] Halley expresses concern that prosecution of rape as torture might increase the use of rape.[90] Her position indicates a very strong belief in the efficacy of law, a belief in law that she herself rejects.[91] Halley has identified the ability to consent to what the ICTY has found to be rape amounting to torture as a core feminist concern that she views as threatened by the torture prohibition.[92] According to Halley, the fact that 'Kunarac inferred non-consent from the 'coercive circumstances' of armed conflict in the Foca region and presumed coercion on the basis of the victims' detention' might affect 'women who want to sleep with men involved in armed conflict—armed conflict which they may well oppose and in which they find themselves'.[93] This was just not the reality of the women and girls in the *Kunarac* case.[94]

FEMINISM DETACHED

Feminism today is in a state that this chapter describes as 'the politics of inevitability'. The politics of inevitability emerge when the power structure is so overwhelming that it is naturalised, although not normatively approved. This moment represents a paradigmatic shift. The shift is away from the contextualisation of power and subjugation and towards detachment and the idea of self-expression as the sole role of agency. This paradigm shift can be seen in Halley's replacement of *power* with *self-expression* in her discussion of the question of rape in the *Kunarac* case. One of the cornerstones of feminist theory has been the idea that rape is about power, not sex. Halley reverses this argument. For Halley, rape is actually about sex, and it is a feminist overreach to not see the sex part in rape. Halley enjoys 'leftist' credentials but her claims more closely mirror those of George Bush's 'compassionate conservatives'. To say that you are for one thing and against another thing, while advocating precisely the reverse,

---

[87] Halley et al, above n 8, 382.
[88] Ibid 383.
[89] Ibid 382.
[90] Ibid 383.
[91] Ibid 378: 'I am interested in these outcomes because they are part of the legal instrumentality of rape in humanitarian law now and because they may well have very different effects in the world than anticipated.'
[92] Ibid 380.
[93] Ibid 380–81.
[94] *Kunarac et al*, above n 19.

has been a hallmark of the post-9/11 era. The politics of inevitability combine an extremely polarised view with an extreme approach to individual agency, with both void of any analysis of the role of power.

Bush's politics and Halley's agency theory have in common the fact that they adopt normative positions mirroring critical theory, for example, racism is bad and sexism is also bad, and then they each detach the structure, racism and sexism, from the individual agency argument, thus leaving the individual a supposedly free agent, not bound by any of the normative values of the structure, or even by the structure itself. On the face of it, Halley's arguments seem provocative, and, in their purely theoretical form, they are a contribution to a wider feminist debate regarding the importance of self-examination, self-criticism and self-expression. However, when one actually reads the material on which Halley relies for her case study, her arguments fail. Indeed, viewed through the lens of the actual content of the *Kunarac* case, Halley's arguments are incoherent, both from a feminist and from a child rights point of view. Post-9/11 politics combine an extremely polarised view (us against them) void of any material substance. Post-9/11, the structure itself becomes a fiction to be replaced by an extreme individualistic view. In the era of permanent war against terror, the American people in their imagined individuality can only see themselves as individually protected by the 'Army of One', a computer game moving image of a soldier with the American flag used to recruit new soldiers.[95] In this era of terror and anxiety, torture prohibitions that have long been seen as protective of civilians and citizens are transformed into threats against national security through the infamous torture memos, and arguments like Halley's begin to make a perverse sense. For Halley, as for the Bush administration, the prohibition of torture is the threat, not torture. One is with them or against them. And to oppose torture is to be with them. As Halley puts it, to presume the actual fact of non-consent to rape is to become a threat against the sexual liberation of women. The war against terror keeps morphing because terror is liquid and does not follow the 'traditional' binaries such as rich/poor, North/South, women/men, and black/white, where the construction of the dichotomy is grounded in material facts. Instead, the war on terror constitutes its own binary: those who feel afraid and those who do not feel afraid; and all of it utterly detached from fixed positions of power or material facts. The liquid structure can explain the use of freedom's denial, such as the PATRIOT Act and torture, as tools to preserve freedom. The fight against terror and anxiety will be fought with terror and anxiety at home and abroad.

---

[95] See the web page by the US Army inviting the viewer to participate in online video games, www.americasarmy.com/ (visited 12 March 2009).

Feminist discourse, post-9/11, is liquid. The politics of inevitability is the site of the new anti-feminism, the liquid feminism that treats unjust structures not as structures to be questioned but as permanent structures to be survived within. In liquid feminism, the divide is between people who believe that rape is a *sexual* and therefore possibly *consensual* act, and people who do not believe rape can ever be consensual. In liquid feminism, torture prohibitions are a threat and an overreach by women against women (and children) and not by the men that raped them. This new feminism of inevitability, liquid feminism, tells women to survive within sexist structures, not to question them. Rather than questioning the binary material fact, such as the war camp, the 'politics of inevitability' focuses on the management of and adjustment to the binary. The structure is seen as so oppressive and so overwhelming that the thing to be fought over is no longer the being or not being of the institutions supporting sexism, but the being or not being of the persons defined within it. The liquidity of the structure is why the Bush administration did not have 'goals' for their invasion of Iraq. The liquidity is also why the political fight takes place over the question of whether the surge worked or did not work, and not over the fact of the occupation and the need to bring the violence and the wars to an end.

Part Three

Feminist Perspectives on Global and Local Justice

From the Margins to the Mainstream and Back Again: Problems and Paradoxes of Feminist Engagement in Global and Local Justice

Reflections on Nesiah, Kouvo, Andersson, and Thomas

ALICE EDWARDS[*]

PERHAPS THE FUNDAMENTAL paradox of feminist engagement with international law is that the more that women work within the mainstream, the more they prop up the structural bias of that same system. As Dianne Otto explains, 'feminist inclusion strategies [reproduce] unequal relations of gender power.'[1] As the editors of this collection make clear, two predominant strategies have emerged to guide feminist activism, each with attendant problems. The first is to push for inclusion within existing structures and frameworks, however, this simultaneously reinforces them, including gender and cultural biases contained therein (which the editors have termed 'compliance'); while the second is to resist those structures and to work outside the boundaries, resulting in potentially less impact, and speaking and engaging only at the margins (that is, 'resistance'). Underlying the specific analyses of the four chapters in this section is direct confrontation with this paradox.

Vasuki Nesiah's concern with transitional justice is that feminist engagement with it 'invariably run[s] the risk that in that effort to impact the transitional justice field, feminism naturalises the field's constitutive biases.' Feminism itself becomes mainstreamed through this process, and although

---

[*] The views expressed in these reflections are not necessarily shared by the United Nations or the UNHCR.

[1] D Otto, 'Lost in Translation: Re-Scripting the Sexed Subjects of International Human Rights Law' in A Orford (ed), *International Law and Its Others* (Cambridge, Cambridge University Press, 2006) 318, 351.

she acknowledges that there are diverse positions taken by feminist groups and scholars engaged with transitional justice, she is concerned that it is the most conservative strand of feminism that prevails. Sari Kouvo's chapter deals with state-building processes in Afghanistan and highlights the dichotomy between women's participation in the mainstream institutions and the erection of women-specific institutions, such as the Ministry for Women's Affairs. She considers the latter to have been rendered largely ineffective due to an intricate mix of 'Western' efforts to prop up women's rights using strategies unadapted to the Afghan context and to the complex political and cultural constraints affecting how Afghan women can and choose to act on behalf of their own and other women's rights. She portrays a system in which feminism at the margins is accepted because it is a safer option for predominant party factions and it 'ticks the box' of the international community's gender equality agenda, but it does not necessarily contribute to the deconstruction of gender inequality. In contrast, there is a sense that women are tolerated in the mainstream as long as they tow party lines. For their part, women are conflicted between representing their own interests as women and their other interests arising from their other affiliations, whether they be political, economic, religious, or ethnic. These findings are confirmed by feminist research about women's political representation: according to Ann Philips, although research suggests that female politicians develop different styles of political engagement, they are wary of speaking *for* women.[2] Other research highlights that there may be a 'numbers threshold' at which women acquire the confidence to speak for their sex.[3] Below this threshold, they refrain from asserting any sexual difference.

A similar struggle with the mainstream legal discourse is set out in the third chapter in this section. Ulrika Andersson scrutinises the 'vulnerability' of the victim of trafficking within international legal discourse and what this means for women, whilst at the same time attempting to reconcile this image of woman with the legal system in which the subject is presumed to be autonomous and rational. She argues that consent-based criminal laws assume the alleged victim to be 'autonomous, free and rational, capable of expressing will and offering resistance'. Under the latest international trafficking instruments, consent is displaced by exploitation; arguably again reinvigorating the image of women as helpless victims without agency. Perhaps the real answer lies somewhere in between these two extremes: that is, is it possible for women to be both vulnerable and autonomous at the same and at different times? This echoes the concept of paradoxical space explored in Pearson's chapter in this collection.

---

[2] See A Phillips, *Engendering Democracy* (London, Polity Press, 1991, 1993 and 1997) 70.
[3] See G Hedlund, 'Women's Interests in Local Politics' in KB Jones and AG Jonasdottir (eds), *The Political Interests of Gender* (London, Sage, 1988), as referred to in Phillips, idem.

For Dania Thomas, the example of the mainstream-margins dichotomy is set against the backdrop of the debt crisis in Argentina in 2001 in which female factory workers assumed the management and ownership of a textile enterprise. True to feminist predictions, the women proved very successful in saving their livelihoods from economic collapse, and in introducing communal ownership and collective management systems. Yet Thomas points out that this example has made no impact on the dominant assumptions that define contemporary economic governance; it has remained on the margins and of passing interest to feminist scholars only. Thomas identifies their interdependence with each other and the integration and support of the community in which they live and work as factors explaining their achievement. She states that 'their relationality allowed the women to increase the range of significant choices available to them collectively as economic agents'. Women thus turned this debt crisis into an economic opportunity; in much the same way as the re-building of post-conflict societies can open up space for gender equality to be mainstreamed into state-building processes (Kouvo) or the ways in which gender can seep into processes of rehabilitation and recovery in transitional justice discourse (Nesiah). However, like both Kouvo and Nesiah, Thomas notes that such opportunities, portrayed as resistance, can themselves be problematic, and, in fact, resulted in what she refers to as 'political compliance' as the state legitimated the takeovers through formal recognition.

It can thus be seen that the language or situations of crisis can open up opportunities to take stock of where women are at, and what remains to be done to advance women's rights, and can be instrumental in raising the profile and participation of women in those processes. However, in spite of the power of the language of crisis, it can also be problematic, as the chapters from Otto, Mertus and Grahn-Farley in this collection identify. In attempting to raise the profile of women and gender, or what Rhonda Copelon calls 'surfacing gender',[4] women can become 'essentialised' in the search for gender entry points.[5] For Kouvo, the singular focus on women's oppression at the hands of the Taliban has contributed to the eclipsing of other factors relevant to their life experience, such as class, ethnicity, and a mix of conflict, poverty and lack of education. Perceived as they are as 'victims', Afghan women have not been expected to have opinions or anything worthwhile to offer the mainstream state-building agenda. Likewise,

---

[4] R Copelon, 'Gendered War Crimes: Reconceptualizing Rape in Time of War' in J Peters and A Wolper (eds), *Women's Rights, Human Rights: International Feminist Perspectives* (New York, Routledge, 1995) 197, 199.

[5] R Kapur, 'The Tragedy of Victimization Rhetoric: Resurrecting the "Native" Subject in International/Post-Colonial Feminist Legal Politics' (2002) 15 *Harvard Human Rights Journal* 1, 2. See also MR Mahoney, 'Victimization Or Oppression? Women's Lives, Violence, and Agency' in MA Fineman and R Mykitiuk (eds), *The Public Nature of Private Violence: The Discovery of Domestic Abuse* (New York, Routledge, 1994) 59.

Chandra Mohanty has pointed out that '[w]omen are constituted as women through the complex interaction between class, culture, religion and other ideological institutions and frameworks. They are not "women"—a coherent group—solely on the basis of a particular economic system or policy.'[6] For Nesiah, the rigid focus on women as victims of rape and sexual violence within transitional justice processes strengthens the image of the gendered victim and loses sight of women's 'authentic voice'. It also narrows possibilities for political solutions and outcomes.

In noting similar difficulties for women moving between legal presumptions of 'vulnerability' and 'autonomy' in the context of rape and trafficking, Andersson proposes that a new category of legal subject needs to be cast, that of the 'contextualised legal subject', an argument that resonates with Grahn-Farley's chapter in this collection. The need for a plurality of vocabularies of justice and redress is put forward by Nesiah, in which women are freed from the constraints of existing rule of law systems and absolute or 'unmediated' 'truths'. In rejecting the one-size-fits-all gender mainstreaming strategies of state-building in Afghanistan, in which women and feminist activists have been complicit, Kouvo similarly calls on us to develop an 'after fear' agenda that takes account of diversity as well as conflicting interests. While not articulating a solution to the dilemma posited in Thomas's chapter, she nonetheless challenges us to engage in a discussion of governance that recognises the 'gender coding' of both abstract and real sources of legitimacy.

In their different ways, these chapters instruct us to reflect on our efforts to renegotiate the gender fault lines of international law. In other words, in taking steps to prioritise gender, we must be conscious of the costs and benefits of moving from the margins to the mainstream and back again. One of the benefits of moving from the margins to the mainstream is certainly the visibility that this gives to women's and gender issues on mainstream platforms. The costs—or challenges—include the danger of giving priority to one model of emancipation and of re-essentialising women and their diverse experiences. Likewise, any reversion back to the margins and to women-specific institutions and enterprises has the benefit of being able to articulate more closely women's needs and interests, and offers a freer, more open and fuller space for dialogue. Yet, at the same time, it risks being sidelined from the main centres of power and decision-making.

---

[6] C Mohanty, 'Under Western Eyes: Feminist Scholarship and Colonial Discourses' (1988) *Feminist Review* 61, 74.

8

Missionary Zeal for a Secular Mission: Bringing Gender to Transitional Justice and Redemption to Feminism

VASUKI NESIAH

INTRODUCTION[1]

'TRANSITIONAL JUSTICE' IS a term that emerged to describe a family of approaches directed at addressing accountability in the aftermath of contexts of large scale human rights abuse—contexts where the scale of crimes, and in some cases, the passage of time, challenges the institutional capacity of routine criminal justice. Thus the field of transitional justice is particularly concerned with 'post-conflict' human rights law and policy initiatives that have currency today—initiatives that include the international criminal court, universal jurisdiction over war crimes, truth and reconciliation commissions and such. This chapter does not engage with the field at large; rather, it explores how we may conceive of feminism's encounter with this field.[2]

---

[1] My thanks to Sari Kouvo and Zoe Pearson for providing the opportunity to develop this paper for inclusion in this volume. An early draft of this chapter was presented in *The Gender and Transitional Justice Workshop* held in Bellagio, Italy, in April 2005 and benefited from those present at that event.

[2] Against the backdrop of the transitional justice field as it has developed, feminists have sought to infuse gender into the canonical approaches of transitional justice. Over the last decade there are many individuals and groups who have been engaging this intersection around the world, be it in local or transnational initiatives. For instance, the work of the Coalition for Women's Human Rights in Conflict Situations (see www.womensrightscoalition. org/) has been pivotal in impacting jurisprudence on rape in the international tribunals addressing war crimes in the former Rwanda; similarly, the interventions of feminist scholars from the University of Witwatersrand in Johannesburg (www.web.wits.ac.za/Academic/Centres/CALS/Gender/GenderTRC.htm) was critical in influencing the gender work of the South African Truth and Reconciliation Commission; Fokupers (see www.timor-leste.org/gender/FOKUPERS_genderprofile_English.pdf), the Timorese Women's Rights NGO was critical in ensuring that the Timor Leste commission investigated gendered patterns of human

There has been a concerted feminist engagement with many dimensions of the transitional justice field over the last two decades. Many feminist interventions have been directed at revisiting and expanding international human rights law and international humanitarian law to better address women's experiences of human rights violations and humanitarian crisis in the interventions of United Nations (UN) agencies and the interpretation of international law in the operation of ad hoc tribunals and other judicial processes. Similarly many groups have worked closely with the International Criminal Court (ICC) process, from the drafting stage to its prosecution of cases today, to design the court's architecture in ways that would maximise the political will and the legal and administrative capacity for the investigation and prosecution of sexual crimes. Many groups have been pushing for the incorporation of gender focused crimes in truth commission mandates, the inclusion of women as commissioners and staff and the mainstreaming of gender into truth commission operations. When engaging with institutions such as the ICC, ad hoc tribunals and several truth commissions, feminists have been developing procedural avenues for women's participation as 'victims'/survivors, witnesses, advocates and practitioners in institutions such as courts and commissions.[3] Other feminist groups have been lobbying government agencies responsible for reparations in efforts to ensure that reparations policies better reflect patterns of gendered harm and better address the needs of women in post-conflict contexts. Similarly, feminist groups have been urging institutional reform efforts to mainstream gender in diverse ways—from developing more 'feminised' holistic approaches to security sector reform to incorporating more women in institutions such as the judiciary and military as a priority in post-conflict state building efforts. The efforts noted above are but a few of a wide ranging and complex series of initiatives that have been undertaken by activists, humanitarian workers, academics, non-governmental organisations (NGOs), the UN and donors seeking to 'engender' the transitional justice field in these and other ways. It is this project of 'engendering' the transitional justice field that serves as the focus of this chapter.

On the one hand, it seems imperative that feminists engage and impact a field that has such momentous consequences for women. However, in doing so, feminists invariably run the risk that in those efforts to impact the transitional justice field, feminism naturalises the field's constitutive biases. This chapter affirms the success of efforts seeking to ensure that explicit attention to gender has become an important dimension of the transitional justice. However, rather than challenge the mainstream of the transitional

rights violations and shaped reparations policy to prioritise female beneficiaries (all visited 21 May 2009).

[3] See discussion on the ICTY in Grahn-Farley, above, this collection. Also see discussion in Andersson, below, this collection, on the notion of victims.

justice field, feminism has become mainstreamed within it. Moreover, while a diverse range of feminists have sought to engage transitional justice processes, when gender had been explicitly taken on board within transitional justice institutions, it has often been the most conservative strand of feminism that has been consolidated.

This chapter maps the constitutive tensions that have run through these engagements to surface the political stakes that have emerged in the encounter between feminism and transitional justice. It does this through a two-part intervention. The first section, *Feminist Critique of Biases in Transitional Justice Law and Policy*, looks at three slices of this encounter by focusing on two key challenges that feminists have brought to the transitional justice field; I engage with these two challenges in relation to prosecutions, institutional reform and truth commissions respectively:[4] biases inherent in dominant constructions of the transitional justice subject; and biases inherent in the methodology through which transitional justice institutions describe, condemn and rectify abuses.

Historically these two topics have both been priority areas in the feminist transitional justice agenda but they are hardly an exhaustive account of feminist interventions in the field.[5] However, feminist engagement with these two 'biases' in different transitional justice institutions and the remedies proposed offer a symptomatic lens into the broader field of initiatives seeking to render transitional justice more inclusive.

The second section, *The Limits of Inclusion*, revisits both of these windows into feminism's engagement with transitional justice to problematise the terms of that encounter as marrying a bounded transitional justice discourse and conservative strands of feminism. I argue that again and again, from prosecutions to truth commissions to institutional reform, the encounter has produced a problematic resolution that has affirmed conventional approaches to gender and mainstreamed hegemonic approach to justice.

---

[4] These are challenges that have been made by a range of feminist critics. For one window into these debates see an account of a discussion by feminist scholars and practitioners in Vasuki Nesiah, 'Gender and Transitional Justice: Reflections on Conversations in Bellagio' (Spring, 2006) *Columbia Journal of Gender and the Law*.

[5] There are many important areas of critique not addressed here—for instance, debates on the notion of 'truth' that inform truth commissions in particular, and transitional justice more generally. Similarly, many strands of contemporary feminist theory would also raise important challenges to the notion of transition itself—the problematic ideas of history, temporality and social change that are implicit (and sometimes explicit) in how the field defines the past, or seeks 'bounded closure' (to use Teitel's term—see R Teitel, *Transitional Justice* (Oxford, Oxford University Press, 2002)).

FEMINIST CRITIQUE OF BIASES IN TRANSITIONAL
JUSTICE LAW AND POLICY

Biases Inherent in Dominant Constructions of the Transitional Justice Subject

The Subject Constituted by 'International Crimes'

Over the last decade the international human rights framework has been consolidating jurisprudence around accountability for what is sometimes referred to as 'international crimes'. These crimes include killings, disappearances and torture. If there is a dominant subject of transitional justice it is one who is interpolated through this category. We 'know' this subject as one who has committed 'international crimes', or been victimised by them; whether prosecutor or victim, this is the subject called forth by efforts to prosecute and redress 'international crimes'.

The mandate of the ICC, the striking down of amnesties for 'grave violations' by the Inter-American court, the weight attributed to effective remedies for 'gross violations of human rights' by the European Court, the establishment of ad hoc tribunals to address 'war crimes' or 'crimes against humanity'—these are all different markers in the development of special targeting of perpetrators of 'international crimes' as warranting more iron clad accountability regimes than other perpetrators. In countries such as Sierra Leone and Timor Leste, the principal institutions for transitional justice in these countries made provisions for a de jure distinction between the legal procedures relevant for 'international crimes' on the one hand and 'less serious crimes' on the other.

If we focus first on perpetrators, this recognition can be tracked in how, increasingly, amnesties are being issued in ways that exclude perpetrators of 'international crimes'—the UN's signature to the Lome Accords explicitly excluded 'international crimes'. In the *Lacan Chaclain* case in Guatemala regarding the appropriate judicial avenues that should be available to 'victims' of international crimes, courts relied on international law to argue that crimes involving serious human rights violations require higher degrees of guarantees for effective redress, including the right to a fair trial by an independent judiciary.[6] Finally, if we look at statutes of

---

[6] See discussion in N Roht-Arriaza and L Gibson, 'The Developing Jurisprudence on Amnesty' (1998) 20 *Human Rights Quarterly* 843, 872.

limitations as a species of amnesty, we also find that there is extensive support for the principle that 'international crimes' are imprescriptable. The Convention on the Non-applicability of Statutory Limitations to War Crimes and Crimes Against Humanity declares that no statutory limitations apply to war crimes and crimes against humanity.[7] The Pinochet trials and other recent developments in Chile and Argentina open the doors to accountability for international crimes that took place decades back by overturning amnesties for international crimes. Finally, coming back to the ICC, we note that Article 29 of the Rome Statute stipulates that genocide, crimes against humanity, and war crimes 'shall not be subject to any statute of limitations'.[8]

If this litany of transitional justice mandates describes how the discourse and institutional practices defining 'international crimes' constitutes the perpetrator of such crimes as its principal target for accountability, the other key protagonist is the victim of these crimes. Transitional justice defines the victim subject as the one who has borne a violation of international crimes—typically the one who has been killed, disappeared or tortured. For instance, as noted above, Pinochet's amnesties were stripped away for international crimes such as disappearances. The distinctive status accorded international crimes becomes clear when one considers that Pinochet's regime victimized people not only through his policy of disappearing dissidents but also his economic policy; yet it is only the former who appear as 'victims' on the transitional justice radar screen. Moreover, while the author of the term genocide and the principal force behind the convention, Raphael Lemkin, defined genocide to include a wide range of offences that may be entailed in the destruction of a people's culture, to date all genocide prosecutions have focused on victims of efforts to physically destroy a group through bodily injury, from rape to mass killings because these are what international institutions consider 'international crimes'. Even in contexts such as apartheid, where the scale and complexity of crimes may channel a broader socio-historical compass regarding the body politic, the 'victim' emerges as the one whose rights to bodily integrity have been violated. These crimes have sometimes been referred to as bodily injury crimes because 'other effects of power' are 'stripped away' and subjectivity

---

[7] See Articles 1 and 4 of *The Convention on the Non-applicability of Statutory Limitations to War Crimes and Crimes Against Humanity*, G.A. Res 2391 (XXIII), annex, 23 UN GAOR Supp (No 18) at 40, UN Doc A/7218 (1968), entered into force 11 November 1970.

[8] Part 3 of the *Rome Statute of the International Criminal Court*, 2187 UNTS 90, entered into force 1 July 2002, laying out the general principles that shall govern its applicability. It clarifies that while the ICC will not have retrospective reach for crimes committed before it came into force (see Article 24), this provision ensures that perpetrators who fall within ICC jurisdiction will be vulnerable to prosecution going forward irrespective of the passage of time (see Article 29). See www.untreaty.un.org/cod/ICC/STATUTE/99_corr/3.htm (visited 21 May 2009). See also RA Kok, *Statutory Limitations in International Law* (Hague, Asser Press, 2007) 119–20.

condensed 'to its traces on the body'.[9] Thus efforts to prosecute and redress 'international crimes' constitute perpetrator and victim of these crimes as the (two-dimensional) subject of transitional justice.

The Feminist Critique of the Privileged Subject of Transitional Justice

Against the backdrop described above, feminists have been concerned with how both protagonists and victims in the international crimes framework carry gendered histories that have foregrounded the male political actor.[10] The iconic 'perpetrator' of political violations of bodily injury is the male political actor. From the front line soldier to the head of state to the guerrilla in the jungles, men are the engines of history who have had the power to direct armies and throw Molotov cocktails as office holders in the state or as aspirants to state power. This is the dominant military history, but even more so than that, it is also the ideological construct of the perpetrator that over-determines the transitional justice framework even in contexts where there have been large numbers of female combatants.[11] From jail conditions to decommissioning initiatives, the notion of the male perpetrator has long shaped UN and state policy.

Interestingly, from popular culture to human rights policy, the iconic 'victim' of international crimes such as disappearances and torture, the dissident targeted by an oppressive regime was, also invariably, scripted as male. Females may suffer such injuries as innocent civilians but typically they are not seen to be targeted for their politics, for the views they hold; rather, their injuries are collateral damage[12]—or at least that is the hegemonic narrative of post-war prosecutions that feminists have long sought to undo.

---

[9] F Ross, *Bearing Witness: Women and the Truth and Reconciliation Commission in South Africa* (London, Pluto Press, 2002) 12. While our particular focus in this section of the chapter is prosecutions, Ross demonstrates how the SA TRCs constituted the victim subject in terms of bodily injury rather than 'the historical constitution of the subject under apartheid', 11.

[10] For instance Patricia Sellers notes that women have been invisible in international criminal law: 'Individuals, unprotected by, or routinely disregarded or marginalized under the Rule of Law, have a tenuous, unsecured membership in their legal community. Under international criminal law, those individuals have traditionally been women.' See P Viseur-Sellers, 'The Rule of Law Applies to Women' in United Nations Department of Humanitarian Affairs News, April/May 1997, No 22, available at www.reliefweb.int/OCHA_ol/pub/dhanews/issue22/lawrule.html (visited 21 May 2009).

[11] When militant groups have recruited large numbers of women and girls (such as the Shining Path in Peru or the Sri Lankan LTTE in Sri Lanka), those cases are flagged and discussed as extraordinary. The very fact that attention is drawn to their gender underscores the extent to which the male subject of transitional justice is naturalised as *the* subject.

[12] Thus feminists have pointed out that when women's injuries were recognised they were marginalised as simply the inevitable casualties of war; for instance, as Sellers notes, in the dominant narrative women are sexually assaulted during wartime because, 'soldiers will be boys and after a long march ...', to paraphrase Stalin's Second World War analysis, or because troops must be 'serviced' for purposes of morale, as attested to by the plight of the Japanese comfort women. See Sellers, above n 9.

Against the dominance of this masculine subject, 'women's rights' activists have focused on how 'international crimes' have not addressed women's experience of human rights violations in many contexts.[13] Highlighting the gender impunity gap inherited from the Nuremberg and Tokyo trials, over the last two decades feminists have gained considerable success revisiting and expanding the jurisprudence regarding international human rights and humanitarian law to 'surface gender'.[14] In particular, they have persuaded transitional justice processes to recognise the female subject as also a 'victim' of bodily injuries that constitute international crimes. As Ariane Brunet and Stephanie Rousseau have argued, 'without recognition there can be no punishment, reparation nor rehabilitation. Worse still there are neither victims nor aggressors.'[15] Thus over the last decade, the dominant story of the international criminal tribunals addressing war crimes in the former Yugoslavia and Rwanda has been the transformation of women's subjectivity so that she too can be written as a 'victim' of international crimes. If the 'victim' or the privileged subject of transitional justice is the one whose rights to bodily integrity are violated, then the raped victim becomes the privileged subject of feminist transitional justice.[16] If the transitional justice field 'stripped away other effects of power' and condensed subjectivity 'to its traces on the body', then feminist transitional justice stripped away other structural and ideological effects of power to focus on the woman who suffered sexual injury.[17] Bodily integrity injuries such as sexual violence have had to be the privileged frame narratives for women's subjectivity. This has meant that those injuries had to be pressed into pre-existing legal categories regarding torture or crimes against humanity for inclusion and full representation within transitional justice's avowed 'emancipatory' promise.

---

[13] See R Copelon, 'Surfacing Gender: Reconceptualizing Crimes against Women in Time of War' in A Stiglmayer (ed), *Mass Rape: The War against Women in Bosnia-Herzegovina* (Lincoln, University of Nebraska Press, 1994) 197–218.

[14] Idem.

[15] A Brunet and S Rousseau, 'Acknowledging Violations, Struggling Against Impunity: Women's Rights, Human Rights', 38, quoted in S Smith, 'Belated Narrating' in W Hesford and W Kozol (eds), *Just Advocacy? Women's Human Rights, Transnational Feminism and the Politics of Representation* (New Jersey, Rutgers University Press, 2005) 126.

[16] There is resonance here with the field of sex work, where the privileged subject is the victim of sex trafficking. As Hesford notes, transnational feminist anti-trafficking campaigns are invested in 'the identification of women as passive and naïve victims lured and tricked into sex work and therefore in need of rescue'. Hesford's chapter analyses how this representation is mobilised in global advocacy, see W Hesford, '*Kairos* and the Geopolitical Rhetorics of Global Sex Work and Video Advocacy' in W Hesford and W Kozol (eds), *Just Advocacy? Women's Human Rights, Transnational Feminism and the Politics of Representation* (New Jersey, Rutgers University Press, 2005) 147. Hesford's article analyses how this representation is mobilised in global advocacy. See also discussion in Grahn-Farley, above, this collection.

[17] Ross, above n 8, 11–12.

The Biases Inherent in how Transitional Justice Institutions Describe, Condemn and Rectify Abuses

Legalistic Institutions, Practices and Discourses

In a preceding section, I looked at how feminist interventions regarding prosecutions addressed the nature of crimes that have been targeted for heightened attention, accountability and redress in courts. In this section, I turn to the methodologies that transitional justice institutions employ in investigating and rectifying abuses. Transitional justice institutions have overwhelmingly employed legalistic institutions, practices and discourses. It is often asserted that the fair application of legal rules to assess evidence and pass sanction represents the triumph of the rule of law over the abuse of power; for many this is the most effective weapon against such abuse. Moreover, it is through such legal engagement that a society establishes norms and consolidates trust. It is frequently argued that, at least since Nuremberg, judicial findings of guilt for mass atrocity have helped unequivocally to testify to the fact that identifiable individuals, not anonymous entities, conduct violations.[18] If the privileged subject of transitional justice was the one who committed or suffered international crimes, the privileged methodology of transitional justice is law and legal process.

A legalistic, judicialised approach has many implications. First, there is the privileging of courts as the forum that is best suited to advance justice goals, and in many ways the crown jewel in the transitional justice tool box. In some contexts (such as Chile in the immediate aftermath of the dictatorship) non-judicial processes such as truth commissions are seen to have arisen only because amnesties had ensured that courts were not a viable option in dealing with the past. In other cases, even when courts and commissions are operating simultaneously (such as in Sierra Leone), the court is perceived to be the more important institution and the one to be prioritised if there is a conflict between the institutional imperatives of the court and commission.

In addition to the field's prioritisation of courts in many contexts, what is key here is not the privileging of courts as such, but the mainstreaming of a judicial approach in transitional justice institutions more generally. The judicial system is geared toward establishing guilt and innocence under due process of law and established standards of proof and truth commission processes, reparation programmes and many security sector reform initiatives often defer to this basic model in the handling of cases. Typically, commissions rely on a civil standard of proof and focus on the balance of

---

[18] See, eg, A Neier, 'The Nuremberg Precedent' in *The New York Review of Books*, 4 November 1993 available at http://www.nybooks.com/articles/archives/1993/nov/04/the-nuremberg-precedent/, last visited 27-01-2011).

probabilities rather than the more strict approach of a criminal standard of proof beyond doubt. However, from South Africa to Ghana, much of the institutional resources of truth commissions have been devoted to an individual case by case determination of who is a victim and who is a perpetrator—ie to a legalized process aimed at what the South African Truth and Reconciliation Commission (TRC) called 'forensic' truth. The statement taking department develops statement taking forms designed to procure information that will be crucial for this determination. Most truth commissions also have large investigative units that are mandated to verify the claims made in these statements. Typically these investigative units shadow the investigative units of courts and employ investigators such as ex-policemen who have experience tracking witness statements in criminal cases. Moreover, as was the case in South Africa, in many commissions, their public hearings also perform an investigative function seeking to shed light on events, consolidate evidence and clarify the witness's story about specific incidents for the official record. Thus commissioners may cross-examine witnesses, and even (as in the Ghanaian case) structure hearings to allow lawyers to lead the questioning of witnesses as a designated part of the process. Reparation programmes often rely on the determinations made by the investigative unit of truth commissions or substitute similar processes to determine beneficiaries of reparation programmes.

The Feminist Critique of the Privileged Methodology of Transitional Justice

Feminists have argued that these judicial processes come with significant costs. On the one hand a forum for testimony is critical. Referencing the public witnessing of comfort women through the language of human rights, it has been argued that this process enabled 'survivors "to awaken" from the social death of the unsharable past'. 'By telling stories of forced recruitment, hunger, confinement, torture, beatings, disease, rape, death and humiliation, the women reconstitute both private and public memories of the past.'[19] However, courts offer particularly inhospitable fora for such testimony. Feminists have argued that criminal justice processes are focused on perpetrators, not the dignity of victims or their priorities for justice. Judicial processes are often alienating for victims, and in some cases may even disempower victims. Specific charges to this effect have emerged from both the International Criminal Tribunal for the former Yugoslavia

---

[19] Smith describes the work done by testimonials in the story of comfort women in the international public sphere by quoting Hyun Sook Kim, 'History and Memory: The Comfort Women Controversy' (1997) 5 *positions* 73–108 and E Van Alphen, 'Symptoms of Discursivity: Experience Memory and Trauma' in M Bal, J Crewe, L Spitzer (eds), *Acts of Memory: Cultural Recall in the Present* (Hanover, Dartmouth Press, 1999). See Smith, above n 15, 130.

(ICTY) and International Criminal Tribunal for Rwanda (ICTR) processes. In both these cases it was argued that hostile cross-examination further exacerbated the injury suffered by victims even in the process of providing accountability.[20] Noting that in the ICTY even Milosevic, acting as his own counsel, was allowed to cross-examine witnesses, Leigh Gilmore comments that in such contexts 'the story of trauma is shaped by legal protocols regulating testimony and evidence, but also by the juridical frame for truth production ... in which the witness to trauma may be discounted.'[21] Tailored as they are to establishing facts regarding the culpability of individual defendants, it is argued that court processes may offer victims little room to discuss the personal and social context of the violation; focused on justiciable indicators of harm, court processes and judicialised truth commission processes may not allow victims to convey the personal impact of the violation.[22]

Concerned that the dominance of the legalistic methodology informs not only courts but transitional justice as a whole, feminists critical of the 'forensic' approach to the tracking of injury have urged that this privileging of the juridical approach fundamentally misunderstands and excludes alternative political vocabularies. In fact, it is argued that from the South African TRC to the tribunals in the Hague, transitional justice institutions have commissioned what Gilmore describes as 'forensic speech acts' that those institutions can traffic in as evidence, evidence that is 'capable of speech.'[23] In exchange for giving legal 'audibility' to testimonials, Gilmore and others argue that courts and official justice exclude history, context and effect. Moreover, in many contexts it is women who are adversely affected by this exclusion, and alienated by the reliance on the legalistic methodologies of transitional justice. Thus feminists have argued that for transitional justice to be more inclusive of women's voices, and more appreciative of a holistic articulation of experience, it needs to be more pluralistic in the political vocabularies it entertains. For instance, Gilmore argues that literary texts such as that of Jamaica Kinkaid or autobiographical speech such as that of Rigoberta Menchu may provide an alternative 'testimonial archive' that is

---

[20] See J Mertus, 'Truth in a Box: the Limits of Justice through Judicial Mechanisms' in I Amadiume and A An-Na'im (eds), *The Politics of Memory: Truth, Healing, and Social Justice* (London, Zed Books, 2000).

[21] L Gilmore, 'Autobiography's Wounds' in W Hesford and W Kozol (eds), *Just Advocacy? Women's Human Rights, Transnational Feminism and the Politics of Representation* (New Jersey, Rutgers University Press, 2005) 107.

[22] Martha Minow describes testifying as an ordeal, which presents the victim with no opportunity to give their narrative directly, in 'Hope for Healing' in R Rotberg and D Thompson (eds), *Truth vs. Justice* (Princeton, Princeton University Press, 2000).

[23] See Gilmore, above n 20, 107. Gilmore herself sees autobiography as opening a space for testimony regarding trauma that is an antidote to the institutional protocols of courts and clinics.

'not bound by the legalistic requirements of courts'.[24] Following Spivak, she describes these forums as producing testimony as 'a wound where the blood of history does not dry'.[25] This alternative testimonials can produce 'the subject of historical trauma' as one 'who is clearly distinct from the autonomous, rational, humanist, neo liberal, rights bearing subject 'that we are familiar with'.[26]

The feminisation of 'experience' rests on an unstated background understanding of women's voice as a priori an articulation of injury. Thus feminine testimony is already always testimony regarding trauma. The sedimentation of 'injury' as the ground from which women enter the transitional justice stage fuels the embrace of the testimonial form and experiential narratives as a project creating 'safe spaces' for the 'traumatised' voice. As already noted, many oral history projects are founded on the premise that these platforms for testimony provide more authentic access to women's experience of injury and more space for the recognition and acknowledgement of 'effect' as the subversive 'other' of law—the feminine that exceeds and spills out of legal categories and judgments.[27]

This approach has informed the transitional justice field in general, and truth commission processes in particular. In discussions with statement takers, psychologists and others working with commissions, one hears repeated discussions about the limits of excessively judicialised mechanisms to fully represent women's experiences and the need to use testimonials or other avenues to better represent women.[28] In some contexts truth commissions have incorporated this model into how they work with testimony— for instance, the Peruvian commission argued that victim testimony was so sacred that it must remain unencumbered by the mediation of the state and that the way to do this was to have victims provide testimony with no engagement by the commissioners—with no cross-examination or follow-up inquiries into the politics of the incident. Even the Ghanaian TRC, a commission that was perceived to be excessively 'judicialised' because it utilised its public hearings for investigating events and cross-examining witnesses, continued to celebrate witness testimony for 'non-judicial' virtues such as personal catharsis. The South African commission famously tried to marry these different goals in the different 'truths' at which it aimed—forensic and social, personal and dialogical. In fact, the creating of a platform where

---

[24] Idem.
[25] Idem.
[26] Idem.
[27] Note the debate on Rigoberta Menchu and contested narratives about the Guatemalan experience of conflict and human rights violations.
[28] Author's ongoing conversations with Adolf Awuku Bekoe and other psychologists and statement takers in the Ghanaian commission 2002–05, and workshop comments by Karen Campbell of the Timor Leste Commission ICTJ's 2005 Bellagio meeting on Gender and Transitional Justice. For more on the Bellagio meeting see Nesiah, above n 3.

witnesses can testify to their experience of injury was itself advanced as a form of reparation.

Interestingly, there has been a reverse flow of influence as it were from commissions to courts on the question of testimony and its role in formal proceedings. Thus in feminist engagements with court processes there has been much discussion about creating institutional avenues to ensure that courts can be more sensitive to the problems of cross-examination and the need to respect victims' voices. The starting point of feminist victim advocacy on procedural reforms in this vein is the notion that victim testimony is sacrosanct, too revelatory of a personal narrative truth to be burdened with dialogue, interpretation and exchange that does not seek to affirm, comfort and redress—let alone be subject to adversarial cross-examination.[29]

THE LIMITS OF INCLUSION

In the preceding section I identified two different kinds of biases that characterise dominant approaches to transitional justice, and the critiques that feminists may bring to the field. Moreover, these critiques were themselves suggestive of alternative conceptual foundations and institutional practices that are more inclusive and representative of women and their human rights agendas, interests and priorities.

But what is the cost of this quest for representation? Judith Butler has argued that, 'It is not enough to inquire into how women might become more fully represented in language and politics. Feminist critique ought also to understand how the category of "women", the subject of feminism, is produced and restrained by the very structure of power through which emancipation is sought.'[30] For instance, let us look at the first bias that we identified above—the bias in the subject of transitional justice, the subject constituted by the laws and norms that are inherent in the notion of 'international crimes'[31]—and the work of feminist lawyers to press crimes such as 'rape' into pre-existing legal categories regarding torture

---

[29] The commission introduced the first public hearings thus: 'a public hearing comprises several aspects of TRC's work. We mainly conceive it, though, as an element to give the victims back their dignity and, in this regard, as a healing and redressing activity. To achieve this we need the activity to take place under a fundamental principle: respect for those who provide testimony. This is why we say it is a solemn session. We want to respect other people's pain and, through us, the country to start expressing consideration to victims. Commissioners shall listen to testimonies. They will be the ears of the Nation.' See www.cverdad.org.pe/ingles/informacion/discursos/en_apublicas01.php (visited 21 May 2009).

[30] J Butler, *Gender Trouble* (New York, Routledge, 1999) 2. For further discussion about the politics of representation and inclusion, see Charlesworth, above, this collection; and Kouvo, below, this collection.

[31] See Andersson, below, this collection.

or crimes against humanity for inclusion and full representation within transitional justice. If the category 'women' may elude and exceed transitional justice, by disciplining that category as a subject of an international crime, that excess is checked and the universality of transitional justice affirmed. Thus the very production of the gendered subject through the jurisprudential 'recognition' of the sexual violence victim as having suffered an international crime is also then the legitimation of transitional justice. That 'recognition' is a constitutive moment: 'There may not be a subject who stands "before" the law, awaiting representation in or by the law. Perhaps the subject, as well as the invocation of a temporal "before", is constituted by the law as the fictive foundation of its own claim to legitimacy'.[32]

It is not that there are no 'victims' of sexual violence, it is that defining women by their sexual violability is no unencumbered victory for feminism.[33] It obscures and constraints understanding of the structures and ideologies that shape subjectivity and social relations outside of that bodily injury. The focus on bodily injury has led to the exclusion of other important dimensions of women's lives and struggles from the human rights radar screen. For example, in Peru, Rwanda, South Africa, Sierra Leone and many other contexts, internal displacement and forced removals were a crucial dimension of women's experience of conflict and the long term socio-economic impact of the war—an impact that is not captured in a focus on sexual violation alone. However, victims of displacement are invisible to the prosecution efforts in all of these contexts; more strikingly however, feminist engagement with these prosecution initiatives has also focused exclusively on bodily injury. Relatedly, reducing rape to its instrumentalisation in war has also obscured attention to the enabling structures of violence. Drawing on Sharon Marcus's critique of justice efforts that posit women as 'inherently rapable', Doris Buss has underscored how contemporary approaches to rape in the context of genocide can produce a decontextualised and thin view of genocide, its causes and consequences.[34]

The way we seek to address rape also has important implications for how agency is configured. For instance, paradoxically, the telescoping focus on the injured body can augment a women's sense of victimisation from sexual abuse. In advocating for recognition of sexual violence as meeting the 'shock the conscience' threshold of an international crime, we also impact how women themselves may invest in a heightened sense of injury

---

[32] Butler, above n 29, 3.

[33] See Andersson, who addresses these issues in the context of trafficking women for sexual purposes, below, this collection.

[34] Doris Buss, 'Rethinking Rape as a Weapon of War' (2009) *Feminist Legal Studies* 17:145–163.

from sexual violation. For instance, when the Category One crimes of post-genocide trials in Rwanda classify rape in the same 'box' as murder, it may actually accentuate women's experience of victimisation from rape as a fate equivalent to death. Sidonie Smith highlights how this 'ur story' of 'abject victimization' flattens our understanding through a juxtaposition of the autobiography of Maria Rose Hensen's *Comfort Women* with the 'script of former sex prisoner' in the public testimonials for recognition of comfort women;[35] Smith's reading highlights how the latter strips away the complex and heterogeneous dimension of women's experiences of war that the former conveys. The autobiography gives Hensen an opportunity to 'write beyond' that script, to tell a story that includes her work with resistance fighters, her marriage to another activist and her community's refusal to be 'passive victims of the Japanese occupation and capitalist oppression'.[36] Smith's reading has interesting resonances with Janet Halley's parallel juxtaposition of *A Woman in Berlin: A Diary* (an anonymously published account of one woman's experiences during the fall of Berlin to the Soviet Army in 1945), and contemporary international feminist jurisprudence.[37] Halley read the diary as holding in tension the experience of rape and the experience of war; the 'meaning' of the former changes and shifts when situated within the dynamics of war, and the multiple ways in which it undoes and reshapes the world of the diary's author such that rape cannot be collapsed into the totality of war, or its injuries. In fact, in some cases, 'rape' may negotiate and hold in abeyance other harms of war. Relatedly, as Karen Engle has argued vis-à-vis the ICTY's interventions, in its effort to protect women through this focus on bodily *injury*, international criminal law may also have the unintended consequence of limiting women's sexual freedom more directly by making all cross-ethnic sexual relationships in times of armed conflict presumptively criminal.[38] Feminists investigating, recording and condemning the crime of rape invest in a heightened sense of injury that needs to explain away a victim's resilience or minimising of injury as false consciousness that needs to be 'corrected' by women's rights and human rights

---

[35] Smith, above n 15, 130–38.

[36] Ibid 136.

[37] J Halley, 'Rape in Berlin: Reconsidering the Criminalisation of Rape in the International Law of Armed Conflict' (2008) 9 *Melbourne Journal of International Law* 78.

[38] For instance, see Engle's analysis of how 'assumptions ... that there are essential ethnic differences between Serbs, Croats, and Bosnian Muslims and that women are powerless victims, incapable of defending themselves or speaking out to defend others, but also of taking sides or participating in war' became embedded in feminists' efforts to render the ICTY's rules of evidence and procedure more hospitable to accountability for rape in K Engle, 'Feminism and Its (Dis)contents: Criminalising Wartime Rape in Bosnia and Herzegovina' (2005) 99 *American Journal of International Law* 778; see also Halley, above n 37.

education.[39] Thus ironically, if a raped woman is not feeling devastated, feminists may find it necessary to 'educate' her regarding the extent of the injury she has suffered.

Our concern here is that feminist engagements in the transitional justice field are so invested in what Brown has termed 'wounded attachments' and that the peculiar dynamic of investment in this identity of injury curbs feminism's political imagination, and limits its ability to stake out more transformative political claims.[40] Unlike engagements that subvert the naturalised priorities of transitional justice, feminism seeks inclusion within its framework. Rather than expose the biases inherent in universalised thresholds of 'shock the conscience' international crime, feminism seeks representation of sexual crimes within that pantheon of privileged rights violations. There is ground for concern here that investment in sexual violability as the entry point for transitional justice blunts the critical edge of feminism.[41] It is worth noting that this contrasts with a different tradition of feminist approaches to rape that emphasised resilience and contestation rather than injury and abjection.[42]

---

[39] For instance, note this Human Rights Watch report regarding rape of Jewish women in camps during the holocaust: 'Thus, an inherent cruel irony underlies the discussion of the rape of Jewish women by Germans and, moreover, it takes no stretch of the imagination to consider that a pervasive and persistent culture of patriarchy "permitted" Jewish men to demand sex for food in ghettos and camps. Just as rape has extensive physical and psychological repercussions for the woman, so does sexual abuse in the form of sex for survival, though perhaps not as much. And just as rape by a friend or relative results in a profound sense of betrayal, so did abuse by a fellow Jew constitute an act of betrayal in the minds of Jewish women. While their need for food was stronger and more elemental than their need to protect their dignity, they were nevertheless victimized and exploited by Jewish men. To be fair, at the same time, we must recognize that women's lack of awareness about their rights prior to the human rights and women's rights movements contributed to their acceptance of a certain amount of exploitation. Clearly, in the ghettos and camps, women's status—or lack of status—"compounded their vulnerability to violence". A vulnerability that included, apparently their own sense that rape was not devastating or that next to the lack of food and other dimensions of the holocaust rape was not the dominant injury.' See M Goldenberg, 'Sex, Rape and Survival' at www.theverylongview. com/WATH/essays/sexrapesurvival.htm (visited 21 May 2009). Goldenberg cites the Human Rights Watch, *Global Report on Women's Human Rights* (New York, 2005).

[40] See W Brown, 'Wounded Attachments' (1993) 21 *Political Theory* 390–410.

[41] There is a need for an historical grounding to appreciating the changing stakes in putting energies on sexual violence/rape as an international crime. The imperatives for drawing attention to the nexus between militarism and violence against women 20 years ago are different from the current context. There is some resonance here with the point Janet Halley makes regarding sexual harassment law in the US—the role of sexual harassment policies today is very different from the role of these struggles some decades back when women were entering the workforce. Paraphrasing Janet Halley we may say that whatever the benefits of arguing sexual violability as an international crime, it also has costs that are not counted. J Halley, 'Sexual Harassment' in J Halley and W Brown (eds), *Left Legalism/Left Critique* (Durham and London, Duke University Press, 2002) 102.

[42] Comments By Janet Halley, Panel on Feminist Interventions: Human Rights, Armed Conflict and International Law, Annual meeting of the American Society of International Law 2009.

In assessing the impact of transitional justice institutions' focus on the injured body, we also need to look at how this focus mediated testimony and produces an investment in a narrative of victimhood. As Sharon Marcus has argued, rape is not a free standing signifier; rather, legal and political interventions regarding rape, consciously or unconsciously deploy a 'rape script' that interpolates the meaning of rape within the grammar of gender inequality.[43] Fiona Ross' story of the South African TRC's handling of rape provides an illustrative, if troubling, incidence of how transitional justice institutions can define women through their injury. In the context of its public hearings, the narrative account of injury was the privileged route to 'truth'; it was the testimonial form that publicly performed verification. The South African commission was troubled that it was not receiving rape narratives yet the commission knew that rape was an integral part of abuses under apartheid and wanted to be able to tell that story. It is against this backdrop that Yvonne Khutuwane came to the commission and came to be the prized rape story. Khutuwane had been an activist from the time she was a teenager and had faced many abuses as a result of her activism—she was imprisoned many times, her house was burnt, she was tortured and harassed and in one of her periods of imprisonment she was raped. The commission asked her many questions about the rape and little else; even when she was trying to talk about the rest of her experience, they kept returning to the rape. Fiona Ross's interview with Khutuwane about her experience with the commission is quite remarkable because Khutuwane herself says she went to the commission because she wanted her grandchildren to know that she fought for the liberation too, that she was part of the country's freedom story—it was a story of activism and resilience that she wanted to narrate. Yet the commission itself needed to see her as a victim and she entered the final report not as an activist but as a rape victim. This becomes the 'truth' of the Yvonne Khutuwane story.

This analysis carries interesting and important resonances with the second of the biases identified above—namely the critique of legalistic methodologies as alienating for women, and the concomitant embrace of the testimonial form as more conducive to the representation of women's experiences. The commission's commitment to testimony as the avenue to truth made it particularly invested in the Khutuwane story to authenticate what other kinds of social and statistical analysis may already have been conveyed regarding sexual violence under apartheid. The South African TRC had institutional hearings and thematic hearings but it was testimony regarding personal injury that was privileged over all else. Where law and judicial methods were seen as mediating voice in ways that obscured truth,

---

[43] See Marcus, 'Fighting bodies, fighting words: A theory and politics of rape prevention' in Judith Butler and Joan Scott (eds), *Feminists theorize the political* (New York, Routledge, 1992) 385–403.

the project became one of creating processes that would render experience and voice more legible and unmediated. Over a decade ago, Joan Scott, Chandra Mohanty and a whole host of others exposed the dangers of pre-critical empiricism, reifying experience, essentialising identity and obscuring the social production of voice.[44] As Scott notes, 'experience is at once always already an interpretation *and* in need of interpretation.' Yet these insights seem obscured in today's efforts to make transitional justice institutions more 'gender friendly' through a return to this nostalgia for a transparent, authentic voice and the faith it seeks to engender in the therapeutic value of participation in these institutions.

In sum then, when feminists advocate for transitional justice institutions to focus on testimonials they buttress claims regarding the therapeutic and emancipatory value of speech that rest on problematic assumptions regarding injury and healing that do not engage with the fraught complex terrain of the speech act. Moreover, they legitimate institutions that are mobilised by objectives that may often be at odds with the very witnesses they are asked to 'nurture' in this way. Most important, the feminist discourse on experience and voice have enhanced the truth value attributed to experiential knowledge in ways that have empowered institutions claiming to 'simply' convey truth by 'accessing' experience. Thus from statement taking forms to truth commission modalities, discussion on whether these create sensitive and therapeutic environments for women's testimony have obscured the 'discursive nature of experience and the politics of its construction.' Thus the very dichotomies advanced by the testimony focused transitional justice institutions, such as social truth and narrative truth, law and experience, may already carry the grammar of that which we criticise in abandoning politics in the name of voice, law in the name of therapy. Debate over whether the official record should be defined by narrative truth versus legalistic truth elides the way the official historical record can itself provide bounded closure over enduring injustice.

CONCLUDING THOUGHTS

I have discussed just two instances where the principal modalities for making transitional justice more gender friendly may not be an unencumbered emancipatory project; this is not intended as a catalogue of the failure of feminist critique, that every critique is a trap, that dystopic post-feminist nihilism is all we have. Rather the effort is to open the conversation to the paradoxes of feminist critique and the challenges of a counter-hegemonic project.

---

[44] See S Stone-Mediatore's discussion of these interventions in 'Chandra Mohanty and the revaluing of "experience"' (1998) 13 *Hypatia* 116.

The tension of institutionalised feminism serving the cause of reform and absorption, rather than subversion and challenge is not confined to the transitional justice field. For instance, there has long been concern that the institutionalisation of women's studies in the academy lost scholars interested in a subversive interrogation of gender as a category of knowledge and performance of the social.[45] Some streams of feminist activism have been directed at inclusion in conservative institutions such as the clergy and the military. When women reached the higher echelons of political power, they invariably advanced positions that maintained and reproduced dominant hierarchies.

These experiences suggests that if feminism is going to enable a counter-hegemonic subversion of transitional justice's naturalised biases/exclusions/hierarchies it may require a reflective, self-critical examination of what becomes naturalised in feminism's own effort to make the project more inclusive, more representative. Feminism may intervene to extend the boundaries of transitional justice, but crucially, it could seek to offer the ground from which to call into question the very terms of those boundary markers.[46] In fact, the story of feminist engagement in many fields is that the very terms through which a debate has been structured are called into question, but that questioning itself often generated a new ground, with a new set of fault lines, from which to situate and shape political engagement.[47] In this case, I worry that rather than breaking new ground that illuminates the limits of transitional justice institutions, and better defines the stakes of alternative discursive practices, feminism reinforces old myths that empower the new face of transitional justice. On the one hand feminist engagements with transitional justice presents as 'cutting edge', as the new frontier of 'women's rights in human rights'—and yet it remains mired in yesterday's embrace of the gendered victim and authentic voice. Tired icons of early feminism that we thought were already put to rest are reinvigorated and resurrected in the transitional justice field.

In my conclusion, I want to suggest that the global backdrop provides at least partial explanation for why feminist transitional justice interventions have not contested the most problematic aspects of transitional justice (such as the focus on bodily injury) but have worked to get entry into transitional justice institutions—and, moreover, that they have done so by resurrecting the most simplistic and problematic approaches to gender. First, there is the dynamic in several fields, from economic development to human rights, that when theories, practices and discourses are exported they get simplified and evacuated of all the complex, thick social histories that shaped their

---

[45] J Scott, *Women's Studies on the Edge* (Indiana, Indiana University Press, 1999).
[46] V Nesiah, 'The Ground Beneath Her Feet: Third World Feminist Debates' (2003) 4 *Journal of International Women's Studies* 31.
[47] Ibid 37.

histories in situ.[48] From the essentialism debates about defining women's subjectivity as sexual victims to fetishising experiential knowledge, many of the very same shibboleths that were unpacked and interrogated in an earlier generation of feminism in many national contexts, from India to the US, have re-emerged on the global terrain of transitional justice as if innocent of those interrogations. Like an Ikea furniture piece, the selling point of transitional justice institutions is that they come in flat packages that are easily shipped, unpacked and set up in new terrain. There is here a canon of knowledge and practice that travels light—where the ease of entry enabled by neoliberalism also frees feminism of any ambivalent baggage, a feminism shorn of complexity and self-interrogation. Even if feminism is wrapped in self doubt at 'home' (whatever 'home' is—be it an academic discipline, a place, a social movement), it can become simplified when taken overseas—it rediscovers a new terrain for redemption, where feminism can once again be an emancipatory project.

Secondly, the ease with which liberal concepts and practices gain dominance (even if not hegemony) also gets re-charged in the post-1989 geo-political landscape. To some extent contemporary transitional justice gets its impetus in the Southern Cone from the truth commissions, reparation programmes, and (at least in Argentina) prosecutions that followed the military dictatorships in the region. The South African TRC learns from that experience but also expands the political work of truth commission in ways that capture the global imagination and launches transitional justice as an international phenomenon. A phenomenon that soon develops institutional legs, resource reach and discursive traction not only in national nation building efforts but also in transnational fora such as the UN, donor budgets, international NGOs and research centres. After that point transitional justice gets incorporated into a North to South trajectory. This is equally true of the dominant strands of feminist engagements with transitional justice; some indicators of this North-South trajectory include the fact that feminist engagements in transitional justice get funded by international donors and get framed in terms of international law and policy (such as Security Council Resolution 1325). While most globally influential feminist NGOs with a transitional justice focus are headquartered in the global North, this is not to say that all feminists involved with

---

[48] Eg, there has long been a recognition that while the economic history of countries such as the UK and the US indicates that market economies have travelled multiple paths accompanied by a range of different subsidies and social entitlements, when 'market economics' gets exported to Eastern Europe or the Global South it gets exported as a singular model that requires the lifting of tariffs, trade barriers and regulatory protections. See S Muralidharan, 'Some heresies of development: An interview with Roberto Unger' in *Frontline: India's National Magazine*, Vol 18, No 18, 1–14 September 2001.

transitional justice are from the global North[49]—this is not a point about identity. Rather, the point is that there is a structurally Northern tilt to the field. It is a tilt that enables and accompanies the founding of feminist initiatives in the field, and the globalised terrain of resources ('discursive' capital) that have been injected into the transitional justice field, including feminist engagements with it. Feminist engagement with transitional justice is mobile and global, travelling from Sierra Leone to The Hague, Geneva to the Democratic Republic of the Congo, working on war crime courts and shaping reparation policies, conducting capacity development workshops and consolidating best practice lists.

It is travel that is lubricated by post-9/11 events. Like human rights groups more generally, gender focused groups that were actively critical of the Bush era invocations of human rights found themselves in a terrain that empowered them even when it complicated their work—a terrain where militarism and human rights were intertwined and liberal principles were mobilised for neoliberal agendas. From Afghanistan to Iraq, human rights/ good governance/rule of law and 'gender sensitivity' were invoked not only to lubricate military interventions in the name of the rule of law, but also to lubricate the sedimentation of neoliberalism into the international community's post-conflict interventions. In some ways the latter had greater significance because human rights' ostensible innocence of power becomes the Trojan horse of naturalised imperial hubris that speaks of victimised women and therapeutic testimony. This is not to set up the 'local' as a venue of oppositional contestation[50] or to devalue transnational solidarities in the name of human rights that contested empire. Rather it is to underscore the complexities of human rights discourse—if human rights violations from Abu Ghraib to Guantanamo Bay helped bring down the empire, human rights discourse also helped to prop it up[51] and transitional justice was the most striking face of the triumphant human rights that empowered neoliberalism. The trial of Saddam Hussein for human rights violations and the formation of the ICC both represent this triumph and mark different faces of international intervention, through the bayonet in one context and the gavel in the other, even when advanced by the US in one context and repudiated by the US in another.

---

[49] In fact many of theses groups are genuinely international in composition. For instance, although the Coalition for Women's Human Rights in Conflict Situations is headquartered in Canada they have a diverse membership and work closely with local partners.

[50] As Hesford and Kozol note, 'the local and global are constituted through each other' and the point here is to come to terms with the 'possibilities and limitations of using rights discourse' for transnational feminist advocacy. See 'Introduction' in W Hesford and W Kozol (eds), *Just Advocacy? Women's Human Rights, Transnational Feminism and the Politics of Representation* (New Jersey, Rutgers University Press, 2005) 19.

[51] V Nesiah, 'From Berlin to Bonn: Militarization and Multilateral Decision-Making' (2004) 17 *Harvard Human Rights Law Journal* 75–98.

Undoubtedly, in many different contexts transitional justice may open opportunities that are critical for women to embrace, extend and make their own. The discursive classification and institutional practices of transitional justice may not all be easily abandoned—as Spivak says of rights more broadly, it may be 'that which we cannot not want'.[52] However, for this to be what Spivak also refers to as an 'enabling violation' requires 'decolonizing the mind through negotiating the structures of violence'.[53] For instance, not merely expanding the received category of international crimes to include sexual violence but to challenge the notion of a hierarchy of human rights violations that can be made universal; not simply to expand the domain of transitional justice to include acts of private or domestic violence but also to challenge the notion of violent acts that can be prosecuted and addressed without also calling into account their enabling structures and ideologies. Moreover to expand and pluralise our vocabularies of justice and redress without reinscribing hegemonic narratives that equate justice with the 'rule of law', or its converse—equating non-legal narratives with unmediated 'truths'.

This may be a moment then for re-orienting critical energies; for recognising the limits of merely reforming transitional justice, of just taking sides in a debate about preferred methodologies, or of simply expanding the scope of the dominant subject to be more inclusive. If we reduce our interventions to the latter, feminist engagements with transitional justice merely contribute to a conservative project of 'bounded closure'.[54] The work we are advocating for may not hold the redemptive promise of an emancipatory project; however, it is work that challenges the imagination of 'justice' within the received repertoire of human rights work.

---

[52] G Spivak, 'Constitutions and Culture Studies' (1990) 2 *Yale Journal of Law and the Humanities* 133–47.
[53] Idem.
[54] Teitel, above n 4.

9

Taking Women Seriously? Conflict, State-building and Gender in Afghanistan

SARI KOUVO*

'God save us always', I said, 'from the innocent and the good'.

G Greene, *The Quiet American*, 2004 [first published, 1955]

INTRODUCTION

Snapshot 1: Gender Mainstreaming

In 2007, I had the opportunity to assess the efforts to mainstream gender and human rights into the projects of a major non-governmental organisation in Afghanistan. I was told by those tasked to deliver gender training that a large part of the training had to focus on undoing misconceptions about gender. 'Six years into President Karzai's internationally supported rule', I was told, '"everybody" in Afghanistan has heard about "gender", but it remains a foreign concept and there's no translation for it in Dari and Pashto. Most people think that it means that Afghan women should become like Western women, that they should leave their husbands.'

While many of those tasked to implement the gender mainstreaming programmes emphasised that the gender training they had received had been an eye opener for them, they stressed that they did not know what to do with their new knowledge, they had not learnt what gender mainstreaming meant for their everyday work. Some said that they now tried to discuss 'gender' as part of their community and rural development work, but that they did not use the language of gender. I was told that 'We do not speak of gender when speaking to villagers; we translate it into village language; we translate it into our language'.

* The writing of this chapter was made possible through a visiting scholarship at the Centre for Law, Gender and Sexuality at Keele and Kent Universities in December 2006 and funding from the Swedish Board of Science within the auspices of the project 'Sexualizing the Public Space—Problematising Law, Market and the Body'.

THE POST-9/11 UNITED States (US) led military intervention came when Afghanistan had been off the international agenda for more than a decade. It also came after a decade's surprisingly successful international advocacy for women's rights. During this decade, one of the rallying points for the international women's movements agenda was bringing an end to the Taliban's 'gender apartheid' in Afghanistan.

The US led military intervention in Afghanistan was justified as an act of self-defence and dominated by a will to oust the Taliban regime, hunt down Osama Bin Laden and bring an end to Al Qaeda. However, additional public legitimacy for the intervention was sought by reproducing the international women's movements arguments about 'bringing democracy to the Afghan people' and 'saving Afghan women'. The United Nations (UN) and the wider international community were brought in to support the state-building efforts, including its softer components focusing on women's and human rights.

Nine years down the track, the US and the wider international community have lost their way in Afghanistan. The Taliban insurgency has returned fiercer than ever, the internationally supported government of President Karzai has lost its public legitimacy due to widespread corruption and links with warlords and narco-traffickers. In this context, the well-meaning, but often naïve efforts to 'save Afghan women' have again been overrun and marginalised.

Against the background of the military intervention and state-building efforts, this chapter analyses the construction of the women's rights and gender discourses in Afghanistan.[1] The analysis in this chapter draws on my previous research about feminist perspectives on international law, and the development of strategies for integrating women's rights and mainstreaming gender as the preferred international strategies for women's advancement and equality during the 1990s. It also draws on my experiences of working on women's and human rights issues in Afghanistan.[2]

This chapter is divided into three parts. The first part, 'Gender, Conflict and 9/11' provides background to the conflict, women's situation and the international intervention in Afghanistan. The second part, 'Women's Rights

---

[1] See generally S Mahmood, *Politics of Piety. The Islamic Revival and the Feminist Subject* (Princeton, Princeton University Press, 2005); A Orford, *Reading Humanitarian Interventions: Human Rights and the Use of Force in International Law* (New York, Cambridge University Press, 2003) and A Orford (ed), *International Law and its Others* (Cambridge, Cambridge University Press, 2006).

[2] See generally S Kouvo, *Making Just Rights? Mainstreaming Women's Human Rights and a Gender Perspective* (Sweden, Iustus Publications, 2004); S Kouvo, 'The United Nations and Gender Mainstreaming: Limits and Possibilities' in D Buss and A Manji (eds), *International Law: Modern Feminist Approaches* (Portland, Hart Publishing, 2005); S Kouvo, 'A "Quick and Dirty" Approach to Women's Rights—A Case Study of Afghanistan' (2007) 16 *Feminist Legal Studies* 363 and S Kouvo and C Levine, 'Calling a Spade a Spade—Tackling the Women and Peace Orthodoxy' (2008) 16 *Feminist Legal Studies* 363.

and Gender in the State-Building Process' discusses the strategies for gender mainstreaming and women's participation in Afghanistan. As the snapshot above seeks to illustrate, the focus has been on mainstreaming gender but without real attempts to understand what gender means in the Afghan context, and on promoting women's participation but without necessarily understanding the complexities of the Afghan political culture.[3] The third part, 'Conclusions: Taking Women Seriously?' pulls together the different parts arguing at the same time for more intrusive and more locally adapted interventions on gender and women's representation.

GENDER, CONFLICT AND 9/11

A History of Conflict and Poverty

Women's situation cannot be advanced in a vacuum. This chapter seeks to show how the overall failure to bring stability and a functioning government framework to Afghanistan has affected the efforts to promote women's rights. It also shows how the complex mix of conflict, custom and poverty has contributed to discrimination and oppression of Afghan women, and how the lack of historical and cultural understanding that plagues the international intervention has led to strategies poorly adapted to Afghan women's needs and the Afghan context.

Kabul-based governments have made repeated attempts to unify and modernise the different ethnic groups and tribes scattered around the mountainous and in many ways inhospitable Afghan territory.[4] To the extent that these attempts have been viewed as serving the political interest of a ruling minority, being ethnically skewed or in conflict with local norms and interests they have been resisted. This does not mean that Afghans are generally backwards, but conflict and repeated changes of government have made Afghans sceptical about directives coming from Kabul—or abroad. The attempts to modernise—or to impose a different order—have also often sought to change the situation of women. The best known reform schemes are those of King Amanullah in the 1930s, Daoud Khan in the 1970s and the Soviet-backed Communist government in the 1980s. The most recent modernisation attempt is that of the ongoing internationally supported stabilisation and state-building effort.

---

[3] For further discussion on the shortcomings of mainstreaming, see Charlesworth; and Nesiah, above, this collection.

[4] See generally R Barnett, *The Fragmentation of Afghanistan* (New Haven, Yale University Press, 2002) and A Rashid, *Descent into Chaos. The United States and the Failure of Nation-Building in Afghanistan, Pakistan and Central Asia* (New York, Viking Penguin, 2008).

In the family-centred and close-knit communities of rural Afghanistan, women are viewed as the carriers of the family honour. The gender codes place the burden of protecting and providing for the family on men, but women bear an equally heavy burden as throughout their lives they have to show themselves deserving of protection through their moral conduct, ability to give birth to male heirs and roles as carers. Women enjoy the privilege of protection, but they are also punished if they fail in their tasks of child bearing, caring and upholding the family honour. A combined result of poverty and the need to ensure that girls' honour is protected is early and forced marriage. In contemporary Afghanistan, over half of all Afghan girls are married at the age of 16. Marrying a girl at an early age provides her father's family with access to a dowry, while the responsibility for the girl shifts to her husband's family. Transgressing the gender codes, especially in poor, rural communities, routinely results in violence against women, including so-called honour-related killings.

The negative effects of conflict on Afghan women's—and men's—lives cannot be overstated. The decades of conflict started with the communist coup and the Soviet occupation in the late 1970s. The Soviet occupiers sought to initiate reforms—including through an emphasis on girls' and women's education—that resonated poorly with the conservative and deeply religious populations of rural Afghanistan. The popular resistance against the Soviet occupation received considerable international support. For the US, supporting the Afghan resistance became a key Cold War strategy. It was a way of attacking the Soviet empire from an unexpected angle. The US financial and military support channelled through Pakistan not only enabled the Afghan resistance to fight the Soviet invaders successfully, but it also empowered a cadre of *Mujahedin* commanders (often called 'warlords')[5] and contributed to sowing the seeds of extremist politics in Afghanistan.[6] While custom and religion is an important part of Afghan life, the international financial and military support to select commanders contributed to strengthening fundamentalist religious politics in Afghanistan.

---

[5] Antonio Giustozzi defines 'warlords' as 'military leaders who emerge to play a de facto political role, despite their lack of full legitimacy', A Guistozzi, '"Good State" vs. "Bad Warlords"? A Critique of State-Building Strategies in Afghanistan', Working Paper, no 51 (London, LSE Crisis States Programme, 2004). However, as Cyrus Hodes and Mark Sedra point out, 'one person's warlord is another person's legitimate political leader', C Hodes and M Sedra, 'The Search for Security in Post-Taliban Afghanistan' (2007) 329 *Adelphi Papers* 7, 10. Legitimacy may also vary over time, and access to public power can be used to legitimise warlords, the process of warlords-turned-democrats or warlord democratisation is by now well known in Afghanistan and elsewhere, B Rubin, 'Peace-Building and State-Building in Afghanistan: Constructing Sovereignty for Whose Security?' (2008) 1 *Third World Quarterly* 177.

[6] S Coll, *Ghost Wars. The Secret History of CIA, Afghanistan and Bin Laden, from the Soviet Invasion to September 10, 2001* (New York, Penguin Books, 2004).

After a brief peace following the withdrawal of the Soviet forces in 1989, a civil war broke out. Unsuccessful power-sharing after the Soviet withdrawal resulted in infighting between the Mujahedeen commanders that soon turned into a civil war. The Soviet withdrawal from Afghanistan coincided with the end of the Cold War. Consequently, as the Soviet forces withdrew and the Soviet empire crumbled, the US lost interest in Afghanistan. The lack of support added to the political challenges inside Afghanistan—and contributed to the civil war. The civil war, maybe more than any other period of the conflict, contributed to the erosion of state structure and community and social cohesion in Afghanistan. Although information remains scarce and anecdotal, this is also the period when sexual violence was increasingly used as a weapon of war.[7]

Under the cover of the civil war, the Taliban movement developed and was able to assert its power in Afghanistan. The Taliban movement consisted of predominantly Deobandi Madrassa educated Afghan Pastuns from the Afghan refugee camps in Pakistan. The Taliban ideology combined Pashtun customary norms (*pasthunwali*) with extreme interpretations of Sharia and, on coming to power in Afghanistan, this ideology was turned into law. The Taliban rule hit hard on Shiite and other religious minorities, and on educated Afghans and women. The Taliban treatment of women included forbidding women's education and work, and forbidding women to leave their homes without being accompanied by a male family member. Already a poor country, the Taliban years forced Afghanistan further into humanitarian crisis and exclusion. The international community's disinterest in Afghanistan continued during the Taliban years (with the exception of increasing concerns expressed for the Taliban's growing ties with international terrorist networks).[8] International women's organisations attempted to break the silence: in the US-based Feminist Majority Campaign 'Stop Gender Apartheid in Afghanistan' Hollywood celebrities joined forces with politicians, academic and activists in calling for a change in Bill Clinton's policies vis-à-vis the Taliban in Afghanistan and demanding intervention in Afghanistan for the sake of Afghan women. In Europe the campaign initiated by Emma Bonino, member of the European Parliament, 'A Rose for Every Afghan Woman' managed to draw the attention of the

---

[7] See generally the Afghan Justice Project, *Casting Shadows—War Crimes and Crimes against Humanity, 1978–2001: Documentation and Analysis of Major Patterns of Abuse in Afghanistan* (Afghanistan, The Afghan Justice Project 2005), Human Rights Watch, *Blood-Stained Hands: Past Atrocities in Kabul and Afghanistan's Legacy of Impunity* (New York, Human Rights Watch 2005) and Amnesty International, *Afghanistan: Addressing the Past to Secure the Future* (London, Amnesty International 2005).

[8] F Ayub and S Kouvo, 'Righting the Course? Humanitarian Intervention, the War on Terror and the Future of Afghanistan' (2008) 4 *International Affairs* 641 and M Fielden and J Goodhand, 'Beyond the Taliban? The Afghan Conflict and United Nations Peacekeeping' (2001) 3 *Conflict, Security and Development* 5.

European Union and several of its member states to the situation of women in Afghanistan.[9] While few women's rights activists would have argued for a full-fledged military intervention as a strategy against the Taliban, feminists and other critical scholars and activists did use experiences from the international intervention in Kosovo and the duty to intervene in cases of humanitarian disasters as arguments for some form of intervention in Afghanistan.[10] The efforts to raise awareness about women's situation under the Taliban was (and is again becoming) important in order to ensure that women are not forgotten in the midst of macro-political often security-related concerns. However, identifying 'The Taliban' as the oppressor with little attention to the effects of conflict, poverty and culture in general, and identifying an international intervention as the solution radically simplified Afghan realities.

The US and its allies launched the 'War on Terror' as a response to the 9/11 attacks on the Twin Towers and Pentagon.[11] Although the US led military intervention into Afghanistan was legitimated as an act of self-defence, the language used to ensure public legitimacy echoed the demands of the 1990s Feminist Majority Campaign and the campaign initiated by Emma Bonino. Through the intervention, the Bush administration set out to succeed where the Clinton administration had failed: it would not only oust the Taliban and eradicate al-Qaeda from Afghanistan; it would also liberate Afghan women. In November 2001, the United States State Department published a short report entitled 'The Taliban's War against Women' and Laura Bush, the wife of the President, delivered a radio address expressing concern for the plight of Afghan women and emphasising the US's commitment to eradicating the 'brutality against women and children by the al-Qaeda and the regime it supports in Afghanistan, the Taliban'.[12] As noted by Vasuki Nesiah, the ground for the military intervention in Afghanistan was not 'laid by the dogs of war, or by macho bombastic talk of the axis of evil and military conquest. Rather, it was established by the soft promise of the intervention's reluctant advocates, in the name of religious tolerance, women's freedom, human rights, and liberal modernity'.[13]

---

[9] Feminist Majority Foundation, *Stop Gender Apartheid in Afghanistan: A Project of the Feminist Majority Foundation* www.helpafghanwomen.com/Global_Petition_Flyer.pdf (visited 16 December 2010) and www.emmabonino.it (visited 27 February 2009).

[10] V Nesiah, 'From Berlin to Bagdhad: A Space for Infinite Justice' (2004) 17 *Harvard Human Rights Quarterly* 75.

[11] See S Kouvo, 'State-Building and Rule of Law: Lessons from Afghanistan?' (2009) 6 *NATO Defence College Forum Papers*. See generally Otto; and Nesiah, above, this collection.

[12] H Charlesworth and C Chinkin, 'Sex, Gender and September 11' (2002) 96 *American Journal of International Law* 600, 602.

[13] Nesiah, above n 10, 95.

9/11 and the 'Liberation of the Afghan Woman'

The campaigns of the international women's movements against the Taliban treatment of women were important for drawing attention to the ongoing human rights violations and humanitarian disaster in Afghanistan.[14] However, the campaigns have also been criticised for failing to take into account the complex interaction between conflict, culture/customs and poverty that contribute to the oppression of women in Afghanistan. The Taliban did not invent women's oppression, they turned it into law. Many of the traditions and practices promoted by the Taliban were already widespread within the rural Pasthun communities in southern Afghanistan and the tribal areas of Pakistan. The Taliban regime forced these traditions and practices onto all Afghans. The socio-economic consequences of the ban on education, healthcare and employment for women were considerable. After years of conflict, Afghanistan has a large number of widows and female headed households and the fact that women were deprived of possibilities to education and work forced women and their dependents further into poverty. Today, after nine years of substantial international support, Afghanistan remains one of the poorest countries of the world. According to UN Development Program (UNDP), Afghanistan has one of the world's lowest Human Development Indexes (HDI).[15]

The post-9/11 images of Afghan women, their oppression and their liberation were not only influenced by the 1990s feminist campaigns and the political needs of the post-9/11 intervention in Afghanistan, they were also influenced by the changing perceptions of gender, culture and religion in the post-9/11 era. The September 11 events and the War on Terror have accentuated a perceived clash of civilisations between the Western world and the Islamic world. It has also dusted off Imperial imagery of 'the civilised' and 'the native', and of men as agents either on the side of good or on the side of evil and of women as mourners and victims. Judith Lorber notes that the 'social construction of heroism, masculinity, and Islamic womanhood are core parts of the gender politics of September 11, a politics deeply embedded in the current debates over the causes and the consequences of terrorism and

---

[14] Life expectancy in Afghanistan is low (44 years for women and 46 years for men). The maternal mortality rates are 16 per 1,000 births and compounded by low marriage age and lack of access to health care. Infant and under-5 mortality rates are high (140 per 1,000 births) and the under-5 mortality is 230 per 1,000 births. Education levels are low (the female literacy rate is estimated to be 16% and the male literacy rate is estimated to be 31%). See *Key Indicators, Asia Development Bank*, 2006, reproduced in *Women and Men in Afghanistan: A Handbook on Baseline Statistics on Gender*, Ministry of Women's Affairs, Kabul, Afghanistan, March 2007, Chs 5–6.

[15] https://hrdstats.undp.org/en/countries/country_fact_sheets/cty_fs_AFG.html (last visited 12 June 2010).

war'.[16] The politicians reassuring their nations, the terrorists and the 'heroes of the day', those engaged in rescue work at Ground Zero, were depicted as mainly men. Women were of course present amongst the fire fighters, the police, the medical personnel and other staff engaged at Ground Zero, but the presence of women 'did little to shake up the pervasive imagery of muscular men in uniform storming up the stairs of the World Trade Centre and burly construction crews in hard hats digging through the night in the smoking rubble, trying to find bodies'.[17] Critical scholars, such as Michael Kimmel, were also caught up in the *éloge* for the old-new male hero. While recognising that traditional definitions of masculinity have 'their imperious sides, brimming with homophobia and sexism', Kimmel stresses that they also contain 'the capacity for quiet heroism, selfless sacrifice, steadfast resolve, deep wells of compassion and caring and, yes, a love that made these men magnificent'.[18] He asks 'Isn't it just like a man to take the feelings of vulnerability, defencelessness, and helplessness—all of which are rational responses to the terrorism of September 11—and turn them into the only legitimate emotion men allow themselves to feel—anger?'.[19]

The construction of the white, working class hero, whether a fire fighter, a police officer or a soldier, is done through differentiating him from the villains of the day, the terrorists and their supporters. In the face of crisis, persuasive dichotomies of the past are dusted off and reapplied: although the heroes and the terrorists seemed to share certain values, including determination, male comradeship, a view of the family as the cornerstone of society and commitment to cultural and religious values, the similarities were suppressed and 'we were presented with a careful construction of two different types of masculinity—the *good-doers* and the *evil-doers*'.[20] Women *as* victims are integral to the construction of both the good-doers and the evil-doers: they are the wives and mothers of the men who called home before toppling the terrorists on board of the United Airlines flight 93, but women are also the victims of the extreme discrimination and violence of the Taliban and militant Islamic extremists.[21]

---

[16] J Lorber, 'A Presidential Address: Heroes, Warriors and *Burqas*: A Feminist Sociologist's Reflection on September 11' (2002) 17 *Sociological Forum* 377, 379.

[17] Ibid 380.

[18] M Kimmel, 'Declarations of War' (2001) *The Chronicle of Higher Education*, at www.chronicle.com/free/v48/i09/09b01801.htm (visited 3 March 2009).

[19] Idem.

[20] Lorber, above n 16, 383.

[21] See especially C Hirschkind and S Mahmood, 'Feminism, the Taliban, and Politics of Counter-Insurgency' (2002) 75 *Anthropological Quarterly* 339 and Nesiah, above n 10, 76; K Engle, 'Liberal Internationalism, Feminism and the Suppression of Critique: Contemporary Approaches to Global Order in the United States' (2005) 2 *Harvard International Law Journal* 427 and SG Khattak, 'Afghan Women—Bombed to be Liberated?' (2002) 222 *Middle East Report* 18.

It is deeply problematic to construct (Afghan) women as needing to be saved. 'Saving from something' always also implies a 'saving to something', and, as feminist third world and postcolonial scholars have emphasised for some time, the 'saving to' tends to be based on an equality norm modelled on Western liberalism.[22] As is noted by Hilary Charlesworth and Christine Chinkin, the 'problem with all types of gendered discourse is that it makes some courses of action impossible to contemplate' as '[gendered discourses and thinking in dichotomies] confines our perspective to simple either- or propositions. It makes certain actions seem inevitable or non-negotiable'.[23] As a consequence of the naturalisation of liberal equality norms alternative forms of equality that seek their legitimacy outside the boundaries of individual agency are often marginalised or overlooked. For example, analysing equality through a (simple) lens of individual agency and resistance to patriarchal practices runs the risk of marginalising ideas of 'equality' that move beyond individual and gender-centred equality and that prioritise kinship systems and community-wide wellbeing. Hence, when embarking on women's rights and gender quests 'feminists, or concerned citizens' should, argues Lila Abu-Lughob, 'be wary of taking on the mantles of those 19th-century Christian missionary women who devoted their lives to saving their Muslim sisters ... One can hear uncanny echoes of their virtuous goals today, even though the language is secular, the appeals not to Jesus, but to human rights or the liberal West'.[24] The next part of this chapter will take a closer look at the implementation of some of the liberal equality strategies focusing on women's representation in Afghanistan.

WOMEN'S RIGHTS AND GENDER IN THE STATE-BUILDING PROCESS

The Early Days of Women's Representation and Participation

A key theme in the efforts to promote women's rights and gender equality within the framework of the post-Taliban state-building process in Afghanistan has been on mainstreaming gender mainly through ensuring women's representation and participation in key political and reconstruction processes.[25]

---

[22] L Abu-Lughod, 'Do Muslim Women Really Need Saving? Antropological Reflections on Cultural Relativism and Its Others' (2002) 3 *American Anthropologist* 783, 788–89.

[23] Charlesworth and Chinkin, above n 12, 605.

[24] Abu-Lughob, above n 21, 789.

[25] See generally H Ahmed-Ghosh, 'Voices of Afghan Women: Human Rights and Economic Development' (2006) 1 *International Journal of Feminist Studies* 110; D Kandiyoti, 'The Politics of Gender and Reconstruction in Afghanistan' *Occasional Paper 4, United Nations Research Institute for Social Development* (New York, UNRISD, 2005); V Moghadam, 'Patriarchy, the Taleban and the Politics of Public Space in Afghanistan' (2002) 1 *Women's Studies International Forum* 19 and C Riphenburg, 'Gender Relations and Development in a Weak State: The Rebuilding of Afghanistan' (2003) 2–3 *Central Asian Survey* 187.

That is, the focus has been on ensuring the physical presence of women at different decision-making forums. Ensuring representation is a basic liberal equality strategy: through decree or law the door to decision-making forums are opened for marginalised or minority groups. Ensuring that women—or other groups—have a seat at the tables where decisions are taken does of course not necessarily equal women's actual participation in decision-making. The formal politics of representation (ensuring *any* women's participation) does not counter the post-conflict political culture, which is often marked by distrust, manipulation and semi-hidden structures of allegiance.[26] This has certainly been true in the peace- and state-building process in Afghanistan where the continued power of 'warlords', politico-military leaders with regional or ethnic powerbases commanding important, often well-armed militias has distorted the post-9/11 political process and where women's loyalties are coloured more by their politico-ethnic allegiances than their gender.

Throughout the state-building process in Afghanistan, the reformist agenda promoted by some international and Afghan actors, including some of the politically active Afghan women, has competed with the predatory politics of the US war on terror doctrine and the new Afghan political elite that is, the old factional commanders. This tension was already apparent at the Bonn conference in December 2001. The Bonn conference aimed at laying the ground for the state-building process, but it became largely focused on power-sharing between the factional commanders ('warlords'). The Bonn conference pulled together representatives of the international community and Afghan leaders with the view of taking initial steps towards forming an Afghan government and state. The Bonn conference was 'hijacked' by the factional commanders. Many of them had been propped up by the US during the Soviet invasion and they had been used as ground forces during the US's and its allies' military intervention against the Taliban government in Afghanistan. The political power of these 'warlords' at Bonn and since is based on their continuing access to armed groups inside Afghanistan and their real and perceived power to destabilise Afghanistan. Consequently, while the two women that participated in the Bonn negotiations were political actors in their own right, their presence became largely tokenistic. The reformist agenda promoted by the women and the civil society representatives did not hold against the regional and ethnic politics of the warlords.

The Agreement on Provisional Arrangements in Afghanistan Pending the Re-Establishment of Permanent Government Institutions (hereafter, the Bonn Agreement), the outcome document of the Bonn conference, included marginal references to women's participation. It emphasised the importance of women's representation in the interim administration (ensured in part

---

[26] For further discussion about gender and state-building, see Charlesworth, above, this collection.

through the establishment of the Department of Women's Affairs as part of the interim administration) and in the commission that was to convene the Emergency *Loya Jirga* ('grand assembly') that was to elect the transitional administration.

In order to counter the poor record of women's representation at the Bonn conference, a side event was organised in Brussels in December 2001. The Afghan Women's Summit for Democracy brought together women decision-makers from the UN and from European institutions, Afghan women, women's rights activists from other post-conflict countries and from international women's organisations. A delegation of the women that participated at the Brussels Summit presented the proclamation adopted at the Summit at the Bonn conference and later to decision-makers in Washington DC and to the UN Security Council. The Brussels Proclamation included a long list of priorities for the reconstruction of Afghanistan, including security, education, health care and economic development.

While women's representation (or lack thereof) at the Bonn conference has received little attention amongst feminist scholars who have followed the peace- and state-building process in Afghanistan, several articles published by feminist scholars in the years following the fall of the Taliban regime have highlighted the importance of the Brussels Summit and the Proclamation. Jessica Neuwirth stressed that the Afghan women delegates 'forcefully dismissed concerns that have been raised about so-called "cultural interference", insisting that Afghan women must be granted their fundamental human rights and that they are ready, willing and able to shoulder the responsibilities of rebuilding their country'.[27] Hilary Charlesworth and Christine Chinkin emphasise that the Brussels Proclamation, the outcome document of the Summit for Democracy, expressed a 'vision of women's future with recommendations across a broad range of issues, including health, education, human rights, participation in government, drafting of the constitution, serving as lawyers and "making all support, including monetary, from the international community conditional on the rights and treatment of women"'.[28] The woman-centred Summit for Democracy was important symbolically: it enabled a shift from viewing women as victims to showing women as actors and allowing their voices about Afghanistan's future to be heard. However, the Brussels Proclamation was a short-lived document, as opposed to the Bonn Agreement that came to guide the state-building process from 2001 till after the Parliamentary elections in 2005.

While women's representation at the Bonn conference and at the Brussels Summit was important, the emphasis on the presence of a few women failed to show how the presence of powerful 'warlords' early on put a lid on any

[27] J Neuwirth, 'Women and Peace and Security: The Implementation of UN Security Council Resolution 1325' (2002) 9 *Duke Journal of Gender, Law and Policy* 253.
[28] Charlesworth and Chinkin, above n 12, 603.

real reformist political agenda. That is, it is difficult—or impossible—to promote an open political debate when some of the parties around the table have access to considerable militia forces and do not hesitate to abuse their power. The focus on women also hid the differences amongst women and the extent to which women are affected by the class-based, ethnic and tribal differences in Afghanistan. The Bonn conference and the Brussels Summit did, as one participant noted, evoke an urgent sense that the engagement for Afghan women needed to be moved into Afghanistan and out to the rural areas—and that that was where the real changes needed to happen.[29]

The state-building process initiated through the Bonn process did bring an engagement for Afghan women to Afghanistan. The donor community, multilateral agencies and international non-governmental agencies have supported mainstreaming efforts ranging from promoting legislative changes to supporting woman-focused income generation and micro credit schemes. It is beyond the scope of this chapter to cover all these areas. Instead the challenges to gender mainstreaming will be exemplified below by a closer analysis of the establishment of the Ministry of Women's Affairs and women's representation in the Parliament.

Gender Mainstreaming and the Ministry of Women's Affairs

The establishment of the Department of Women's Affairs through the Bonn Agreement and its subsequent consolidation to a Ministry of Women's Affairs as part of the transitional administration and later in the permanent government structures of Afghanistan, has been symbolically important. However, the challenges faced by the Ministry are illustrative of the difficulties in developing coherent and systematic approaches for women's rights and gender equality in Afghanistan. Discussing the challenges can also provide useful lessons on the longer term perspective and careful planning needed when seeking to establish and support woman-focused institutions in conservative, fragile and volatile country contexts.

The Ministry is widely perceived as an international invention. Sippi Azerbaijani-Moghaddam notes that 'Afghan leaders, being consummate negotiators and traders for centuries, did not miss the nuances that [the establishment of the Ministry of Women's Affairs and the emphasis on women's rights and gender] was all at the painless level of rhetoric. They were happy to accommodate international desire to see women in prominent positions, as long as they remained powerless'.[30] The fact that the Ministry

---

[29] Discussion between the author and a participant at the Summit for Democracy in Brussels (Kabul, June 2007).

[30] S Azarbaijani-Moghaddam, 'On Living with Negative Peace and a Half-Built State: Gender and Human Rights' (2007) 1 *International Peacekeeping* 127, 134.

(like most Afghan ministries) receives considerable technical and financial support from the international community is seen as proof of 'women's affairs' being an international rather than national agenda. The Ministry of Women's Affairs has been used as a pawn in negotiations between the Afghan government and its international partners. When the donor community (currently funding most of the Afghan government apparatus) has called for a leaner government structure, the Ministry of Women's Affairs has been one of the ministries that the Afghan government has suggested abolishing, knowing full well that the international community would not be willing to accept the abolishment of this ministry.[31]

The political power of the Ministry has been undermined by frequent changes of Minister (five changes during seven years). The political power of the Ministry is also undermined by the overall challenges of the Afghan political context. While the Ministry of Women's Affairs was established to appease the international community, other concessions were made to appease the many politico-ethnic factions with real or perceived ability to destabilise Afghanistan. As a consequence, the Ministry of Women's Affairs finds itself locked between demands for decisive action by the international community and fear of upsetting more conservative elements in Afghan government and society. Azarbaijani-Moghaddam notes that 'women and the institutions set to protect and further their rights know that they are fair game if they cross the line and challenge conservative elements—knowledge that keeps them in a state of paralysis'.[32] Factional politics also influence the day-to-day work inside the Ministry and its provincial departments: When a Minister is changed, staff are sacked and reshuffled depending less on their qualities than on their political and ethnic allegiances. Unsurprisingly the lack of clear career opportunities affects the morale of the staff.[33]

Lack of capacity affects the types of interventions made by the Ministry and its ability to contribute to systematic reform processes. The Ministry receives extensive technical and capacity-building support from several international agencies,[34] but low initial capacity and frequent staff reshuffles have hampered the long term effects of technical and capacity-building support. The major policy interventions made by the Ministry, such as the development of the National Action Plan for the Women of Afghanistan and ensuring gender mainstreaming in the Afghanistan National Development Strategies, have relied primarily on the work of international consultants and only marginally

---

[31] Discussions between the author and key Afghan and international stakeholders (Kabul, 2006).

[32] Azaraijani-Moghaddam, above n 30, 134.

[33] This author has followed the changes in the Ministry after the two last changes of Minister.

[34] The United Nations Development Fund for Women (UNIFEM), the United Nations Development Program (UNDP), the Asia Foundation are amongst the international agencies that have offices inside the Ministry of Women's Affairs.

on the work of Ministry staff. Both these documents have also been criticised for corresponding poorly with the realities of Afghan society and for being too complex for Afghan policy-makers to implement. The Ministry itself has tended to focus on projects that will bring visibility to donors and key individuals within the Ministry, such as International Women's Day celebrations on 8 March, and on infrastructure projects. At the provincial levels, Departments of Women's Affairs remain primarily project implementing bodies that focus on educational and income generation projects, they also occasionally serve as women's shelters in extreme cases of abuse.

It is worth noting that relevance of the Ministry of Women's Affairs has also been questioned by some of its strongest defenders.[35] International gender advisers working in Afghanistan interviewed by this author have argued that having a specific Ministry for women's issues in a country where it is still viewed as non-permissible for women to raise concerns outside their family can do little but further marginalise women's concerns.[36] However, while the Kabul-based Ministry may not have fulfilled donors' expectations, several gender advisers have also stressed the importance of the Ministry's provincial departments. The provincial offices remain in many cases the only places where women can seek refuge in cases of extreme violence or poverty.

The establishment and work of the Ministry of Women's Affairs illustrates well the clash between the intention of women's representation and the reality. The Ministry has not managed to become a key player due to difficulties inherent to promoting women's rights and gender concerns in conservative and conflict-ridden Afghanistan, but also because the strategies of mainstreaming have not adequately taken into account the political context in which Afghan women's rights advocates operate, their capacity constraints and how gender relates to other mechanisms of inclusion and exclusion in Afghan society. The Ministry has also been unable adequately to address the ethnic and social variations of Afghan society. Afghanistan is a multi-ethnic society, where ethnic belonging seems, in most cases, to trump gender-based solidarity. These issues will be further explored below in the analysis of women's representation in the Parliament.

Women's Representation and the Afghan Parliament

In late-2003, a Constitutional Loya Jirga was organised in Afghanistan with a view to adopting a new Constitution for Afghanistan. The 500 elected delegates of the Loya Jirga, included 64 women elected at the provincial

---

[35] Ibid.
[36] Ibid.

levels and women representatives from the minority communities.[37] During the Loya Jirga, Malalay Joya, one of the women candidates, criticised the proceedings for being dominated by warlords and war criminals, as a result her microphone was silenced and she was temporarily thrown out from the Loya Jirga tent. However, Joya's concerns were well-founded: the Constitutional Loya Jirga was used by many as an opportunity to further entrench the power of their politico-military factions rather than to participate constructively in the establishment of a founding document for the Afghan state. The consequence of this is that the Afghan Constitution adopted in January 2004 is an eclectic document based on many compromises: some of the inherent conflicts in the Constitution have only been unearthed when Afghan prosecutors and judges have used it in convictions for blasphemy and conversion.[38]

The Constitution includes a general equality clause.[39] Most importantly perhaps, from an equality perspective, the Constitution includes a quota for women's representation in the upper and lower houses of Parliament and in the provincial councils. The inclusion of a sizeable quota for women, about 27 per cent of the seats in the lower house and one sixth of the seats in the upper house, is an important milestone for women's representation and participation in decision-making in Afghanistan.[40] The Constitutional quota did influence many women to put themselves forward as candidates, and in some cases it influenced the women's families, tribes or networks to choose a woman rather than a man to run for Parliament.[41]

Although the Constitutional quota did ensure women's presence in the Parliament, it has not been able to ensure that women are able to use the political space of parliamentary politics. The 2005 parliamentary elections were marked by corruption, fraud and less than democratic campaigning by warlords-turned-democrats. The presence of parliamentarians with known records of human rights abuses and war crimes and continuing links to illegal armed groups in Parliament has resulted in Afghan parliamentary politics being marked more by a culture of fear and intimidation than by political debate.

---

[37] Presidential Decree of the Constitutional Loya Jirga, art 2, at www.cic.nyu.edu/peacebuilding/oldpdfs/TextofPresidentialDecreeonConstitutionalLoyaJirga1.pdf (last visited 15 May 2009); NA Shah, 'The Constitution of Afghanistan and Women's Rights' (2005) 13 *Feminist Legal Studies* 239.

[38] N Shah, 'The Constitution of Afghanistan and Women's Rights' (2005) 13 *Feminist Legal Studies* 329, 224ff. It should be emphasised that the priority given to Islamic principles becomes a challenge only due to lack of Constitutional interpretation and follow-up legislation on key issues, which has given a conservative and powerful clergy an extensive 'right' of interpretation.

[39] Constitution of Afghanistan, art 6.

[40] Ibid arts 83–84.

[41] The author interviewed several women candidates in the run-up to the parliamentary elections in 2005. Many of the women stated that the fact that the Constitution specifically addressed women's participation had influenced their decision to put themselves forward as candidates.

This culture has also influenced the women parliamentarians both through dividing them, as women are equally influenced by factional politics as male parliamentarians, and by silencing them. Anne Wordsworth notes that contrary to the often 'romanticised portrayals in Western media', Afghan women parliamentarians do not constitute a homogenous group but are divided 'across ethnic, class, linguistic, political and regional lines'.[42] Using the notion of 'multiple identities', Wordsworth emphasises that women may have common interests, but other loyalties and interests may be more important for women parliamentarians.[43] The international efforts to establish a women's caucus in the parliament and to establish a women's resource centre have run up against the challenge of women viewing their common interests as secondary to the ethno-political affiliations, the initiatives to support women's rights have also been tainted by the affiliations of the women that have come to dominate these initiatives.[44] Although it may seem surprising to a non-initiated observer that Afghan women parliamentarians do not use the political space that they have been provided to further their common interests, it is not surprising when considering the conflict-induced differences in Afghan society. Afghan women (no differently from Afghan men) demand convincing evidence before choosing to trust anybody outside their family, community or network.[45] At the same time the conflict has fostered a culture of manipulation, or as noted by Wordsworth, the 'patronage-based and zero-sum nature of Afghan politics' contributes to a system 'where one person's gain is another's loss'.[46]

The presence of women in the Parliament has been an important symbolic marker of change. Over time, women's presence may also contribute to building solidarity and issue-specific networks amongst the women in the Parliament and affect political decision-making. The establishment of women-centred institutions or ensuring women's presence in decision-making forums does not in itself constitute change. It is only a first step, and it is a first step that can be constructively used or abused. Nevertheless, women's presence in the Parliament has 'been used as a rubber-stamp, confirming outwardly a commitment to increasing their political participation'.[47] The Islamic Republic was 'sold' to donors and their constituencies as a 'broad based, multi-ethnic, politically balanced, freely-chosen Afghan Administration'.[48] In the 'new' Afghanistan a democratically elected president and legislator would take gender-sensitive, ethnically balanced and 'moderate' decisions with a view to stabilising Afghanistan and ensuring its long term peace. This Afghanistan never existed except on paper.

---

[42] A Wordsworth, *A Matter of Interests: Gender and the Politics of Presence in Afghanistan's Wolesi Jirga* (Kabul, AREU, 2007) 3.
[43] Idem.
[44] Ibid 18.
[45] Ibid 1.
[46] Ibid 19.
[47] Ibid 9.
[48] Nesiah, above n 10, 92.

CONCLUSIONS: TAKING WOMEN SERIOUSLY?

Snapshot 2: Silenced by Threats and Treats

In 2007, I had the opportunity to follow a group of 'Afghan women leaders' on a tour of the European Union institutions. The group of women consisted of Afghan business women, government officials and civil society activists. They had been invited to Brussels by an international non-governmental organisation specialised in organising encounters between policy-makers and women from post-conflict and developing countries. In my address to the women, I shared my concerns with them, I stressed that 'everybody will be impressed by you, they will be so impressed that they may not listen to what you are saying'. This was a heartfelt comment, based on my experiences of working in Afghanistan.

At a well-attended hearing at the European Parliament, the women delivered several well-informed speeches about the role of the European Union in the state-building process and about the worsening security situation in Afghanistan. They also received many questions, but next to none of these questions picked up on the discussions about the European Union's role in Afghanistan or the very pressing security concerns. Instead the women received several questions about the situation of Afghan women's and girls' education.

The international community's perception about Afghan women continues to be coloured by the snapshots of burqa-clad women hurrying down dusty streets in Taliban-governed Afghanistan. Although not a primary objective of the US led military intervention of the internationally supported state-building process, these women were to be 'saved from' oppression under the Taliban and 'saved to' freedom and individual agency in a democratically governed Afghanistan. Very quickly it became apparent that the 'saving exercise' was more complicated than expected. This chapter has attempted to show that Afghan women's situation cannot be advanced in a vacuum and that naïvely and poorly construed strategies are at best ineffective and at worst counterproductive.

Afghanistan remains an inherently patriarchal society, and continued efforts are needed to end harmful cultural practices and to enable women to contribute to their own and their family's economic situation. The steps taken in the state-building process have fallen short of delivering sustainable results. This chapter has attempted to pinpoint some of the fault lines that well-meaning, but naïve engagement for Afghan women has resulted in, including inadequate attention to ensuring that women's rights and gender discourses are Afghan-owned, inadequate attention to differences amongst Afghan women and the shortcomings of women-centred schemes in a family and community-based system and a failure to understand how, and in what context, politically active Afghan women operate.

The fact that it is the international community that has emphasised the importance of women's participation and gender mainstreaming, has resulted in a backlash against women's and gender issues. Although there is a small and fragile women's movement inside Afghanistan and although concern also by broader constituencies is expressed for the need for girls' education, widows' economic opportunities and action to stop violence against women (especially outside the family), critics have been able to rally support against the women's rights and gender agenda through claiming that it was forced on Afghanistan by foreigners and that it is against Afghan culture and Islam.

Although an understanding of conflict-induced, ethnic and cultural differences has influenced much of the international political decision-making on Afghanistan, women are often approached as one group. While there is an understanding that the agendas of politically active women, women entrepreneurs and women in rural communities differ, there is not necessarily an understanding of what consequences these differences should have on the gender analysis in the Afghan context or on strategies employed to overcome discrimination and oppression.

The singular focus on Afghan women has been based on the presumptions that one or a few Afghan women will speak for all women, and that the women who are enabled to participate will also be able to influence decision-making. As was shown in the analysis of women's representation in the Afghan Parliament and the establishment of women-centred institutions, women—although they have been only marginally involved in the Afghan conflicts as combatants—are not immune to the conflict-induced differences in Afghan society. Women's political loyalties will vary depending on what issues are debated. On occasion, their loyalties will be with the 'cause of Afghan women', but when stakes are high their loyalties are likely to lead them to vote as encouraged by their political patrons and in line with the interests of their ethnic group, region or tribe. Given the dominance of former commanders (many of whom continue to have active links with illegal armed groups), it is also unrealistic to expect that women are ready to take the risk of challenging the dominant political culture of patronage and governance by force.

The shortcomings of the women's rights and gender strategies should not be viewed as an excuse for more limited engagement, but they should be viewed as a call for strategies that are based on cultural and local knowledge, and consultations with different constituencies, and that take women—and their many different agendas—seriously.

10

Trafficking in Human Beings: Vulnerability, Criminal Law and Human Rights

ULRIKA ANDERSSON*

INTRODUCTION

THE STORY IS familiar. She is poor, unemployed and lives in the suburbs of one of the towns in the former Soviet Union or another part of Eastern Europe. Often she puts her trust in her boyfriend or a relative. She is persuaded to go to Sweden, Germany, Holland or another country in Western Europe to get a job and a new life. Instead of a job in a restaurant, however, a life in prostitution awaits her once she reaches the new country.[1]

This typical story of trafficking is commonly associated with gender and sexuality. The vulnerability of the victim in connection with trafficking is also clearly related to the broader structural factors, such as poverty and unemployment. The vulnerability of the trafficking victim is a key aspect emphasised in international law as well as in criminal law.[2] This chapter scrutinises the vulnerability of the victim in criminal and international legal texts on trafficking.[3] Trafficking in human beings is considered to be a

---

* I would like to thank the editors for valuable comments.

[1] A similar story is told in the film *Lilja forever* (2002) by Lukas Moodysson.

[2] See, eg, Council Framework Decision 2002/629/JHA of 19 July 2002 on combating trafficking in human beings (OJ L 203, 1 August 2002, 1); United Nations Protocol to Prevent, Suppress and Punish Trafficking in Persons, Especially Women and Children, supplementing the United Nations Convention against Transnational Organized Crime, A/Res/55/25 of 15 November 2000, and Proposition 2003/04:111, Ett utvidgat straffansvar för människohandel (Swedish Governmental Bill: An extended criminal legal responsibility in terms of trafficking). See also Council of Europe Convention on Action against Trafficking in Human Beings.

[3] I do not intend to make a complete exposition; my intention is rather to apply my thoughts on legal subjectivity in relation to trafficking. For further discussion on violence and women's subjectivity, see Grahn-Farley, above, this collection. For interrelated discussion on gender and international law, see Nesiah, above, this collection.

serious violation of human rights requiring international action in national and international documents that discuss how trafficking should be defined and addressed.[4] The measures mentioned in these documents to prevent and punish the crime of trafficking are, inter alia, a focus on improved circumstances for particularly vulnerable groups, and the development of legislation, especially criminal legislation.[5]

The criminal justice system in modern western democracies is built on the rights of the accused, the subject of criminal responsibility, in relation to the repressive power held by the state. The entire system rests upon rules and principles aimed at ensuring the rule of law in relation to this subject. The subject is presumed to be autonomous and is placed before the law according to the legal doctrine of criminal responsibility, presupposing that this subject makes free and rational choices.[6] The human rights system was founded on the same theoretical principles, with a key focus being on the relationship between the individual and the state. Not until the 1990s did this perspective shift, and the relationships between individuals started to fall under the scope of human rights.[7] This change was of great importance for questions on gender-based violence, which are discussed here in the context of trafficking in human beings.[8] In relation to criminal law, as well as human rights and law in general, several authors have highlighted and questioned the autonomous subject.[9]

The aim of this chapter is to look more closely at the subject of criminal protection, the one who may claim protection from a certain criminal provision, as well as the subject of human rights, in the context of the crime of

---

[4] See n 2 above.

[5] For a critical discussion on criminalisation of trafficking in human beings, see J Berman, '(Un)Popular Strangers and Crisis (Un)bounded: Discourses of Sex-Trafficking, the European Political Community and the Panicked State of the Modern State' (2003) *European Journal of International Relations* 37. See also J Westerstrand, *Mellan mäns händer. Kvinnors rätts-subjektivitet, internationell rätt och diskurser om prostitution och trafficking (Between the hands of men. Legal subjectivity of women, international law and discourses on prostitution and trafficking)* (Uppsala, Uppsala University, 2008) 256, fn 781.

[6] See N Lacey, *Unspeakable Subjects: feminist essays in legal and social theory* (Oxford, Hart Publishing, 1998).

[7] J Niemi-Kiesiläinen, 'Våld mot kvinnor och mänskliga rättigheter' ('Violence against women and human rights') (1999) *Retfaerd, Nordisk juridisk tidsskrift (Nordic Legal Journal)* 49. See also H Charlesworth and C Chinkin, *The Boundaries of International Law. A feminist analysis* (Manchester, Manchester University Press, 2000).

[8] For a discussion on gender and human rights in a wide sense, see eg, K Engle, 'International Human rights and feminisms: When Discourses Keep Meeting' in D Buss and A Manji (eds), *International Law: Modern Feminist Approaches* (Oxford, Hart Publishing, 2005). See also R Cook (ed), *Human Rights of Women: National and International Perspectives* (Philadelphia, University of Pennsylvania Press, 2005).

[9] See, eg, N Naffine and RJ Owens (eds), *Sexing the subject of law* (Sydney, Sweet and Maxwell, 1997); Lacey, above n 6; N Lacey, 'Feminist Legal Theory and the Rights of Women' in K Knop (ed), *Gender and Human Rights* (Oxford, Oxford University Press, 2004); N Naffine, 'Can Women be Legal Persons?' in S James and S Palmer, *Visible Women: Essays on Feminist Legal Theory and Political Philosophy* (Oxford, Hart Publishing, 2002) and J Niemi, 'What we talk about when we talk about buying sex' (2010) 16 *Violence against Women* 2.

trafficking. Apart from gender and sexuality, trafficking is commonly associated with poverty and shortage of work in criminal legal documents as well as in international human rights documents. For example, the definition of trafficking is discussed in connection with the grounds of trafficking. These are in turn related to different structures, presupposed to cause certain practices by individuals.[10] Drawing on the concept of discursive power put forward by Michel Foucault, I analyse legal documents as discourses.[11] My question is how these discourses construct, or produce, the subject of trafficking. The materials I explore are official legal documents, in particular Swedish criminal legal documents and international legal documents on trafficking,[12] which consist of descriptions and analysis of trafficking, as well as discussions on the formulation of the criminalisation. My method is based on a notion of the subject as being relational or contextualised; individuality is explicitly related to structural and discursive factors. Structural factors here refers to an overall context that creates conditions such as poverty or unemployment, while discursive parts refers to what is said and done in and through language, symbols and normative concepts. In this study, it is thus possible to make visible how the documents relate the vulnerability of the subject to the individual, structure and discourse.

INDIVIDUAL, STRUCTURE AND DISCOURSE

The notion of the contextualised or relational subject emerges from three theories of gender, put forward by philosopher Sandra Harding,[13] historian Joan Wallach Scott[14] and political scientist Iris Marion Young.[15] Apart from emphasising the individual and structural dimension of gender, these

---

[10] Proposition 2003/2004:111, above n 2, at 9 and 15.

[11] About this method, see U Andersson, *Hans (ord) eller hennes? En könsteoretisk analys av straffrättsligt skydd mot sexuell övergrepp (His (word) or hers? A gender theoretical analysis of criminal protection against sexual abuse)* (Lund, Bokbox Publishing, 2004). See U Andersson, 'Vara till salu. Utsatthet vid människohandel. Individer, strukturer och diskurser' ('Being for sale.Vulnerability in relation to human trafficking' (2009) *Tidskrift för Genusvetenskap (Journal of Gender Studies)* 4.

[12] In addition to the documents lists above n 2, see also the Reports by the National (Swedish) Investigation Department, *Handel med kvinnor (Trafficking with women)*, reports 2003:1, 2005:4, 2006:4 and 2007:6.

[13] S Harding, *The Science Question in Feminism* (Ithaca and London, Cornell University Press, 1986).

[14] JW Scott, 'Gender: A Useful Category of Historical Analysis' in JW Scott (ed), *Feminism and History* (New York, Oxford University Press, 1996).

[15] IM Young, 'Genus som serialitet. Tankar om kvinnor som ett socialt kollektiv' ('Gender as seriality: Thoughts on women as a social collective') in IM Young, *Att kasta tjejkast. Tankar om feminism och rättvisa (Throwing like a girl. Thoughts on feminism and justice)* (Stockholm, Atlas, 2000). See also M Albertson Fineman, 'The Vulnerable Subject: Anchoring Equality in the Human Condition' (2008) 20 *Yale Journal of Law and Feminism* 1. Fineman promotes the idea of the vulnerable subject in relation to equality in the state and its institutions.

scholars all use discursive perspectives of power stressing language, symbols and normative concepts. Thus, for these authors, individuality is linked with structural and discursive factors, while also illuminating how different analyses of gender might be useful for interrogating other relevant aspects of power, such as class or ethnicity.

Harding talks of three different aspects of gender: the symbolic, the structural and the individual.[16] Amongst other things, the symbolic refers to language and other representations, where symbols and metaphors refer to gender through dualisms and dichotomies. The symbolic constructs the framework for the structural, where social activities and relations are organised through gender. Individual identity is also formed through the symbolic. As a result, Harding argues that gender is produced by all three:

> It is the result of assigning dualistic gender metaphors to various perceived dichotomies that rarely have anything to do with sex differences; it is the consequence of appealing to these gender dualisms to organize social activity, of dividing necessary social activities between groups of humans; it is a form of socially constructed individual identity only imperfectly correlated with either the 'reality' or the perception of sex differences.[17]

A central part of Harding's analysis is that gender is asymmetric in all these parts.[18] She stresses that this concept of gender makes is possible to highlight how these three different aspects of gender coincide and interact.[19] It is the symbolic, which I call discursive, that forms the foundation of her analysis.

In a similar vein, Scott claims that both the individual subject and the structural perspective are necessary to understand how gender works and how change can occur.[20] Scott sets out two basic premises for gender as an analytical category: first, gender produces social relations as it is channelled through the lived differences between the sexes; and second, gender thoroughly marks relations of power.[21] Scott argues that there are four interrelated aspects integral to the production of gender: first, symbols, culturally available, producing multiple and often contradictory representations; second, normative concepts, interpretations of the meaning of symbols, thus restricting their metaphorical possibilities, third, social institutions and organisations, for example, family and relatives, the labour market, teaching and politics; fourth, the subjective identity. Through engaging with Michel Foucault's concept of power and the importance of language, Scott emphasises symbols and normative concepts, in other words the discursive part of gender, and makes the agency of the individual visible:

[16] Harding, above n 13, 18, 'gender symbolism, gender structure and individual gender'.
[17] Ibid 17–18.
[18] Ibid 55.
[19] Ibid 56.
[20] Scott, above n 14, 157–67.
[21] Ibid 167. See also 170.

Within these processes and structures, there is room for a concept of human agency as the attempt (at least partially rational) to construct an identity, a life, a set of relationships, a society within certain limits and with language-conceptual language that at once sets boundaries and contains the possibility for negation, resistance, reinterpretation, the play of metaphoric invention and imagination.[22]

Finally, Young, through her approach to gender, illustrates how the individual, structure and discourse work together in the construction of the subject, even if this is not her explicit aim. Young considers, as with Jean Paul Sartre's theory, gender as seriality, which concerns the relation of the individual to practices in different structures. Seriality consists of individuals' way of acting or being exposed to others' actions. The actions are directed towards the same object and depend on material surroundings being caused by certain structures. The structures are in turn a consequence of collective actions and practices. Belonging to a series is not a deliberate choice even if the separate actions in a series take place deliberately. A series is 'a social collective whose members are passively united by the objects which their actions are directing and/or by the objectified results by the material effects from others' actions'.[23] Young separates series from groups, by stressing that in a series there is no mutual recognition that the individuals together constitute a unity.[24] In a series, however, everyone is aware of how their own actions may be part of a kind of collective, which is constituted by certain structures and discourses. The structures and discourses give the series boundaries and restrictions.[25] It is the focus on the social practices or actions that I see as part of Young's discursive approach. Young also applies a discursive perspective of power, stressing language and norms in her reasoning on what factors that affect different practices.

In the context of trafficking, the individuals that are victims of trafficking can be described in relation to a series. The incidences of trafficking of women can be seen as practices in this series. Structural factors include poverty, limited education, or unemployment, which the individual cannot influence alone. People in a series may feel powerless in relation to material conditions and be aware that others in the series also have this incapacity.[26] Discourses include language, symbols and norms, which make certain actions possible and prevent others. This seriality is demonstrated by analysing how the practice of trafficking might rely on certain structures and conditions being in place, on the practices of trafficking that respond to and occur within those structures, and on individuals' reactions to such practices, structural conditions and the discursive conditions that might make people more disposed to change their

---

[22] Ibid 167.
[23] Young, above n 15, 232.
[24] Ibid 231.
[25] Ibid 233.
[26] Ibid 235, with reference to JP Sartre.

lives. It is the concept of seriality that makes it possible to move away from the construction of the liberal individual subject, and consider women as a sort of collective without saying that all women are the same.[27] This analysis could also be used in relation to other aspects of power, such as class or ethnicity. Thinking of women or other groups as a collective is important for interrogating how they are oppressed in systematic, structural and institutional processes. In my view, these processes include the discursive parts of gender.[28]

While these theories of gender all have slightly different emphases, they are useful points of departure for my analysis of how the subject exposed to trafficking is constructed. Harding's analysis is the theory that most explicitly stresses the discursive nature of gender. Moreover, her theory most strongly stresses the advantages to studying how the different parts interact. Scott, on the other hand, emphasises the importance of structures, but at the same time stresses the importance of illustrating individual agency, which she introduces through the discursive perspective of power. Young's use of the concept of seriality, finally, allows us explicitly to relate the individual to the structural and discursive hierarchies of power.

Before looking more closely at the vulnerability of the subject of trafficking, I will first discuss Swedish discourses on rape, because rape crimes raise similar questions about the vulnerability of the subject. The force and exploitation on the part of the offender are central elements of the crime of rape, replaced with the will and resistance of the victim in practice. The subject of rape is presumed to be autonomous, free and rational, capable of expressing will and offering resistance. Despite the structural factors that are associated with the causes or the vulnerability of particular individuals to trafficking, as put forward in various legal documents, a person exposed to trafficking is also expected to offer resistance or other expressions of non-consent. Accordingly the subject of trafficking is also presumed to be autonomous, free and rational.

SWEDISH DISCOURSES ON RAPE, FORCE AND CONSENT

Defining Rape Through Force or Consent?

In Swedish law, sexual offences are constructed as sexual acts connected with force or exploitation.[29] Sexual acts are defined from a perspective of mutual sexual relations. This means that the elements of force or exploitation draw the legal boundary of these offences. Historically, definitions of

---

[27] Ibid 230.
[28] Ibid 223.
[29] See Andersson, above n 11, 93. See also U Andersson, 'The unbounded body of the law of rape' in K Lundström, J Niemi-Kiesiläinen, E-M Svensson, K Nousiainen (eds), *Responsible Selves: Women in the Nordic legal culture* (Oxford /Cambridge, Ashgate, 2001).

rape have focused on the male perpetrator's force. When women started to be considered as legal subjects in this context, during the eighteenth century, the female will—or consent—was included in the legal definition of rape. However, in contemporary Swedish and Nordic legislation, the decisive criterion in the provisions on rape is force, whereas, for example, British law focuses on the victim's will, or lack of consent.[30] In the latest amendment, the question of whether Swedish legislation should use lack of consent instead of force was discussed, but the Commission on Sexual Offences eventually decided to keep force as the decisive criterion. Some ambivalence about this can be seen, however, because the Commission also chose to place incapacitation of the victim (due to certain conditions, such as intoxication, sleep and illness) in the same category as force. Despite this, a focus on force and exploitation, consent and will dominate in practice.

Focus of the Courts

In previous work, I have analysed cases on sexual offences from Swedish courts of appeal. I identified three main discourses regarding the victim's expression of will, technical evidence and the sexual character of the act respectively.[31] The main discourses focused on the victim's expression of will. Focusing on a victim's expression of will in the legal reasoning produced the body of the subject of criminal protection as open and accessible. If the victim did not defend his or her body, by offering resistance or showing other kinds of rejection, the body was considered accessible for others. This was the case in the discourse on technical evidence as well. Here, different 'bodily expressions', such as injuries, were related to the victim's action or verbal statement, which in turn produced an open body. The open body was also expressed in the discourse on the sexual character of the act, where the victim had to accept involuntary contact or verbal abuse.

In the discourse, the victim was only given the possibility of reacting to the perpetrator's action. Circumstances that could be interpreted as lacking potential sexual activity of the victim were excluded from the discourse. The sexuality of the subject of criminal protection was therefore produced as passive. Until the victim objected, he or she could be used sexually, which produced an accessible sexuality. The case was the same with the discourse on technical evidence, which related to the statement of the victim, and the discourse on the sexual character of the act, where the victim had to accept involuntary contact and verbal abuse.

---

[30] See, eg, Andersson (2001), above n 29 and J Temkin, *Rape and the legal process* (Oxford, Oxford University Press, 2002). As for European legislation on rape, see the European Court of Justice case, *M.C. vs Bulgaria*, 39272/98, 4 December 2003.

[31] Andersson, above n 11, 216.

The Heterosexual Matrix

The open, accessible body and the accessible, passive sexuality have obvious links to the notion of the feminine body and the feminine sexuality. The subject of criminal protection produced in the dominant discourses in the cases from the courts of appeal was therefore clearly defined as feminine. These discourses may be seen as a clear expression of the heterosexual matrix that Judith Butler argues is the foundation for the construction of gender.[32] The notion of sexuality that produces the subject of criminal protection as having an open body and an accessible sexuality is obviously heteronormative. In this reasoning, the feminine body becomes accessible at the discursive level, through the feminine passive (hetero)sexuality. In the few examples in the study where the subject was in fact male, the discursive subject was produced as feminine, with an open body and a passive, accessible sexuality. The gender of the discursive subject was thus superior to the 'real' one.[33] Accordingly, the criminal legal discourses produced the body of the subject of criminal protection as open and the sexuality as accessible and passive. The subject of criminal protection was produced as feminine, despite the gender-neutral subject being the starting-point of the criminal provisions on sexual offences.

The focus on the victim's will rather than force or exploitation of the victim's vulnerable position also seems to be central in relation to the crime of trafficking in human beings, as will be discussed below. Here a problem in practice seems to be the difficulty of proving the victim's vulnerability. How this vulnerability is constructed will be discussed below.

TRAFFICKING IN HUMAN BEINGS

Elements of the Crime of Trafficking

Trafficking in human beings was criminalised in Sweden in 2002, with the focus on trafficking in human beings for sexual purposes.[34] The criminalisation was based on a United Nations (UN) protocol and a framework-decision from the European Union (EU), with both documents presupposing a widespread traffic in human beings, above all women and children, as sexual merchandise.[35] Because of the evidence that the trafficking of human beings for

---

[32] J Butler, *Gender Trouble: Feminism and the Subversion of Identity* (New York/London, Routledge, 1990).

[33] Andersson, above n 11, 240. See also N Fairclough and R Wodak, 'Critical Discourse Analysis' in TA van Dijk (ed), *Discourse as Social Interaction, Discourse Studies: A Multidisciplinary Introduction*, vol 2 (London, SAGE Publications, 1997).

[34] Proposition 2001/02:124 (Swedish Governmental Bill).

[35] UN Protocol, EU framework decision, above n 2.

non-sexual purposes, such as for organs or for labour, is extensive, the Swedish legislative provision was later considered as unsatisfactory, and was amended to also include trafficking without sexual purposes.[36] The legislative provision now includes the transporting, recruiting and lodging of a human being with the intent to sell him or her for sexual purposes, as labour or for removal of his or her organs.

To be considered as a criminal act this has to take place with force, or by misleading or exploiting someone's vulnerable position.[37] As in rape, the criterion of force or exploitation is central to this crime. Consent is here explicitly linked to force in the provision. For victims under 18 years old, consent is presumed not to be at issue; children's consent is irrelevant in this situation.[38] Law here considers a child's body and sexuality as bounded and impossible to interfere with. The situation is the reverse when the victim is over 18. When trafficking involves an adult victim, his or her non-consent must be proved, more or less, in terms of force or other exploitive criteria. In practice, criteria often relate to structural factors and are considered extremely difficult to prove. As a result, the crime of trafficking is used very rarely, at least in Sweden, when the victim is over 18.[39] An adult's body and sexuality is thus indirectly produced as open and accessible to trafficking.

Factors Affecting Practices of Trafficking

In the UN protocol, the criminalisation of trafficking covers 'recruiting, transporting, housing and receiving' that takes place through force, fraud, misleading, abuse of power or someone's vulnerable position.[40] The Swedish criminal provision on trafficking largely corresponds to the UN protocol.[41] Such texts outline a number of factors that are thought to affect the practice of trafficking. One factor is the demand for human beings to exploit.[42] The causes of this demand are not explored any further in the documents,

---

[36] Proposition 2003/04:111, above n 2, 7–8. The provision has once again been changed, see proposition 2009/10:152, Förstärkt skydd mot människohandel (Swedish Governmental Bill: A stronger protection against trafficking in human beings). The perpetrator no longer needs to control the victim. The crime is however constructed in the same way and questions of structural power are not focused.

[37] The provision on trafficking in human beings is in *brottsbalken* (the Penal Code) ch 4 para 1a.

[38] Penal Code ch 4 para 1a. In relation to consensual sexual relations, the age of consent is 15.

[39] This is confirmed in the latest governmental report on trafficking. However, while the report widens the scope of situations that could be considered as creating vulnerabilities in particular groups, it does not look closely at structural factors. SOU 2008:78 (Swedish Parliamentary Report).

[40] UN Protocol, Art 3A, above n 2. See also Prop 2003/04:11, above n 2, 16.

[41] Penal Code ch 4 para 4:1a.

[42] Proposition 2003/04:111, above n 2, s. 8.

though it seems that it is the demand for sexual services that is referred to. This is shown in the focus on descriptions of women and children being recruited and transported for the purpose of being exploited 'in prostitution and in other ways'.[43] Other forms of exploitation are also discussed:

> Another reason for children being sent to other countries is that they have been victims of trafficking to be exploited for sexual services or as cheap or free labour, above all in home environments as servants. The aim might also be to force them to be engaged in begging.[44]

Another factor that is said to affect the practice of trafficking is ethnicity. The National (Swedish) Investigation Department states that pimps often look for customers, buyers that is, within their own 'ethnic group'.[45] The explicit focus on ethnicity in this document is a distancing technique: those involved in trafficking in Sweden are not Swedes but belong to another ethnic group.[46] I will return to how ethnicity relates to the recruiting of women and their pimps below.

TO BE A SUBJECT OF TRAFFICKING

Vulnerable Individuals

A central point of departure in the documents is that trafficking with human beings is an exploitation of the individual. Trafficking is repeatedly described as a complex phenomenon and a 'cruel and cynical exploitation of other human beings'.[47] These individuals are largely referred to in gender neutral terms. When the exploited individuals are described in more detail, it is in terms of gender or age, as will be discussed below. Individuals that are subjects of trafficking are also vulnerable. In the UN protocol it is, for example, stressed that member states should act to 'protect victims of trafficking of *human beings* from repeated vulnerability'.[48] Further factors of vulnerability will be discussed below.

In the framework decision from the European Council, an ambivalence about how victims of trafficking should be named is apparent. The Council

---

[43] Ibid. The National Investigation Department also discusses trafficking in a more practical sense. The most common way of entering the country is 'via ferry or by car', report 2003:1, above n 12, 23. Compare with report 2005:4, n 12, 31–32.

[44] Report 2003:1, above n 12, 24.

[45] Ibid 23.

[46] About the making of 'otherness', see eg P de los Reyes and L Martinsson (eds), *Olikhetens paradigm: intersektionella perspektiv på o(jäm)likhetsskapande* (*The Paradigm of Difference: Intersectional perspectives on the Production of (In)Equality*) (Lund, Studentlitteratur, 2005) and CT Mohanty, 'Under Western Eyes: Feminist Scholarship and Colonial Discourses' (1988) 30 *Feminist Review* 65.

[47] Prop. 2003/04:111, above n 2, 8.

[48] UN Protocol, Art 9(1)(b), above n 2.

refers to what is stated in other documents, noting that 'in the fight against trafficking with *women* legislation against trafficking with *human beings* is mentioned'.[49] Thus, in one sentence trafficking is both mentioned in general and specific terms. Thereafter trafficking is described as 'a serious violation of fundamental *human* rights and *human* dignity'.[50] Once again, exposed human beings are mentioned in gender neutral terms. Later in the text, the importance of the UN protocol is stressed when it comes to 'fighting and punishing trafficking with *human beings*, particularly *women* and *children*' and then it is stated that '*children* are more vulnerable and exposed to higher risks of becoming victims of trafficking'.[51] Apart from gender, age is supposed to be an important factor; particularly vulnerable are children, only mentioned (if at all in terms of gender) as girls.

Accordingly, it is believed that trafficking is more likely to affect women and children. On the individual level men are not mentioned, vulnerability is intimately associated with women. Those guilty of this trafficking are then implicitly men. Furthermore, as I will explore below, the Swedish Governmental Bill states that individuals exposed to trafficking are living under unequal conditions in terms of gender.[52] However, a distancing technique is again employed: the unequal gender conditions are discussed only in relation to other countries. As discussed above, the Swedish Government cannot imagine the possibility that demand for trafficked women could exist among Swedish men; this is not, therefore, related to gender inequality in Sweden. Whether there is a demand among women or what else distinguishes individuals demanding the sexual services in question is also not discussed or problematised.

Discussion of women is also related to ethnicity, though not necessarily in terms of their own ethnicity; rather, the ethnicity of women is often related to the origin of the pimps. For example, the report from the National Investigation Department notes that the 'women and the pimps do not always have the same ethnic background. The reason for this might be that the women are recruited in their countries of origin by their fellow-countrymen but are sometimes sold on the journey'.[53] In the view of the National Investigation Department, trafficking is thus committed in other countries by 'others'.[54] Here, both the vulnerable women and the ones

---

[49] EU Framework Decision, above n 2, reasoning in (1).

[50] Ibid, reasoning in (2), my italics. Considering human trafficking a violation of human rights is not uncomplicated and has been discussed by several authors, see eg, G Noll, 'Globalisation, migration and human rights: international law under review' in *Collection of the Geneva Academy of International Law and Human Rights* vol II (Bruxelles, Bruyant, 2007). For a discussion on the criminalisation of trafficking, see above n 5.

[51] EU Framework Decision, above n 2, reasoning in (3) and (5), my italics.

[52] Proposition 2003/3004: 111, above n 2, 15.

[53] Report 2003:1, above n 12, 23.

[54] I would like to thank Monika Edgren who drew my attention to this.

committing the recruitment are seen as strangers.[55] The underlying message is that women from other countries are recruited by men from other countries. This connects trafficking with the 'other' at the same time as creating a distance from the problem. In a later report there is a certain change in this message. Here '[p]ersons that the police earlier suspected of having recruited foreign women to Sweden for prostitution have [also] recruited vulnerable domestic women and girls for the same purpose'.[56] It is stressed that Swedish women are recruited by 'persons' earlier suspected of recruiting foreign women. Instead of describing the women as Swedish, they are described as 'domestic', which partly hides that they are Swedish. The men, as already mentioned, are made 'persons'.

Structural Conditions

According to the various texts, the circumstances that are supposed to promote trafficking with human beings are poverty, unemployment and other structural situations of inequality.[57] In the documents there are clear connections made between trafficking, and the living conditions associated with certain countries or areas. In countries where recruitment takes place, the population is supposed be poor, unemployed and live under serious forms of inequality, such as oppression due to gender or racism.[58] In the UN protocol, the member states are encouraged to relieve 'circumstances that make people, particularly women and children, exposed to trafficking, for example, poverty, underdevelopment and lack of equal opportunities'.[59] Economic conditions are seen as a strong contributory cause for people being exposed to trafficking: 'Low standards of living and poverty are well-known push-factors for persons risking to be victims of trafficking. They are attracted by a life in the west and believe they will earn a lot of money'.[60]

In the reports from the National Investigation Department, written from a Swedish perspective, there is, as mentioned above, an obvious distancing, a sort of dissociation from the presence of trafficking in Sweden. The countries associated with these circumstances and in which the recruitment takes

---

[55] See, however, Report 2005:4, above n 12, 29. Here it is stressed that trafficking with human beings for reasons of sexual exploitation in Sweden, also is demanded in small towns where 'local men buy sexual services'. Thus trafficking is not only a phenomenon in large cities, as discussed below.

[56] Report 2005:4, above n 12, 30.

[57] See UN Protocol and EU Framework Decision, above n 2.

[58] Proposition 2003/04:111, above n 12, 15.

[59] UN Protocol, Art 9(4), above n 2, my italics. See also Proposition 2003/04:111, ibid 18–19.

[60] Report 2003:1, above n 12, 22.

place are reported as being the Baltic States and the rest of Eastern Europe, together with the Balkans.[61] Why there is a demand in Sweden, and who leads the demand, is not problematised; this may be interpreted as attempting to dissociate Sweden from involvement in trafficking. As mentioned, this view is slightly more nuanced in the latest report where 'domestic' women are reported as being recruited. This report also states that 'local' men buy 'sexual services' and that trafficking not only is a phenomenon in the big cities.[62] By using the terms 'domestic' and 'local', however, the National Investigation Department hides that these women and men are Swedish. Therefore, while there are strong connections made between trafficking and structural living conditions in the national and international texts that seek to address trafficking, the involvement of the countries in the West is not problematised; rather it is hidden. There is thus a distinct distance created between the phenomenon of trafficking and the West's implication in the causes of trafficking.

Discursive Conditions

One discursive condition that is thought to affect the practice of trafficking is Swedish criminal legislation, which is talked of in positive terms. It is claimed that the law prohibiting purchase of sexual services has affected trafficking in human beings in Sweden.[63] In court hearings, and through investigations using telephone tapping, it has emerged that Sweden is said not to be such a good market for trafficking because money is not earned fast enough: women have to be escorted in order not to be seen, thus they have time for fewer clients. Criminal organisers are heard complaining of the need to organise business better in Sweden to reach profitability.[64] Whether this means that the women are exposed to worse or better conditions is not discussed. Accordingly legal concepts and discourses in legislation and case law that restrict the purchase of sexual services are supposed to affect the practices of trafficking. However, this can be seen as another dissociation; ignoring ethnicity and celebrating the 'success' of domestic legislation is another way of dissociating 'Swedishness' in relation to trafficking. The problems are not as serious for 'us' because of the robustness of our legal responses.[65]

---

[61] Ibid 23.

[62] Report 2005:4, above n 12, 29.

[63] I choose to look at this as a discursive factor since I see legislation primarily as normative discourses in this context.

[64] Report 2003:1, above n 12, 26.

[65] Compare, however, with what is said above about 'domestic' women and 'local' men.

TOWARDS A NOTION OF A CONTEXTUALISED LEGAL SUBJECT?

The criminal justice system, as well as the system of human rights, is built upon the individual subject and its relation to the state. The subject is supposed to be autonomous, free and rational. Difficulties arise when it comes to protection of a subject who is exposed to crimes related to structure, for example, trafficking and other gender-based crimes. Some subjects fall out of the scope of criminal law and human rights respectively. It is therefore necessary to modify the notion of the legal subject.[66] Drawing on theories of gender, I suggested we look at the individual in connection with structural circumstances as well as discourses.

In the documents I have analysed, the subject presumed to be exposed to trafficking is related to different structures and discourses. It is claimed that structural factors such as poverty, unemployment and inequality promote an exposed situation. Also discursive factors, such as legislation, are said to affect patterns of trafficking. The Swedish Law prohibiting purchase of sexual services, for example, is said to decrease the presence of trafficking in Sweden. Accordingly, the subject exposed to trafficking is not only connected to a specific delimited situation. Rather it is highly dependent on practices that relate to certain structures and discourses, which in a way extends the meaning of being exposed to a crime. Every situation is therefore a result of structural and discursive practice. Being in a vulnerable position and thus exposed to trafficking is not a bounded situation.

This perspective on vulnerability is implicit in the official documents analysed above, and affects both the Swedish criminal provisions on trafficking and the international concept of and documents on trafficking. However, this perspective is not explicit, either in the documents or in the definition in the Swedish penal code. This lack of recognising the subject as contextual affects the possibility of proving this complex vulnerability in practice. To look at vulnerability as contextual may improve the individual's chances of making a demand for legal protection. When a specific situation is explicitly connected to structural and discursive aspects of power, such as poverty, unemployment or legislation, this may clearly affect legal practice. The chances of proving that the individual is in an 'exposed position' would thus be appreciably improved. This concept is often crucial in proving that the particular act of trafficking is criminal. Possibilities to take structural or discursive factors into account might then shed some new light on a specific situation. An extended notion of the legal subject would contextualise the subject, without denying the individual agency.

---

[66] This also affects questions related to criminal responsibility, something I will not discuss here.

The girl from Russia might be seen as an independent individual trying to improve her standards of living at the same time as being abused under certain circumstances. Thus she is not only a young woman who decided to go to Western Europe as she trusted her boyfriend and wanted a better life. Instead a *possibility* emerges of accusing the boyfriend and his assistants for having abused her vulnerable position.

11

Women Workers Take Over Power at the Margins: Economic Resistance, Political Compliance

DANIA THOMAS

INTRODUCTION

IN DECEMBER 2008 the workers of the Republic Windows & Doors Company, Chicago seized control of their employers' factory. Their takeover forced the company's banks to pay for severance pay legally required in a plant closure.[1] This takeover was not reported or discussed as widely as the credit crisis and has been marginal to the ongoing 'credit-crisis' governance debate. This is reminiscent of the governance debate that followed the Argentine debt crisis in 2001 in which similar social responses to the crisis there were marginal. On 18 December 2001, workers (mainly women) of the Brukman textile factory in Buenos Aires took over their factory, continued production during the crisis and even doubled their wages. The women still legally occupy the factory as a worker-run cooperative. This is remarkable as at the time Argentina was going through what was widely viewed as 'one of the most spectacular [debt crisis] in modern history'.[2]

The crisis was triggered entirely by Argentina's failure to repay its debt owed mainly to its foreign (mainly US) creditors. Given the success of the takeovers, it is therefore even more remarkable that creditor interests dominated the debate at the time. In fact, even after the crisis the same assumptions still dominate the contemporary governance of sovereign debt which include inter alia that the sovereign is an 'individual' debtor who enters into individual contractual relationships with several thousand creditors and

---

[1] C Black, 'What the Republic Victory Means' *The Huffington Post*, 15 January 2009, www.huffingtonpost.com/curtis-black/what-the-republic-victory_b_151169.html (accessed 21 May 2009).

[2] P Blustein, *And the Money Kept Rolling In (and Out): Wall Street, the IMF and the Bankrupting of Argentina* (New York, Public Affairs, 2005) 1.

that private law contractual doctrine and notions of property can resolve debt crises and regulate the sovereign bond market.[3] This chapter clarifies that the assumptions by which the sovereign debt market is governed silences the contribution that alternate responses such as the Brukman worker takeovers can make to contemporary debates on governance. This is especially so since, like any foreign creditor, they managed to turn the crisis into an economic opportunity.

The sovereign bond market (defined in the literature inter alia as the sum of bond contracts between a debtor and each of its creditors) is spread over several jurisdictions and involves several hundreds of thousands of creditors and several sovereign debtors. However, the effects of sovereign borrowing (and a debt crisis) are not confined to market actors and are felt by several thousands more, such as the workers who lost their jobs (and prompted the takeovers in Argentina). The current situation in Greece is another example of the widespread and inevitable social costs of a sovereign debt crisis. Clearly, sovereign debt crises are very public events but the sovereign debt market is governed by a private law commonsense, institutionalised through doctrinal contract law and notions of private property. Sovereign debt market actors have consistently resisted proposals to introduce a multilaterally negotiated, international bankruptcy law. This chapter clarifies the nature of this private law commonsense and the mechanisms that ensure its dominance.

For the purposes of this chapter, the private law that defines the governance of sovereign borrowing is viewed as an object of analysis and not as a framework of analysis within which Brukman for instance is examined.[4] I use the term governance (instead of law or regulation) to refer to the ad hoc, informal 'commonsense' that informs the actions of participants which, inter alia, include: debtor governments; private investors (hedge funds, investment banks, pension funds); official lenders (the International Monetary Fund (IMF), the World Bank); significant policy-makers (the United States (US) Administration and Treasury, the Argentine state); debt rating agencies; Creditor Clubs such as the Paris and London clubs; the US courts with jurisdiction to enforce sovereign bonds and the law firms that represent the debtors and creditors. I confine my attention to the 2001 Argentine debt default and the policy interventions that followed.

---

[3] This is a reflection of mainstream economic theory. See TI Palley, 'Sovereign Debt Restructuring: What is the Problem' (2003) at www.imf.org/external /NP/EXR/seminar/2003/ sdrm/pdf/palley.pdf. Also B Herman, 'The Players and the Game of Sovereign Debt', Background Note, Ethics and Debt Project, New School University and the Carnegie Council on Ethics and International Affairs (2005).

[4] This avoids an assumption made in the literature that the social costs of a debt crisis are dealt with either by the sovereign or by protecting creditors' interests. The assumption made here is that the takeovers have both economic and political interests that are distinguishable from the interests of both market actors: the sovereign as debtor and creditors. See Palley, above n 3, 4; Herman, above n 3, 12.

The aim is to develop a framework of analysis to understand why social responses to a sovereign debt crisis, in this case Brukman, are marginal to the concerns that dominate contemporary governance. In fact, the private law commonsense that defines governance in this area uncritically segues into either International Economic or Financial Law,[5] which by definition overlooks the political and social impacts of a sovereign debt crisis. In the absence of a formal, multilaterally negotiated, sovereign, bankruptcy law, the term 'International Economic Law' and its assumptions about legitimacy and privacy to describe governance in this area is a misnomer. This literature inadequately describes (and mostly ignores) what are overlapping and intersecting frameworks of legitimacy, some dominant and others marginal, some local and some global.[6] The mainstream literature normalises a dominant framework and erases alternative frameworks of legitimacy.[7] This chapter relies on a feminist perspective to reveal why this kind of erasure is a problem.[8]

However, the Brukman takeover complicates feminist perspectives on law[9] premised on a firmly demarcated public/private divide to locate vulnerability and justify critique. It blurs the boundaries between public and private domains in interesting ways.[10] Privacy for instance, represents a distinct, discursive, value system and as such is distinct from privacy as a location—the domestic sphere in which women are oppressed, for instance.[11] Further, the term 'public' is partly an empirical measure that refers to the impact of a debt crisis on a large number of creditors in several legal jurisdictions and on a significant number of non market actors. The term 'public' is also partly defined by exclusion and subjection to state authority. It is not a location where women are emancipated.[12] In addition to its nuanced engagement with

---

[5] P Wood, *The Law and Practice of International Finance*, University edn (London, Sweet & Maxwell, 2008) 12–16; A Quereshi and A Zeigler, *International Economic Law* (London, Sweet & Maxwell, 2007) 7–16.

[6] There is at present no multilaterally negotiated sovereign debt restructuring court or framework. For the main governance options that followed the Argentine debt crisis see P Bolton and O Jeanne, 'Structuring and Restructuring Sovereign debt: The Role of a Bankruptcy Court' IMF working paper No 72/192 (2007).

[7] H Charlesworth and C Chinkin, *The Boundaries of International Law: A Feminist Analysis* (Manchester, Juris Publishing, 2000) 60.

[8] For some examples, see C Dalton, 'An Essay in the Deconstruction of Contract Doctrine' (1985) 5 *Yale Law Journal* 94; and on economic policy, see I Bakker (ed), *The Strategic Silence and Economic Policy* (London, Zed Books, 1994).

[9] The exception is JA Nelson, 'Ethics and International Debt: A View from Feminist Economics' Global Development and Environment Institute, Working Paper No 06-04, (2006) which provides an ethical critique of international debt.

[10] These issues arise in the international political economy literature, see, eg, Stoker, 'Locating and Understanding the Marketplace in Financial Governance' in A Baker, D Hudson and R Woodward (eds), *Governing Financial Globalization: International Political Economy and Multi-level Governance* (Oxford/Cambridge, Routledge, 2005) 63.

[11] M Allen, 'Women, "Community" and the British Miners' Strike of 1984-85' in S Rowbotham and S Linkogle (eds), *Women Resist Globalization: Mobilizing for Livelihood and Rights* (New York, Zed Books, 2001).

[12] Ibid.

the sovereign debt market, the spatial location of Brukman itself does not fit into the private/public divide. The embeddedness of the takeover in the local community that supported and sustained them through the crisis was not 'private' and though there were other factory takeovers at the time, each was confined to a factory and thus not 'public'.

Finally, the absence of an obvious[13] 'gendered coding of binary oppositions'[14] also limits a feminist critique with governance in this context: for example, it destabilises a dominant reading of the feminist preoccupation with uncovering the male domination of women. Brukman demands an inquiry that negotiates the terms private and public as spatial locations, as intersecting value systems and competing sources of legitimacy. In the context of the contemporary governance of sovereign debt, Brukman is public and marginal while the concerns of the creditors private and thus central. The 'private' is included and thus privileged as legitimate and the 'public' marginal and of no consequence. This chapter does not aim to identify whether one system is gendered and the other is not. It seeks instead to use a feminist framework to signify the dominant framing of the contemporary governance of sovereign debt. Is the legal reasoning that defines governance an instance of doctrinal erasure? Why is this significant? Does this neutral private law commonsense explain the persistent failure of existing market-driven strategies to both avoid sovereign debt crises and mitigate its social effects?[15]

The marginality of social responses to debt crisis is even more perplexing as the Brukman workers were and remain anything but silent. They not merely responded to the debt crisis, but actively resisted the factory closures, faced up to law enforcement and still did not stop. They channelled their resistance and anger into innovative management practices and successful legal arguments to subvert the frameworks that made the closures inevitable. In fact the economic achievements of these 'non market' 'non state' responses to the debt crisis were pretty spectacular too. The women peacefully appropriated the property owned by their employers, managed their factory collectively, achieved fairer working conditions and even increased their wages! Finally, Brukman was one of a series of worker-takeovers that began in 2000, mainly in response to cessation of production by employers in the period leading up to the crisis, bankruptcy proceedings and consequent stoppage of wage payments. In the aftermath

---

[13] Hence the need for 'an archaeological dig' approach, as set out by Charlesworth and Chinkin, above n 7.

[14] Ibid 49.

[15] For a discussion on the recurring debt crises in Argentina, see E Borensztein, E Levy Yeyati, U Panniza (coordinators), *Living with debt: How to Limit the Risks of Sovereign Finance*, Economic and Social Progress in Latin America 2007 Report (Washington, Inter-American Development Bank, 2007) 63–77. For a critique of the existing regulatory paradigm, see J Stiglitz, *Globalization and Its Discontents* (London, WW Norton & Company, 2002) 22–36.

of the Argentine debt crisis, 10,000 employees controlled production in 170 to 180 factories ranging from ceramic firms to printing presses.[16]

Their marginality is also perplexing from the perspective of mainstream economic theorising about debt crises, which views the takeovers (namely unaccounted social costs of a crisis or external effects) as market failures. They lost their jobs and in the absence of markets where such costs can be traded off they have borne the inevitable 'social costs' of a debt crisis. If not then private investors will have no incentives to risk lending to emerging economies such as Argentina. The onus of 'cleaning up the messy [social costs]' thus naturally lies with the defaulting state. This reasoning overlooks the fact that the social costs of a crisis are inevitably borne by a constituency that did not take the decisions to either issue or buy the debt. In other words, the financial risks are taken privately while the consequences are borne publically.

Further, it appears that Brukman's location on the responsibility side of this governance paradigm is inevitable. This is counterintuitive as the Brukman workers did not lose their jobs; instead they resisted the impact of the debt crisis and subverted the market mechanism to achieve their own goals. The takeovers are not market failures as conventionally described. Instead it is clear that the workers and society as a whole, and not the debtor government nor the creditors, were eventually responsible for the financial risks of excessive sovereign lending. They remain excluded from having an independent interest in the sovereign debt market and its governance.

The following section describes the Brukman worker takeover and the Argentine state's attempt to regulate the takeovers in the aftermath of the debt workout. This is followed by a description of the discursive dominance of a private law commonsense in the context of sovereign debt governance. The final section views the responses to the debt crisis through a feminist lens to both clarify and signify the nature of the interface between them. This is followed by conclusions.

THE BRUKMAN WORKER TAKEOVER: A CASE-STUDY

The Context

In the decade leading up to the Argentine debt crisis in 2001, the country was the 'spoiled child of the Washington Consensus'.[17] Its economy 'hewed to the "Washington consensus"'.[18] Inflation was eradicated, industry privatised, its

---

[16] AC Dinerstein, 'Workers Factory Takeovers and the Programme for Self-Managed Work: Towards an Institutionalisation of Radical Forms of Non-Governmental Public Action in Argentina' NGPA Working Paper Series (2008) at www.lse.ac.uk/ngpa/publications, 6.

[17] Blustein, above n 2, 5.

[18] Ibid 4.

economy deregulated, trade barriers lifted and its currency (the peso) was pegged to the US dollar. This changed rapidly after it defaulted on its foreign debt repayments.[19] In late 2001, after the IMF refused to rollover their debt,[20] the 'second largest economy in South America with a population of 38 million'[21] ground to a halt. This left 'a quarter of its workforce unemployed and a majority of the population under the poverty line'.[22] Prices for basic food items such as bread, noodles and sugar soared leaving a rising number of children suffering from malnutrition, with a number dying from it.[23] The social costs of the debt crisis were extensive and deep. It is this context that makes the Brukman takeover truly exceptional. This section describes the takeover, the nature of their collective, economic resistance through changes in their decision-making structures and working ethos after the takeover and the state's response to them.

The Beginning

Following the Argentine debt crisis, workers across the country took over their factories on account of the factory closures precipitated by the crisis. In most cases, the takeovers were supported by the local community who for instance, volunteered childcare, set up communal kitchens, etc and thus made it possible for workers to restart production. The 'embeddedness' of the takeovers in the local community played a crucial part in sustaining them during the debt crisis and even after the debt workout. The Brukman textile factory was one such factory. It manufactured hand-sewn fine silk suits for men. This particular takeover was initiated by a group of 30 workers, (mostly) middle-aged women, with 13 male workers. All the workers had children and the women work primarily to support their families. In the period leading up to the default in 2001, their wages had decreased from $100 in 1995 to between $5 and $2 a week towards the end of 2001. They asked the management of the factory for a portion of their unpaid wages to travel home and back to work the next day. The management left the factory on the pretext of getting their unpaid wages from the bank and did

---

[19] Its mainly US creditors only lend in US dollars to minimise their risk, this means that Argentina has to repay the interest and capital it owes in US dollars. It is widely believed that the debt crisis was triggered by the refusal of the IMF to help with its loan repayments, though there is no similar consensus on the reasons for the debt crisis. ibid 1–12.

[20] Ibid.

[21] Ibid 7.

[22] Ibid 4.

[23] Ibid 2.

not return.[24] The workers stayed on in the factory, returned to their sewing machines, continued to process outstanding orders.

Initially, as a source of cash to travel home, they created a makeshift store on the ground floor.[25] A few weeks after the takeover, a client offered to pay them if they could finish the 200 suits he had ordered before the crisis. They took up his offer and successfully executed it. Four months later they were finishing up old orders, selling suits and even taking in new orders. Gradually each worker received an equal wage and all workers were paid weekly in cash. Workers were not paid for the days that they did not work.[26] At the time of the takeover in 2001, a part of their profit came from exporting finished garments to China[27] but their main market was local.[28] This local market sustained the takeover through the economic downturn and was another aspect of their 'embeddedness' in the local community.

After the debt crisis settled the owners of the factory and the municipal police tried to evict the workers from the factory twice. The workers decided to consult workers in other factories[29] to plan how to proceed. They filed a suit demanding that the city government expropriate the factory and let them work there legally as a cooperative. At the end of a lengthy trial, in October 2003, they convinced a judge to rule that the city could expropriate the factory and to recognise them as a cooperative.[30] However they operated the factories and organised production in very distinct ways as discussed below.

Economic Resistance

Officially there are no set administrative positions at Brukman. Instead the workers have created different internal *commissones* (committees) to oversee different aspects of the factory's operations. There are committees for administration, quality control procedures, organisation, accounting,

---

[24] MC Spieczny, 'When Workers Take Over: Reclaimed factories in Argentina' Unpublished thesis presented in partial fulfillment of the requirements for the degree of Bachelor of Arts, Department of Sociology, Princeton University (2004) www.cmd.princeton.edu/papers/Thesis%20Molly%20Spieczny.pdf (accessed 10 March 2009).

[25] The fact that they could sell any suits at the time of a severe downturn reflects their innovative ability to tap the local market.

[26] Spieczny, above n 24, 32.

[27] Though information on what extent of their profits came from exports is sketchy, this outlet would have been significant at the time of the debt crisis where local market conditions where depressed.

[28] This again is surprising as the workers relied on their 'embeddedness' in the local community to generate their income at a time when the economy was in a severe downturn. Spieczny, above n 24, 14.

[29] Ibid.

[30] Ibid.

selling and other matters.[31] After the takeover, the workers held weekly meetings with extra meetings scheduled in case of emergencies. At the meetings workers could bring up any topic or issue, and everyone ensured that each had a say and a vote in decisions. Votes were cast by show of hands. All workers were required to attend weekly meetings, and if for some reason several workers were absent, the meetings were cancelled or rescheduled. All decisions made at these meetings were recorded. Outsiders were not allowed to attend these meetings, though specialists were occasionally admitted for specific purposes.[32]

Within the factory, the workers rearranged the way the workplace was set up by their former employers, where their sewing machines, for instance, were in rows facing the same direction. After the takeover many of the machines faced each other. This new setup created an environment more conducive to learning and performing tasks differently from those that workers generally perform. So for instance, a worker who usually sewed jacket collars could easily go to a machine on the other side of the room and have a co-worker teach her how to sew inseams. Without an employer and the absence of an organisational hierarchy, an important aspect of their viability was that workers were required not only to do their jobs, but also to look around them and make sure everything was running adequately and that nobody was shirking their duties.[33] This strengthened their social relationships.[34] Their innovations on the shop floor for instance, engendered an interdependence that subsidised their economic activity.

It is clear that the Brukman workers sustained their economic enterprise on account of their relationality and their interdependence with each other and with the communities in which they functioned. This is distinguishable from the pre-takeover factory where their interdependence had to be 'legally' geared to become economically useful. This was usually done through the employer's reliance on externally imposed formal, legal institutional forms (for example, incorporation) and through the provision of individual incentives (for example, wages) to cooperate in ways that furthered the economic enterprise. Characteristically, this takeover was successful as workers were performing functions beyond those required by their individual jobs. They 'learned how to step in for one another for the job to get done'.[35] Their interdependence or relationality[36] sustained the production and made the unit economically viable despite extremely difficult economic circumstances.

---

[31] Ibid 36.
[32] Ibid 40.
[33] Ibid 46.
[34] Ibid 22.
[35] Ibid.
[36] C Mackenzie and N Stoljar, *Relational Autonomy: Feminist Perspectives on Autonomy, Agency and the Social Self* (New York/Oxford, Oxford University Press, 2000) 22.

In Brukman, their relationality allowed the women to increase the range of significant choices available to them collectively as economic agents. Their successful management of the factory was not an involuntary or inevitable response to the debt crisis but a distinctive form of economic resistance through the formulation of shop floor innovations that allowed for the exercise of a rich and nuanced relationality. This—contrary to positioning them as a market failure—sustained their enterprise and turned the debt crisis into an economic opportunity. Further and significantly, as they were embedded and sustained in their local communities, they gained the authority and the (perceived) *right* to both occupy and continue production. They acquired legitimacy independent of the state. Their economic savvy changed their political relationship with the state.

By successfully managing the factory through the crisis, the worker takeovers were also successfully dealing with the impact of the debt crisis and the financial risks taken by private investors and the debtor state in the sovereign debt market. The worker takeovers were not a market failure. They were creating and managing the transition to new markets locally and globally. More to the point and contrary to doctrinal orthodoxy, the worker takeovers indicate that the dominant concerns about the governance of sovereign debt cannot be confined to private investors, debtor governments and their interests. The Argentine debt crisis was a public event, not a private contractual dispute. The takeovers were responses to factory closures which were consequences of the risks taken by private market actors. This challenges their erasure from the debates on governance that followed the Argentine debt crisis.

Crucially, their authority to act and their legitimacy was derived from their local community. Their resistance was a response to the consequences of how the sovereign debt market functions in which the state as a sovereign debtor was a significant actor. The political significance of the takeovers was that through their resistance they indicated that their interests as 'non market' participants differed from that of the sovereign debtor (the Argentine state) and its creditors. What began as an act of economic resistance soon exposed a disjuncture between the concerns of the state, the market and the workers. The success of the takeovers challenged the political authority of the state to represent their economic interests. However, this resistance was short-lived and they were not allowed to stake their claim as market actors in the sovereign debt market as the following analysis of the state's response to the takeovers indicates.

Political Compliance

In 2002, the authorities sought to dismantle the takeovers with the aim of re-establishing order, 'to control the high degree of social mobilisation unleashed by the crisis and depoliticise them'.[37] This initially offensive response changed under President Nestor Kirchner, whose government launched new programmes to support the workers' cooperatives. The state instituted a programme for Self-Managed Work (PTA). The PTA offered the enterprises that were taken over or recuperated, different kinds of financial and other forms of assistance: monetary help to individual workers, to workers in 'productive units for technical assistance and training, raw materials etc in exchange for formalising/legitimising the cooperatives'.[38] The majority of the assisted companies 'became co-operatives' under the aegis of the state, as cooperatives were deemed 'more compatible with the need to reach consensus and set common goals'.[39] Secondly, this legal form was encouraged by new bankruptcy legislation, where magistrates were given the power to allow workers to continue with the takeovers 'on the condition that the workers present a project and organisation plan under the form of worker's cooperatives'.[40]

It is clear that 'institutionalisation' de-politicised the takeovers 'in exchange for the recognition of their practical aspirations'[41] and guaranteed them 'institutional help to secure financial and technical support in order to pursue their stated objectives of attaining solidarity, autonomy and self-management through factory takeovers and recovery'.[42] It was also true (and overlooked) that 'institutionalisation' as state policy converged with the contemporary governance of the sovereign debt market as explained below.

The main thrust of the state's response was to bring the factories back into the market economy through a process of 'institutionalisation' to create a demand for capital. It was a macroeconomic policy that sought to legitimise (and thus regulate) economic and political resistance to state authority or the discipline of the market.[43] This was achieved through a gradual process of 'disembedding' of the workers' dependence on the local community from which they derived their authority, legitimacy and their right to occupy the factories. This was achieved by the imposition of legal structures of state authority such as the formal recognition of takeovers as cooperatives, as discussed above.

Convergence

The state policy of 'institutionalisation' as described by Ana Dinerstein above is premised on the assumption of non-negotiable political compliance.

---

[37] Dinerstein, above n 16, 6.
[38] Ibid 28–36.
[39] Ibid.
[40] Ibid.
[41] Ibid, 6.
[42] Ibid 37–38.
[43] Ibid.

This re-establishes the private law commonsense that defines the governance of sovereign debt as it diffuses the economic resistance of the workers by subjecting them to state policy. As far as the governance of the sovereign debt market is concerned it remains focused on putative transactions between the creditors and the debtor (who oversees the interests of its politically compliant citizens). This ensures that in the event Argentina regains access to primary capital markets the 'politically compliant' are again made responsible for the social costs of the sovereign crisis while the creditors and the policy elite in Argentina that typically engage in high risk financial speculation are insulated from these costs. Further, this outcome was deemed inevitable, a recognition of worker autonomy. In fact, 'institutionalisation' saw the worker takeovers as natural 'subjects' of public policy while market participants were naturally shielded from responsibility by their privacy. The potential for economic resistance to private capital that the takeovers represented was silenced by the state's demand for their political compliance.

Is this silence a function of the convergence of state policy with the governance of sovereign debt ('convergence')? Convergence as a reflection of market regulation is graphically portrayed by Thomas Friedman in his book *The Lexus and the Olive Tree,* where the 'Electronic Herd', the world's investors, 'can impose pressures [for good policy] that few governments can resist ... The Electronic Herd turns the whole world into a parliamentary system, in which every government lives under the fear of a no-confidence vote from the herd'.[44] This is consistent with the post-crisis scenario described in the preceding paragraph when it appears that the Argentine state had no option but to ensure that 'institutionalisation' was consistent with the framework that socialised the risks of sovereign borrowing and lending. This would signal to the market that Argentina as debtor was taking all the steps needed to bolster the confidence of private creditors and maintain their incentives to invest in Argentina. Contrary to the doctrinal orthodoxy, which assumes the debtor acts to further the interests of its citizens, convergence indicates that the interests of the sovereign debtor as a market actor are distinct from the interests of its citizens. More specifically, for Argentina to regain access to primary capital markets as a private debtor it would have to ensure that its worker-citizens were accountable only to it as a sovereign state.

Convergence legitimises the actions of market participants and delegitimises the actions of non market participants. In the absence of a multilaterally negotiated regulatory bankruptcy framework to resolve sovereign debt crises, there is a private law commonsense that ensures the convergence of state policy and the governance of sovereign debt. This commonsense is

---

[44] As quoted in Blustein, above n 2, 6.

informal, ad hoc and market defined. The following section clarifies the nature of this private law commonsense.

GOVERNANCE OF SOVEREIGN DEBT: THE PRIVATE LAW COMMONSENSE

The Orthodoxy[45]

Typically, a sovereign wishing to borrow from capital markets issues bonds which are then bought by several hundred thousand creditors in different legal jurisdictions. A bond contract is a debt instrument that specifies the terms on which the debtor borrows capital. In the event of a debt crisis (when a sovereign fails to fulfil its debt obligations) the terms[46] of the debt contract usually allow for the debt to be 'restructured'—this is when the sovereign negotiates a write-down (or 'haircut') with its creditors reducing its original debt obligations.

The haircut is a reduction in the face value of the debt specified in each bond contract and is 'technically' based on the sovereign's financial ability or capacity to repay its outstanding debt. The negotiations between the sovereign debtor and its many creditors (represented by creditor associations) eventually leads to the restructuring of the defaulting sovereigns debt obligations. The debtor then issues new debt in exchange for its defaulted debt instruments and the debt settles. This re-establishes the debt cycle (and sustains the debt market). Argentina is in the process of repaying its debt to regain access to private capital markets and avoid the possibility of defaulting on its existing debt obligations.[47]

The debt contract is viewed as a private transaction between an individual debtor and several (individual) creditors. Each debt contract can be individually enforced as such by the US courts (debt issued in New York). Further, sovereign debt contracts are individually insulated from the 'social costs' of a debt crisis by the private law doctrine of sanctity.[48] Finally and most significantly, each creditor's 'contractual right to repayment' is viewed

---

[45] See generally Wood, above n 5, 12–16; Quereshi and Zeigler, above n 5, 7–16.

[46] LC Buchheit, 'Changing Bond Documentation: The Sharing Clause' (1998a) 17 *International Financial Law Review* 7, 17; LC Buchheit, 'The Collective Representation Clause' (1998b) 17 *International Financial Law Review*, 9; LC Buchheit and M Gulati, 'Exit Consents in Sovereign Bond Exchanges' (2000) 48 *UCLA Law Review* 13, 59, 83; LC Buchheit and M Gulati, 'Sovereign Bonds and the Collective Will' (2002) 51 *Emory Law Journal* 4, 13, 17.

[47] J Attwood and D Benson, 'Argentine Bonds, Stocks Sink as Takeover Fuels Default Concerns' (2008) www.bloomberg.com/apps/news?pid=20601087&refer=home&sid=aDuA9 V2SI6GY (accessed 10 March 2009).

[48] For the relevance of sanctity in doctrinal scholarship see JT Gathii, 'The Sanctity of Sovereign Loan Contracts and Its Origins in Enforcement Litigation' (2006) 38 *George Washington International Law Review* 251.

by the courts as 'property' in US law.[49] On default, the protection of a creditor's property interests skews the governance of sovereign debt in favour of creditors. Property and contractual sanctity are the frameworks that define the private law commonsense by which the sovereign debt market is currently governed. This commonsense socialises the costs of a sovereign debt crisis (or using economic jargon) as 'externalities' or 'the external effects' of sovereign borrowing. The external effects of a sovereign debt crisis are inter alia a natural consequence of missing markets. It follows that the non market constituents affected by a debt crisis are not entitled to any redress by market actors themselves and in the absence of the state developing mechanisms to offset the costs of sovereign debt they naturally pay the costs of a debt crisis.

Further, the private law commonsense ensures that responsibility for sovereign borrowing and lending is limited to individual debt contracts. In this context, the debtor as a market actor is naturally responsible for the costs of profligate borrowing as the responsibility of each creditor is defined by its contractual obligations as specified in the bond document. Socialising the costs associated with the risks of sovereign lending increases the profitability of debt transactions and as such acts as an incentive for creditors to lend excessively. The absence of a framework of responsibility that holds creditors and debtor governments accountable for the social costs of profligate lending (and borrowing) increases the volatility associated with sovereign lending and entrenches the cyclical nature of debt crises. This is inter alia attributable to the private law commonsense that ensures the 'public'—the non market constituency which includes the worker takeovers—ultimately suffer the consequences of a debt crisis.

It is not surprising therefore that in the aftermath of the Argentine debt crisis with its extensive and deep social consequences, poverty, hunger, loss of well-being and even loss of life, the central issue that dominated the governance debate at the time was the collective action problem—what are the ways in which creditors can be induced to cooperate, curb their individual instincts to collect full payment and accept a write-down? The governance debate at the time was focused on working out an optimum procedure to maintain the incentives for creditors to act appropriately (in a way that sustains the viability of the sovereign debt market) after sovereign default. This was sought to be achieved in part by contract modification. Henceforth all bond contracts (issued under US law) now contain collective action clauses that specify the requisite threshold (number of creditors who must agree to the write-down) for the debt to settle as quickly and as efficiently as

---

[49] *NML Capital Ltd v The Republic of Argentina*, Judge Greisa (SDNY) (13 March 2005).

possible. The proposal to set up an IMF-sponsored international 'sovereign debt restructuring mechanism' was vehemently rejected by the market.

A central (often overlooked) assumption in the doctrinal orthodoxy that governs sovereign debt is that the sovereign as private debtor (a legal fiction), is represented by a government that upholds the interests of its citizens in its borrowing decisions. The market's reliance on this fiction 'normalises' the following. It ensures that the social costs of a debt crisis do not raise any concerns about governance as these are generally attributed to the conduct of a defaulting individual debtor—the refusal of the sovereign debtor to borrow less, or default, the poor reputation of a debtor on account of its historical track record of default, etc.[50] It normalises the view that since the debt incurred by the sovereign will be used to benefit its citizens (as was the case with Argentina in the decade leading to the debt crisis) technically there is no constituency that was not involved in the decision to borrow.[51] The market's reliance on the legal fiction that the sovereign is a private debtor satisfies a certain notion of corrective justice, as it is fair or efficient[52] that in exchange for access to capital, the debtor (rather than each individual creditor) is ultimately responsible for the social costs of a debt crisis. The market's reliance on a legal fiction ensures that the risks associated with sovereign debt transactions are rightly borne by a sovereign's subjects who ultimately benefit from them. It is also fair that the creditor's right to repayment is protected as property in exchange for the benefits that a sovereign's subjects receive on account of its access to private capital markets.

The fiction of sovereign as private debtor insulates the concerns of governance from the social costs of a debt crisis. It ensures that risks are taken privately and responsibilities for the social costs that follow are thus naturally borne publically. The private law commonsense ensures the convergence between 'institutionalisation'—the state's response to the worker takeovers and the assumptions that dominate the governance of sovereign debt. In the aftermath of the Argentine debt crisis the worker takeovers are formally recognised through 'institutionalisation' as acts of political compliance. At the same time, their compliance insulates market actors in the sovereign debt market (both the debtor and its creditors) from responsibility for the social costs of the debt crisis.

---

[50] AC Porzecanski, 'From Rogue Creditors to Rogue Debtors: Implications of Argentina's Default' (2005) 6 *Chicago Journal of International Law* 311–32.

[51] This commonsense has been challenged by the view that elites in a defaulting country may be responsible for decisions to borrow and this may be an explanation for default. However this literature generates arguments for debt write-downs on account of the illegitimacy of the state. See the Jubilee Debt Campaign on Iraqi debt at: www.jubileeiraq.org/odiousdebt. htm (accessed 10 March 2009); LC Buchheit, M Gulati and RB Thompson, 'The Dilemma of Odious Debts' (20070 56 *Duke Law Journal* 1201–62.

[52] Quereshi and Zeigler, above n 5, 4, 7–16.

The role of the private law commonsense in sovereign debt clarifies the nature of what Philip Cerny refers to as 'neo-liberal convergence'[53] with the state policy of 'institutionalisation'. This convergence is underpinned by private law doctrine as manifested in the market's reliance on the legal fiction of the sovereign as private individual debtor, contractual sanctity and sovereign bonds as property. This convergence is bridged by the assumption that the sovereign debtor acts in the interests of its citizens. It turns out that the sovereign may be acting in a way that furthers the interests of its creditors, or its influential elites first before considering its sovereign obligations to its citizens. The following section uses a feminist perspective to examine what contribution the worker takeovers make towards an alternative reading of governance in the context of convergence.

GOVERNANCE THROUGH A FEMINIST LENS

The Argentine debt was large, its default spectacular and as discussed above, the social costs of the crisis remain unaccounted. This section examines new work in this area of governance that reveals the problems with the current reliance of the sovereign debt market on the private law commonsense discussed in the preceding section.

Social not Legal

In a significant piece of work in the period following the adoption of collective action clauses in sovereign debt contracts (contract modification), Anna Gelpern and Mitu Gulati reveal that contractual terms may not matter in the resolution of a debt crisis in the way doctrinal orthodoxy assumes they should.[54] In their analysis of the responses of market actors to contract modification, they found the latter indifferent about the benefits of this change. It appears that contracts were being relied on to signal information publicly to other market actors, or third parties. Through their empirical work, the authors trace a disjuncture between two views of the same market actors: the predominant and publicly voiced recommendations for a market approved legal fix to resolve the problem of sovereign debt and the privately voiced view that this per se would not have any impact on the resolution of a debt crisis in the future. This work raises an obvious question: if the contracts do not work in the way they

---

[53] PG Cerny, 'Power, markets and accountability: the development of multi-level governance in international finance' in Baker, Hudson and Woodward, above n 10, 45.

[54] A Gelpern and GM Gulati, 'Public Symbol in Private Contract: A Case Study' (2007) 84 *Washington University Law Review* 1627–715.

should, and in the absence of a formal regulatory framework then what are the mechanisms that actually resolve a crisis? Following on from a reading of Gelpern and Gulati's conclusions it appears that as far as creditors are concerned, the social contexts (their local creditor coalitions and groups) invest the bond contract with a symbolic meaning. Thus factors such as the social positioning, influence, identity and reputation of creditors are key determinants of debt workouts. In any event, it appears from this work that the determinative influences in a resolution of a debt crisis are social variables and market constraints that operate independent of the market's reliance on private law doctrine.

The symbolic role that sovereign bond contracts (and arguably private law doctrine) play in regulation was apparent during the Argentine debt restructuring. This was a situation where creditor coalitions had different agendas and given that their large numbers were spread in eight different jurisdictions, the lack of access to reliable information was a significant problem. It was clear that creditors were watching what other creditors were doing with their contracts to obtain information about how they should act. So for example, in the lead up to the debt workout most creditors were looking to the big, influential creditors to decide how to move (sell their bonds, exchange them for new bonds from the debtor or sue). This strategy paid out for slightly over seventy five percent of creditors as they eventually exchanged their debt for new bonds on extremely favourable terms. The Italian pensioners (a sub-set of Argentina's creditors) chose instead to sue the debtor in the Italian courts and sought repayment of the face value of their debt. In other words, they did not respond to the signals from the big creditors and were sticking to their contracts. They were consequently excluded from the debt settlement and have so far got nothing at all from the Argentine Government. The outcomes for different creditors were clearly very different, even though their contracts were identical.

Thus the variables that influence sovereign debt workouts are clearly social not legal. This is also evidenced by two specific creditor-initiated changes that followed the Argentine debt crisis: one mentioned earlier— contract modification and the other involving the formulation of voluntary creditor codes of conduct that inter alia rely on good faith, a socially embedded norm recognised domestically in common law jurisdictions such as the United Kingdom. This reliance on good faith reinforces the idea that in debt workouts, a creditor's social positioning in the sovereign debt market will matter as much as (maybe even more than) their contractual rights. Of course, contract modification and the adoption of socially embedded norms such as 'good faith' reinforce the private law common-sense described above and as such the adoption of this norm displaces the need for a more formal framework to regulate the sovereign debt market. In other words, recent changes further entrench a private law commonsense that inter alia shields the market from accountability for the social costs of a debt crisis.[55]

A Slippage between the Doctrinal and the Real

The fact that social variables such as good faith, informal networks and creditor identity are key factors to resolve a debt crisis indicates a 'slippage' between the doctrinal and the 'real'. This reaffirms a view contrary to the doctrinal orthodoxy, that social variables matter as much as (and sometimes even more than) contractual rights when it comes to sovereign debt regulation. This goes even further as a creditor's position in a workout is determined by their allegiances to specific creditor coalitions (or networks) as the Italian pensioners realised to their disadvantage. This is further confirmed by the fact that a debt workout is typically reliant on thresholds to indicate fair outcomes instead of, a priori, multilaterally negotiated contractual notions of substantive fairness. This increases the symbolic value of the contracts. The evidence that the social context has a determinative influence on debt restructurings raised an obvious question—if the law is marginal as indicated in recent empirical work then what role does the private law commonsense *still* play in the governance of sovereign debt?

A quick answer (consistent with the evidence) to this question refers back to Gelpern and Gulati's paper discussed above where they found that international lawyers and law firms play a pivotal role in maintaining the doctrinal orthodoxy that frames the private law commonsense.[56] They maintain the orthodoxy because it is in their interests to do so.

Another answer consistent with the preceding section reflects the view that the doctrinal orthodoxy is a dominant discourse. More specifically, a particular discourse—private law legal reasoning—dominates the governance of sovereign debt. This orthodoxy is discursive as it relies on abstract categories and fictions such as sovereign debtor, bonds as property, private contract and sanctity. To maintain its relevance to the messy 'reality' of a sovereign debt crisis, the doctrine relies on several fictions—the individual sovereign debtor, the bond contract as property. These categories are abstractions distinguished from the 'real' social context that actually governs sovereign debt as described above.

The worker takeovers challenge the legitimacy of their exclusion by a doctrinal boundary in the following way. The economic success of their rich, textured relationality subverts the holdall category 'social costs'. Through

---

[55] D Thomas and J Garcia-Fronti, 'Good faith in sovereign debt restructuring: mapping a shift from enforcement to voluntary compliance' (2007) 28 *Zeitschrift fur Rechtssoziologie* Heft 2, 201–11.

[56] Gelpern and Gulati, above n 54, 1700.

their resistance they changed the crisis into an economic opportunity. This makes them market participants with equally legitimate interests in participating in the resolution of a debt crisis, independent of the sovereign debtor and its creditors. As the 'real, material subjects of their collective resistance' the worker takeovers challenge their discursive exclusion by the doctrinal orthodoxy.

Further—and significantly—their authority, their right to take over the factories is derived from a legitimacy grounded in their local community in contrast to the doctrinal legitimacy derived from the markets reliance on legal fictions as described above. The grounded legitimacy of the takeovers is a counter point, an alternate discourse to the abstract and contrived fictions that legitimate existing governance based on private law doctrine. In the multiple social spheres of governance that influence the resolution of a debt crisis, this makes the doctrinal orthodoxy just another sphere of governance. In the absence of a conceptual framework of the kind developed below the dominance of the doctrinal orthodoxy erases its real impact.

The private law that dominates governance discursively defines a socio-cultural domain: the sovereign debt market. It is the 'cultural and ideological composite Other'[57] that filters 'through different domestic political and social systems', by a process of gradual convergence, as described in the preceding section. In the Argentine debt crisis, the private law commonsense ensures the convergence between 'institutionalisation' and the governance of sovereign debt. This reasoning privatises risk-taking and externalises or makes the public responsible for the social costs of private risk-taking. As explained in the preceding section, (almost inevitably) the constituency (the state government and creditors) that takes the financial risk to lend is not the constituency that bears (and deals with) the consequences of a default.

The functionality of private law commonsense as a mechanism of convergence is one reason why it maintains its dominance. When viewed through a feminist perspective, the other reason for this discursive dominance is that private law commonsense represents a socio-cultural domain in which its subjects, a consistent rationale and the values that legitimate its processes, are realised.[58] In this domain, the worker takeovers are not market actors. Moreover, convergence ensures that as such 'non-private persons' they remain illegitimate in the absence of the imprimatur of state recognition ('institutionalisation'). Once recognised as sovereign subjects, the takeovers slot into the fictional 'box' labelled 'sovereign debtor' and the private law defined sphere of governance is complete.

---

[57] CT Mohanty, 'Under Western Eyes: Feminist Scholarship and Colonial Discourses' in CT Mohanty, A Russo, and L Torres (eds), *Third World Women and the Politics of Feminism* (Bloomington and Indianapolis, Indiana University Press, 1991) 49.

[58] For a good description of the domain of private law see W Lucy, *The Philosophy of Private Law* (Oxford, Oxford University Press, 2007).

The 'abstract', contrived legitimacy of market actors and the 'grounded' legitimacy of the worker takeovers represent conceptually different sources of legitimacy. However, the dominance of the private law commonsense discursively erases the latter. This erasure is partly explained by the functionality of private law in socialising the costs associated with risky lending and borrowing decisions taken privately. It is also partly explained by 'convergence' necessitated by the state's demand for political compliance.

This is a view of governance through a feminist lens. It is informed by the work of Chandra Talpade Mohanty who demarcates two distinct constructions of 'Women': 'a cultural and ideological composite Other constructed through diverse representational discourses (scientific, literary, juridical, linguistic, cinematic etc.)—and ... — real, material subjects of their collective histories'.[59] According to Mohanty (and in a different context) the first discursively erases the second.

The further questions that arise from the discussion on governance (and not dealt with here) are whether the recognition of 'abstract' and 'real' sources of legitimacy in governance is gender coded? Do the distinct sources of legitimacy and the dominance of one satisfy the feminist preoccupation with uncovering 'the male domination of women'?

This analysis of the governance of sovereign debt is also distinguishable from existing critiques of international law. Balakrishnan Rajagopal[60] for instance, accepts the position taken by Dianne Otto and Julie Mertus who have both engaged with the elitist bias of rights theories discourses. They have also attempted to 'formulate general conceptions of law that could accommodate the role of subaltern communities and individuals'.[61] Rajagopal's work extends these conceptions by using a 'social movements perspective [that] emphasises the importance of extra-institutional forms of mobilisation for the "success" or "failure" of institutional forms'.[62]

Rajagopal's critique does not capture the distinctive nature of the private law commonsense, its persistence and the implicit assumptions about legitimacy that underpin its dominance. In a modified reading of the elitist bias in international law, the analysis of governance that this chapter offers specifies how distinct frameworks of legitimacy simultaneously emerge from different sources to resolve a debt crisis—one a creature of 'governance in a private law framework as recognised by market participants', the other more conventionally a creature of 'state recognition' and the third that challenges the first two—the grounded legitimacy of worker takeovers such as Brukman.

---

[59] Mohanty above n 57, 49–50.
[60] B Rajagopal, *International Law From Below: Development, Social Movements and Third World Resistance* (Cambridge, Cambridge University Press, 2003) 234.
[61] Ibid.
[62] Ibid, 235.

This analysis indicates that Brukman occupies the space between economic resistance and political compliance. As far as the governance of sovereign debt is concerned, their economic resistance does not count and their political compliance is non-negotiable. Fortunately, for the Brukman workers the takeover had a wider geo-political impact with linkages to other takeovers in Argentina and beyond across Latin America. The social disruption in the aftermath of the debt crisis did have a political consequence as the unrest (initially) informed the Argentine state's reluctance to access primary capital markets. Moreover at the time, it moved away from its reliance on the IMF by paying off its official debts with a loan from its neighbour Venezuela. The Argentine state sought instead to rely on commodity barter and other arrangements to satisfy its capital requirements. The lasting significance of takeovers like Brukman on the governance of sovereign debt is still unfolding.

CONCLUSIONS

In the aftermath of the Argentine debt crisis, the chapter describes the convergence between the state's response to the worker takeovers that arose as a response to the crisis and the private law commonsense that defines the governance of sovereign debt. This convergence marginalises alternative, distinct and conflicting sources of legitimacy. The private law commonsense derives its legitimacy from abstract categories. It functions as an ideological value system that discursively erases and silences alternative, grounded, socially located sources of legitimacy. This may explain its ineffectiveness in the resolution of a debt crisis but when viewed through a feminist lens its impact is 'real' as it demarcates a boundary of legitimacy that erases (and thus delegitimises) the responses of the worker takeovers. It also diminishes the possibility of political resistance to the continuing cycle of sovereign debt crises and the inevitably unaccounted social costs that follow in their wake.

12

Concluding (or Beginning?) Thoughts: Postcards to the Future

SARI KOUVO AND ZOE PEARSON

P
ROVIDING CONCLUDING THOUGHTS for an edited collection as diverse and rich as this one is a task that we undertake with some ambivalence. On the one hand, the subject matter, the themes of the collection and the reflection in the chapters themselves seem to caution against providing any grand narrative or summary. This 'stock-take' of where feminist perspectives on international law are today vis-à-vis women of the world and the mainstream of international legal scholarship and practice has highlighted once more the diversity of feminisms, and of their locations at the margins, the mainstream and elsewhere. The collection has reflected on the strengths of interdisciplinary knowledges, exercises in recontextualisation and connections between feminist theorising and politics. The chapters have explored the many ways in which feminists negotiate the tensions between resistance and compliance that seem inherent in our work as we try to maintain the apparent momentum of feminist discourses while also responding to the demands of self-reflective methodologies as well as the crisis-driven hegemonies of international law that threaten, but make increasingly important, any spaces for contestation. Any summary cannot do these collective undertakings justice.

This was also our thought at the end of the workshop. Therefore, we gave the task, and the final words, then and now, to the contributors at the workshop, asking them to send a postcard to the future and in doing this to 'think beyond the full stops'. As 'real' postcards, these postcards were bought in the village of Oñati, where the workshop had been held, and they showed pictures of the village, the surrounding countryside and the people of Oñati.

Postcards presented an interesting medium for the task. Postcards are directly linked to location. They capture the fleeting coincidence of a particular time and space. They are a memento to send to loved ones (or to yourself) to capture the magic (or misery) of a particular moment and place. The connection with location and time in the social history of postcards is one that has been important for less flippant reasons; postcards have been used as propaganda mechanisms to support colonialism, shore up nationalism and champion various social debates.[1] Historical and contemporary postcards often borrow from and reinforce cultural or gender stereotypes, 'images complicit in the advancement of empire and the "norms of gender, sex and race that empire underwrites"'.[2] Postcards have also been thoroughly linked with women, both in terms of those who, at the height of the early postcard craze in Britain, sent such cards; and those whose bodies were appropriated for the images presented by these cards.[3] Cynthia Enloe and Gillian Calder et al note the use of women's bodies in these postcards in ways that reflected and reinforced gender and race stereotypes and eroticised indigenous women.[4] The use of postcards to represent stereotyped pictures of the location and its inhabitants persists today. Indeed, two of the Oñati postcards contained 'typical' pictures of locals from the area: one picture of a happy looking woman dressed in traditional dress, carrying a basket while walking in the hills; another of a serious male figure, again in traditional dress, shown directing his dog to herd sheep.

Postcards are also linked to location in another important way, as Calder et al note, they 'trade on the notion of "away" or of the margin—they are self-conscious communications from the edge to the centre or "home"'.[5] In this way, postcards, as well as being intricately linked with location and with preservation of boundaries of these locations, the maintenance of geopolitical borders, distances between home and the 'other', the exotic, the dangerous/backward/aberrant,[6] are also thoroughly imbued with notions of movement across and transgression of borders. Postcards also complicate the public/private divide, occupying both spheres simultaneously, with private messages for the intended addressee able to be read on the back of the postcard by anyone during its journey through the postal system.[7]

These understandings of postcards strengthen the usefulness of our postcard exercise: discussions in this collection show careful reflections from contributors not only about the many different locations of feminist thinking but also the simultaneous occupation of feminist international law

---

[1] See, eg, E Adjin-Tetley, G Calder, A Cameron, M Deckha, R Johnson, H Lessard, M Maloney, M Young, 'Postcard from the Edge (Of Empire)' (2008) 17 *Social & Legal Studies* 5, 14–16, noting the role that postcards have played in Britain's colonies, debates over suffrage, tariff rates, elections, war propaganda.

[2] Ibid 14, quoting M Wollaeger, 'Woolf, Postcards and the Elision of Race: Colonizing Women in *The Voyage Out*' (2001) 8 *Modernism* 43, 44.

[3] Ibid 14–15.

[4] See esp C Enloe, *Bananas, Beaches and Bases. Making Feminist Sense of International Politics*, 2nd edn (Berkeley, University of California Press, 2000) 42–44, with discussion about the use of postcards for colonial propaganda, but also giving examples of the sexualised, eroticised and exoticised postcards featuring indigenous women. Calder et al, above n 1, 15.

[5] Calder et al, above n 1.

[6] Idem.

[7] Ibid 16.

scholars and practitioners on the margins of the discipline, as well as in the mainstream, in sites of resistance at the same time as sites of compliance.

As you see from the postcards reproduced below, some of the participants chose to write to particular addressees—they wrote to daughters, the future United Nations *Madame* Secretary General; others chose to direct their message to all feminist scholars and practitioners of international law in the future (and possibly themselves). The postcards are full of hope and possibility; some are practical, some are prescriptive, some are philosophical. Some signal the self-reflective nature of feminist projects in international law, in terms of individual motivations, interdisciplinary methodologies and opportunities to engage and connect, within and outside of the potentially limiting world of academia and international legal practice. Others imagine a world that accommodates the diversity of feminisms to the extent that the silences and violences that are the focus for many feminist engagements with international law are rendered memories, manifestations of 'times gone by', when 'gendered divisions of labour and thought' are undermined. They leave us with strong and hopeful messages for the future of feminist engagements in international law.

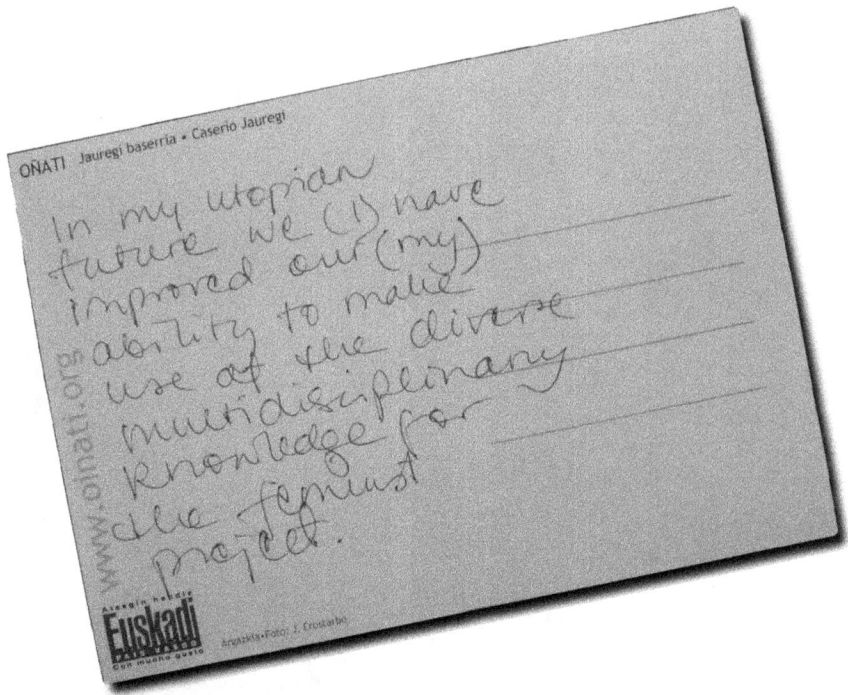

ONATI
23.5.
08
Ubao erreka gainean eraikitako Kloustroa (Mikel Goiangeruaren Parrokia)
Claustro construido sobre el río Ubao (Parroquia San Miguel Arcángel)

for the future —

In 2008, we start too late in trying to change the way we understand international law. We should start in homes, in primary + high schools and undermine/challenge gendered versions of labour + ttaught.

www.onati.org

EUSkadi

11253.- TIPICO VASCO

5-POINT GOAL PLAN :
ANNUAL REVIEW

1. Numerical equality achieved in all positions + at all levels

2. Diversity accepted as positive + 'normalized'

3. Categories + Dichotomies transcended

4. Equality understood

5. Humanity fully understood

Transformation complete ▽

Exclusivas San Cayetano - Bilbao

MADAME SECRETAIRE-GÉNÉRAL

UNITED NATIONS

PALAIS DES NATIONS

?

Ed Besson
BV

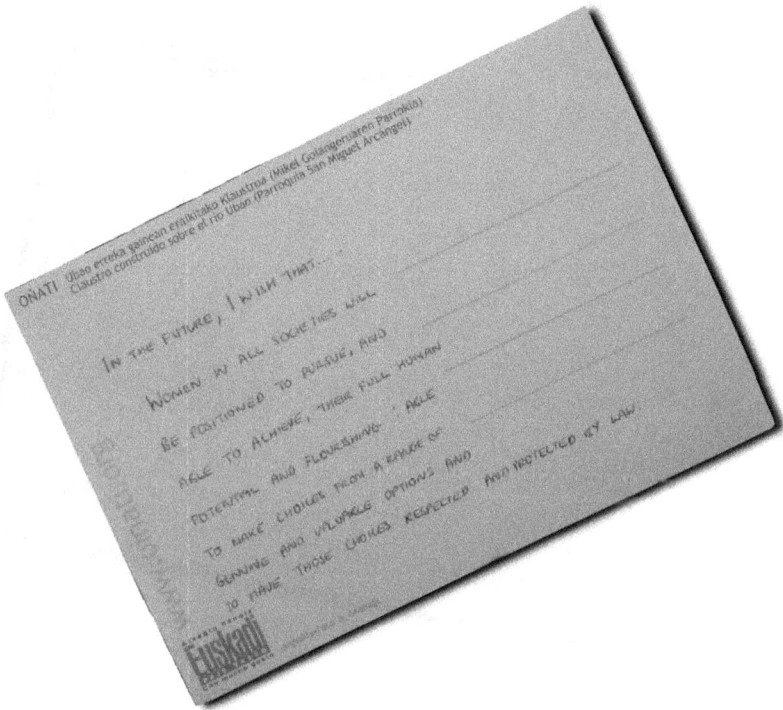

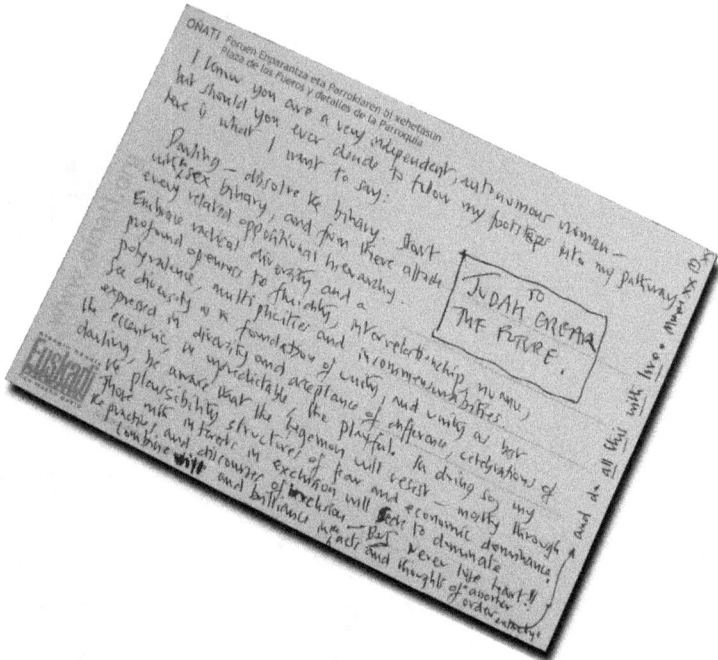

BILBAO

23rd May, 2008   Onati to the future

Is this a time when injury, suffering, indignity, symbolic, material violence, injustice, hunger, poverty are terms that conjure up times gone by? Is this a time of beautiful chaos?

Nº 205 Fotografía: Peio Arrúa

OÑATI   Nazioarteko artzain txakur txapelketa
Concurso Internacional de Perros de Pastor

www.onati.org

in the future
we have finally learned to listen and read
across and over the disciplinary boundaries

I have had time to read all the essential books
without anymore missing those that are most central for
the development of my own thinking

I have had most of the eye/ear opening experiences
which help me to understand the limits of my own
seeing & 'hearing' and partly overcome them.

The feminist project has remained as controversial
as it was in the past but there has been a serious
spill-over towards all theorizing/analyzing in the
social sciences

it is not more concentrating on the imagined
binary men vs women

Euskadi

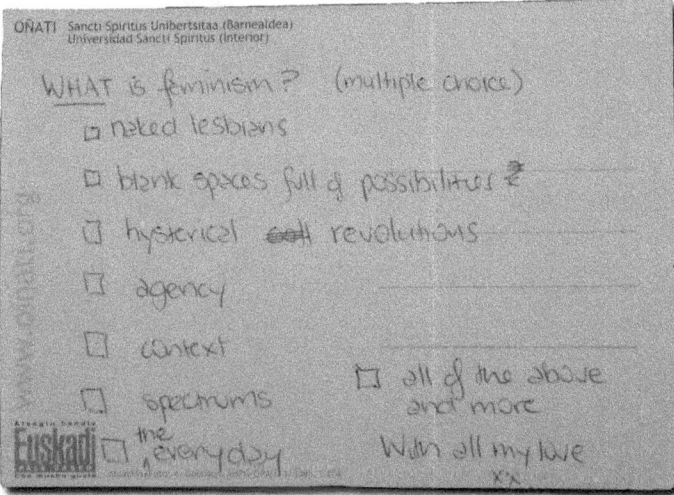

OÑATI Sancti Spiritus Unibertsitaa (Barnealdea)
Universidad Sancti Spiritus (Interior)

WHAT is feminism? (multiple choice)

☐ naked lesbians

☐ blank spaces full of possibilities ?

☐ hysterical ~~call~~ revolutions

☐ agency

☐ context

☐ spectrums   ☐ all of the above
                                        and more
☐ the
   ￪ everyday   With all my love
                                          xx

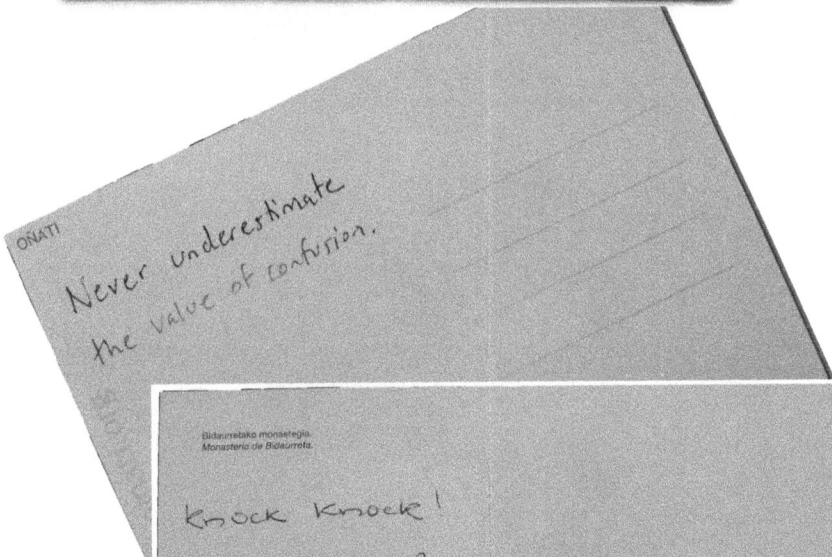

OÑATI

Never underestimate
the value of confusion.

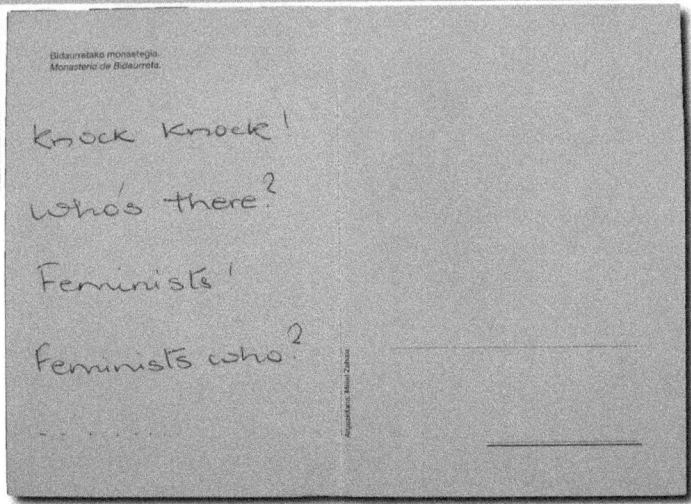

Bidaurretako monastegia.
Monasterio de Bidaurreta.

Knock Knock!

Who's there?

Feminists!

Feminists who?

Index

Aboriginal communities in Australia, intervention in 80, 82, 83
Abu-Lughob, Lila 167
accountability 137, 140–1, 144
acknowledgment of influence of feminism 21, 31
activism
    ad hoc criminal tribunals 22
    experts 22
    feminism 20, 22, 76, 83, 89, 95
    identity, giving activists an 102
    scholars and activists, divide between 20
    Sierra Leone 144
ad hoc criminal tribunals
    activism 22
    International Criminal Tribunal for Rwanda 4, 143, 150
    International Criminal Tribunal for the former Yugoslavia 4, 19, 111–17, 119–20, 126–7, 143
    Nuremberg Military Tribunal 143, 144
    Tokyo Military Tribunal 143
    transitional justice and international crimes 138, 140
    war crimes 111–17, 120–1, 127, 140, 143
Afghanistan, state-building in 25, 159–76
    Afghan Women's Summit for Democracy 169–70
    'after fear' agenda 136
    Bonn Agreement 2001 168–70
    Brussels Proclamation 169
    civil war 163
    civilised and uncivilised 165
    clash of civilisations 165
    Cold War 162–3
    Constitution 172–3
    co-option of feminist ideas 84, 88–9
    corruption 160, 173
    crisis, language of 78, 84, 86–9, 91–4
    culture 161, 164–5, 169, 173–6
    custom 161, 163
    decision-making, involvement in 167–70, 172–6
    Department of Women's Affairs 169, 170
    Department of Women's Affairs at regional level 172
    diversity 136
    education of girls 162–3, 165, 169, 172, 175–6
    ethnicity 161, 168–72, 174, 176
    European Union 163–4, 169, 175

factions 168, 171, 173–4
forced marriages 162
gender mainstreaming 88, 134, 135–6, 159–61, 167–8, 170–2
General Assembly of the UN 84
general equality clause in Constitution 173
history of conflict 161–4
honour killings 162
honour, women as carriers of the family 162
human rights 156, 160, 164–5, 167, 169
inequality, increase in 87, 91–2
inevitability, politics of 91
international crimes 93
liberal equality strategies 167–74
life experience 134, 135–6
local women's groups, failure to engage with 88–9
mainstream/margins dichotomy 134, 135–6
military intervention on behalf of women 8, 25, 78, 84, 87–9, 94, 156, 160, 164–7, 175–6
Ministry of Women's Affairs 170–2
modernisation 161
Mujahedin/warlords 162–3, 168, 169–70, 173–4
National Action Plan for Women 171–2
National Development Strategies 171–2
oppression 161, 164–5, 175
orientalist mythologies 94
Parliament, women's representation and 172–4, 176
participation in mainstream institutions 134, 167–76
Pashtun 163, 165
patronage and manipulation in politics 174, 176
political participation and representation 86–8, 93–4, 134, 167–76
politics of inevitability 91
post-9/11 era 134, 160, 165–76
poverty 161–2, 164–5
protectors, men's role as women's 162
quotas 173
religion 162, 165, 176
representation and participation of women 86–8, 93–4, 134, 167–76
Revolutionary Association of the Women of Afghanistan 88

saved, Afghan women as needing to be 94, 167, 175
Security Council of the UN 84
sexual violence used as weapon of war 163
Soviet occupation 161, 162–3
specific institutions for women 134, 169, 170–2
stabilisation 161
state-building process 25, 167–70
Taliban 84, 87, 135, 160, 163–6, 169, 175
terrorism 165–6
tokenism 168
transnational justice 155–6
United States 160, 162–8
veiled women needing rescue, orientalist mythologies about 94
violence
    increase in 87, 91–2
    sexual violence used as weapon of war 163
war on terror 164, 165–6, 168
Western liberalism 167
women's organisations 88–9, 163–5, 169
women's rights 160–1, 164, 167–76
Agamben, Giorgio 79, 81–2, 90
agency theory
    choice 121
    crisis-hegemony 72
    critical theory of agency 123–6
    decontextualised agency 72–4, 123
    identity-based movements 125–6
    inevitability, politics of 121
    interpretation 117–18, 121, 123–4
    liquid feminism 121
    location of interpreter 123
    objectification 124–5
    oppression 123–4
    politics of inevitability 121
    power 111–12
    rape and sexual violence 111–13, 115, 117–18, 120–8, 149–50
    self-expression 123, 127
    sexism and anti–feminism 121
    sexual agency during conflicts, denial of 19–20
    slavery 124–5, 126
    social death argument 124–5
    terror and anxiety 123
    torture 72
    trafficking 134, 180–1
    United States 121
aggressive masculinity, language of crisis and 72, 76–7, 82
Al Qaeda 160, 164
Allott, Philip 63
Alvarez, Jose 100–1

Amanullah, king 161
American Society of International Law 93
amnesties 140–1, 144
Andersson, Ulrika 8, 134, 136
Ankara, Turkey 47–8, 66–7
anti-sex 21
Anti-Terrorist Financing Guidelines: Voluntary Best Practices for US charities 107
anxiety *see* terror and anxiety
Aoki, Keith 63
Argentina *see* Argentina, debt crisis and takeover of factories by workers in; sovereign debt market and Argentina
Argentina, debt crisis and takeover of factories by workers in 193–212
    binaries 195–6
    Brukman textile factory 193–204, 211–12
    case study 197–204
    committees, formation of 199–200
    context 197–8
    convergence 202–4, 207, 210
    definition of sovereign bond market 194
    economic resistance 199–201
    expropriation 199
    feminist scholarship 134, 195–6
    gender coding 136, 196
    governance 193–7, 201, 212
    institutionalisation 202–3, 206, 210
    interaction 135
    interdependence 135, 200
    legitimacy 201, 210–12
    local community, embeddedness of factories in 198–9, 202, 210
    mainstream/margins dichotomy 134
    market failure 197, 201
    political compliance 201–3
    private law commonsense 194, 197, 203–12
    Programme for Self-Managed Work 202
    public/private boundary 195–6
    relationality 135, 200–1
    restructuring of debt 208
    social costs 197, 198, 203–6, 209–11
    sovereign debt market 193–7, 201–12
    Washington Consensus 197–8
    workers' cooperatives, support for 202
armed conflicts *see* wars and conflicts
Asian tsunami 81
Askin, Kelly 3
Australia, intervention in lives of Aboriginals in 80, 82, 83
autonomy 134, 136, 177, 182, 190
Azerbaijani-Moghaddam, Sippi 170–1

bad faith 20, 21 *see also* good faith
bare life 79

Berman, Nathaniel 18–19
biases
    dominant constructions 140–3
    institutions describe, condemn and rectify
        abuses, bias in how 144–8, 152–4
    naturalising constitutive bias, feminism as
        133–4, 138–9
    subject constituted by international
        crimes, bias in 140–4, 148–9
    transitional justice and international
        crimes 133–4, 139–44, 148–9, 151
Bin Laden, Osama 160
binaries *see also* resistance/compliance
    binary
    Argentina, debt crisis and takeover of
        factories by workers in 195–6
    civilised/uncivilised 1, 165
    insider/outsider 54–5
    political resistance 51
    public/private dichotomy 28, 57, 59–60,
        195–6, 214
    spaces of international law 49, 51, 54–62,
        65–8
    war on terror 128
    West 51
blind spots 1, 4, 5, 6, 21, 62, 73, 98,
    101–5, 108
bodily injury crimes 141–2, 143, 147–53
Bonino, Emma 163–4
Bonn Agreement 2001 168–70
Borgen, Chris 100
break from feminism, taking a 7, 13–16,
    20–4, 33–4
Breuer, Josef 38
'brief for women, carrying a' 24
Brown, Vincent 124, 126
Brown, W 151
Brukman textile factory, Argentina, takeover
    of 193–204, 211–12
Brunet, Ariane 143
Brussels Proclamation 169
Bush doctrine 74
Bush, George W 72, 74, 82, 84, 86–7,
    102–3, 105–6, 110–11, 118–23,
    127–9, 156
Bush, Laura 84, 164
Buss, Doris 4, 59, 65, 149
Butler, Judith 126, 148, 184

Calder, Gillian 214
Cerny, Philip 207
charities, Anti-Terrorist Financing
    Guidelines: Voluntary Best Practices for
    United States 107
Charlesworth, Hilary 2, 4, 5, 7, 13–16,
    33–5, 48, 81–2, 112–13, 125,
    167, 169
Chicago School 81

children
    Aboriginal children in Australia, abuse
        of 80
    rape as torture, criminalisation of 115–17,
        119–20
    trafficking 185–6
Chile 81, 141, 144
Chinkin, Christine 2, 4, 5, 167, 169
Churchill, Ward 122–3
civil and political rights 28
civilised and uncivilised binary 1, 165
civilising mission of international law 57
Cixous, Hélène 38
clash of civilisations 1, 6, 165
Clinton, Bill 163–4
Cold War 3, 25, 162–3
collective action clauses 205–6, 207
colonisation and auto-colonisation of
    feminism 71–3
comfort women 145, 150
compliance *see* resistance/compliance binary
conflicts *see* wars and conflicts
consent
    rape 73, 113–17, 119–21, 127–9, 182–3
    torture 119
    trafficking 134, 185
conservative feminism, consolidation of
    134, 139
contestation, space and 51–2, 56
context
    agency 72–4, 123
    Argentina, debt crisis and takeover of
        factories by workers in 197–8
    decontextualisation 72–4, 112, 120,
        123, 149
    genocide 149
    rape as torture, criminalisation of 73–4,
        112, 120
    sovereign debt market 208, 209
    terror and anxiety 74, 123
    torture 120
    trafficking 179–80, 190–1
convergence 202–4, 207, 210
Cook, Rebecca 3
Copelon, Rhonda 135
co-option of feminist agenda 72, 78, 83–92,
    94–5
creditor codes of conduct 208
crime *see* ad hoc criminal tribunals;
    international crimes; rape and
    sexual violence; terrorism; transitional
    justice and international crimes; war
    crimes
crimes against humanity 140–1, 143, 149
crisis, language of 75–95
    Aboriginal communities, intervention in
        80, 82, 83
    activism 76, 83, 89, 95

Afghanistan, women in 78, 84, 86–9, 91–4
agency theory 72
aggressive masculinity 72, 76–7, 82
colonisation and auto-colonisation of feminism 71–3
colonisation of politics 72
critical legal theory 83
development of international law 81–2
disaster capitalism 81–3, 95
domesticated womanhood 72, 76–7, 82
economic liberalisation 81
emergencies, declarations of 75–8
essentialism 135
everydayness of crisis 79–83
exception, state of 79–80, 82–3
experts in crisis management 76
feminism 71–3, 76–9, 83–92, 94–5
gender hierarchy, revitalisation of 76–8, 82
gender mainstreaming 85, 88
governance 72, 78–80, 82–91, 95
hegemony 71–4, 78
human rights 77–8, 80
inclusive security 86, 92
inevitability, politics of 82, 91, 95
Initiative for Inclusive Security 76
international economic institutions 81
Iraq 78, 80, 81, 85–9, 91–4
language of feminism 78, 89–92
local women's groups, failure to engage with 88–9
management of crises 72, 84
masculinity, language of aggressive 72, 76–7, 82
mapping 86–8, 94–5
militarism 76, 91–2
non-governmental organisations 85, 88
Northern Territory, reduction of rights of Aboriginals in 80, 83
partnership model 73
politics 79, 82–3, 85–6, 88, 91, 93–5
post 9/11 era 71–3, 77–8
pre-emptive self-defence 78, 80
racial stereotypes, resurgence of 82
re-mapping emergencies 92–5
resistance/compliance hegemony 73
security agenda 72–3
Security Council 76–8, 80, 82, 85–6, 93, 95
September 11, 2001 terrorist attacks on the United States 75–7
sexual abuse during armed conflict and post-conflict peace-keeping 89–90
shock therapy stabilisation programmes 81
state of exception 79–80, 82–3
structural inequalities and disadvantages 82
surfacing gender 135
terrorism 75–7
torture, use of 78
un-crisis thinking 72, 94
water 80
Women Waging Peace 76–7, 85, 86
critical legal geographies 14, 49–57, 61–2
critical legal theory
 agency theory 123–6
 crisis, language of 83
 feminist scholarship 18, 20, 33–4
 first wave feminist approaches 34
 geographies 14, 49–57, 61–2
 New Approaches to International Law 18
 politics 20, 33
 post-structuralist theory 34
 second wave feminist approaches 34
 third wave feminist approaches 34
cross-examination 146, 148
culture
 Afghanistan, state-building in 161, 164–5, 169, 173–6
 East Timor, state-building in 14, 26–7
 imposition of women's rights 14, 26–7
 postcards 214
 sexuality 21

Dallmeyer, Dorinda 3
de Beauvoir, Simone 118
debt crisis *see* Argentina, debt crisis and takeover of factories by workers in
deconstruction of international law 5, 15
decontextualisation
 agency 72–4, 123
 rape 73–4, 112, 120, 149
 terror and anxiety 74, 123
 torture 120
Democratic Republic of Congo 156
democratisation 2, 6, 14, 17, 26
Derrida, Jacques 44
Dershowitz, Alan M 122
Dinerstein, Ana 202–3
disappearances 141
disaster capitalism 81–3, 95
discrimination *see* equality and non-discrimination
displacements and forced removals 149
distancing techniques 186, 187–9
diversity 63–6, 136, 213
Dobriansky, Paula 86–7
domestic labour, unequal balance of 28
domesticated womanhood 72, 76–7, 82

East Timor, post-conflict state-building in 14, 26–7, 140
Eastern Europe, trafficking and 177, 189, 191
Economic and Social Council (ESOSOC) 29–31

economic institutions 81
economic, social and cultural rights 28
ECOSOC (Economic and Social Council)
   29–31
education of girls in Afghanistan 162–3,
   165, 169, 172, 175–6
El Salvador, amnesties in 140
Emanuel, Rahm 80
emergencies, declarations of 75–8
employees *see* workers
England, Kim 53
Engle, Karen 3, 5, 19, 94–5, 112–13, 150
Enloe, Cynthia 214
equality and non-discrimination *see also*
   ethnicity and race
   Afghanistan, state-building in 167–74
   definition 24
   domestic labour, unequal balance of 28
   equal pay 28
   human rights law 3
   language of discrimination 28
   liberal equality strategies 167–74
   Northern Ireland 26
   political conflicts as springboard for
      equality 26
   procedural non-discrimination 27–8
   stereotypes 82, 91, 214
   structural inequalities and
      disadvantages 82
   trafficking 179, 181, 188
   undervaluation, language of 28
equality of States 99–100
Erturk, Yakin 112
essentialism 34, 54, 135–6, 153, 155
ethnicity and race
   Afghanistan, state-building in 161,
      168–72, 174, 176
   crisis, language of 92
   father, as determined by biological
      94–5
   hierarchies, creation and utilisation
      of 57
   human rights law 3
   marriage along ethnic lines 27
   partitions model 27–8
   rape as torture, criminalisation of 113
   sexual relations across ethnic lines as
      criminal 150
   stereotyping 91, 214
   trafficking 186, 187–9
European Union
   Afghanistan, state-building in 163–4,
      169, 175
   membership 48
   trafficking 184, 186–7
exception, state of 79–80, 82–3
experiences of women 134, 135–6, 143,
   147–8, 152–3, 155
experts 22, 27, 76, 115

factories, takeover of 193 *see also*
   Argentina, debt crisis and takeover of
   factories by workers in
facts, war against 121
Faludi, Susan 76–7, 92
Falwell, Jerry 77
financial markets *see* Argentina, debt crisis
   and takeover of factories by workers in
financial support for terrorism 106
Fineman, Martha 15
first wave feminist approaches 34
force
   governance 34
   marriage 87, 162
   rape 182–3, 185
   removals 149
   trafficking 185
former Yugoslavia *see* International
   Criminal Tribunal for the former
   Yugoslavia
Ford Foundation Annual Reports 105
Ford, Richard 49
Foucault, Michel 67, 179, 180
framing 73, 101–2
freezing of assets 106
Freud, Sigmund 37
Friedman, Milton 81
Friedman, Thomas 203
Fukuyama, Francis 77

Gardam, Judith 112–13
Gelpern, Anna 207–9
gender coding 136, 196
gender hierarchy, revitalising 76–8, 82
gender impunity gap 143
gender mainstreaming
   Afghanistan, state-building in 88, 134,
      135–6, 159–61, 167–8, 170–2
   competition policy 30
   crisis, language of 85, 88
   head counts 30
   human rights 29–30
   institutions 13, 23, 29–30
   International Court of Justice 30
   International Criminal Court 30
   International Law Commission 30
   Iraq 85
   mainstream/margins dichotomy 134,
      135–6
   policy development 30
   Security Council 85
   sex and gender, distinction between 30
   state-building 29–31, 35, 135
   synonym for women, gender as 31
   transitional justice and international
      crimes 138
   UN Economic and Social Council
      (ESOSOC) definition 29–31
   women's organisations 29

genocide 141, 149
geographies 14, 49–57, 61–2, 86, 89
Ghanaian Truth and Reconciliation
    Commission 145
ghetto, feminist scholarship as being in a
    13–14, 18–19, 33
Gibbings, Sheri 85
Gilmore, Leigh 146
Goldsmith, Jack 122
good faith 208–9 *see also* bad faith
governance
    Argentina, debt crisis and takeover of
        factories by workers in 193–7, 201, 212
    crisis, language of 72, 78–80, 82–91, 95
    feminism 21
    force 34
    legitimacy 195
    meaning 194–5
    sovereign debt market 194–7, 201,
        203–12
Grahn-Farley, Maria 7–8, 71–4, 82, 135–6
Grear, Anna 66
Greece, sovereign debt crisis in 194
Grosz, Elizabeth 19
Guantanamo Bay, bare life in 79
Guatemala, guarantees for redress in 140
guilt or innocence model 144–5
Gulati, Mitu 207–9
Gusmão, Xanana 26–7

Halley, Janet 7–8, 13, 14–15, 17, 20–4, 31,
    33, 72–4, 111–23, 126–8, 150
Hannah, Matthew 53
Harding, Sandra 179–80, 182
Harris, Angela 111–12, 125
Hartman, Saidiya V 124, 126
Harvard Law School, torture and 122
Hegel, GWF 126
hegemony
    agency theory 72
    colonisation and auto-colonisation of
        feminism 71–3
    crisis, language of 71–4, 78
    hegemonic States 100–1
    hegemonic security agenda 72
    non-governmental organisations 100–1
    partnership model 73
    post-9/11 71–3
    security agenda 72–3
    September 11, 2001 terrorist attacks on
        the United States 71
    spaces of international law 51–2, 54–6,
        59, 61–2, 66, 67
Hensen, Maria Rose 150
Heyzer, Noeleen 87
homosociality 37
honour 162
hosting, ethics of 43–4

Howard, John 80
human rights
    Afghanistan, state-building in 156, 160,
        164–5, 167, 169
    civil and political rights 28
    crisis, language of 77–8, 80
    definition 27–8
    economic, social and cultural rights 28
    experience of violations, women's 143
    feminist scholarship 3
    framing 101–2
    human wrongs 101
    Iraq 156
    military intervention 25
    national discriminatory laws 3
    neoliberalism 156
    non-governmental organisations 98–9,
        102, 105
    post-9/11, co-option of agenda after 72
    power of feminism 23
    rape as torture, criminalisation of
        111, 119
    security agenda 77–8
    state-building 25, 27–9
    Third World feminism 19
    trafficking 178, 187, 190
    transitional justice and international
        crimes 137–8, 140, 143, 148
    United States 105–6
    victimisation rhetoric 19
humanitarian law 111–12, 116, 119,
    126, 138
humanity, crimes against 140–1, 143, 149
Hunter, Rosemary 28
Hyndman, Jennifer 53
hysteria 37–9

identity-based movements 125–6
inclusive security 86, 92
inequality *see* equality and non-discrimination
inevitability, politics of 8, 74, 82, 91, 95,
    120–1, 127–9
Initiative for Inclusive Security (formerly
    Women for Waging Peace) 76–7, 85, 86,
    103–4
Injury Triad 14–15, 21, 23
insider/outsider binaries 54–5
institutions *see also* transnational justice
    institutions
    Afghanistan, state-building in 134, 169,
        170–2
    Argentina, debt crisis and takeover of
        factories by workers in 202–3, 206, 210
    bias in how institutions describe, condemn
        and rectify abuses 144–8
    feminism, institutionalisation of 21
    gender mainstreaming 13, 23, 29–30
    head counts 30

international economic and financial
institutions 28, 81
legalistic institutions, practices and
discourses 144–5
reforms 139
ritual incantations 23
security agenda 72
specific institutions for women 134, 169,
170–2
state-building 25, 27, 29–30
terror and anxiety 121–3
transitional justice and international
crimes 139, 144–8
interdependence 135, 200
inter-disciplinary insights for feminist
reform 14
internal displacement and forced
removals 149
International Conference on Population and
Development 3
International Court of Justice (ICJ) 30
international crimes *see also* ad hoc criminal
tribunals; international crimes; rape and
sexual violence; terrorism; transitional
justice and international crimes; war
crimes
Afghanistan 93
crimes against humanity 140–1, 143, 149
genocide 141, 149
trafficking 177–9, 184–90
universal jurisdiction 157
International Criminal Court (ICC) 30, 138,
140–1, 156
International Criminal Tribunal for Rwanda
4, 143, 150
International Criminal Tribunal for the
former Yugoslavia
rape 4, 19, 111–17, 119–21, 126–7
transitional justice and international
crimes 143
war crimes 4, 111–17, 120–1, 127, 143
international economic and financial
institutions 28, 81
international human rights *see* human rights
international humanitarian law 111–12,
116, 119, 126, 138
International Institute for the Sociology of
Law workshop, Oñati, Spain 1, 213–14
International Law Commission (ILC) 30
interpretation
agency theory 117–18, 121, 123–4
location of interpreter 118, 120–1, 123
neutral interpreters, influence of 74
politics of inevitability 120–1
rape as torture, criminalisation of 123–4
silenced women, interpretation for
117–18, 123
terror and anxiety 118

intersectionality 91, 94–5
Iraq
crisis governance, justification for 78
crisis, language of 78, 80, 81, 85–9, 94
disaster capitalism 81
gender mainstreaming 85
human rights 156
imposition of women's rights 27
masculine traditionalism, assertion after
invasion of 26
non-governmental organisations 85
orientalist mythologies 94
political participation of women 85–8, 93
post-conflict state-building 14, 25–7, 78,
80–1, 85–9, 91–4
pre-emptive self-defence 80
religion 27, 87–8
secular approach to personal status
laws 26
Security Council 85
surge 87–8
tokenism 14
UN measures of gender empowerment 26
veiled women needing rescue, orientalist
mythologies about 94
violence and disadvantage, increase in
87–8, 91–2
Women, Peace and Security resolution
85–6, 93
Women's International League for Peace
and Freedom 85
women's organisations 26
Irigaray, Luce 34, 36–8
Ivory Coast, amnesties in 140

Joya, Malalay 173
jurisdiction of international law 43
justice 6, 18–19, 24 *see also* transitional
justice and international crimes

Kapur, Ratna 19
Karzai, Hamid 159, 160
Kennedy, David 18, 79–80
Khan, Daoud 161
Khutuwane, Yvonne 152
Kimmel, Michael 166
Kincaid, Jamaica 146–7
Kirchner, Nestor 202
Klein, Naomi 81, 95
Koenig, Dorean 3
Koskenniemi, Martti 18
Kouvo, Sari 8, 67, 88, 125, 134–6
Kristeva, Julia 15, 3, 34, 36, 38–40, 44
Kunarac, Dragoljub, conviction of 111–17,
120–1, 127

Lacan, Jacques 38
Langton, Marcia 83

language of crisis *see* crisis, language
    of Latin America, disaster capitalism
    in 81, 95
Law's cardboard walls 15
Lefebvre, Henri 50–1, 55, 59–61
Lemkin, Raphael 141
liberal equality strategies 167–74
liberalisation 81
limitation periods 141
liquid feminism 7–8, 74, 121, 129
lived space 50–1, 55, 62–3, 66–7
lobbying 85, 138
local women's groups, failure to engage
    with 88–9
Lome Accords 140
Lorber, Judith 165
Lorde, Audre 14

MacKinnon, Catharine 21, 24, 25, 90–2,
    111–13
mad women in the attic, imagery of 15
mainstreaming *see* gender mainstreaming
males and masculinity
    aggressive masculinity and the language
        of crisis 72, 76–7, 82
    bias in international law 3, 35
    heroism 165–6
    power, focus on 21
    perpetrators and victims, as 142–3
    traditionalism, assertion of masculine 26
    sovereign state relations, masculinist
        constructions of 35
    sovereign subjectivity of masculinist
        constructions 35–7
Manji, Ambreena 4
mapping 86–8, 94–6
Marcus, Sharon 149, 152
marriage
    ethnic lines, across 27
    forced marriages 87, 162
masculinity, crisis language of aggressive 72,
    76–7, 82
Massey, Doreen 52, 61
maternal feminine 36, 40–2
men *see* males and masculinity
Menchu, Rigoberta 146–7
Mertus, Julie 7, 71–3, 76, 135, 211
Mieville, China 83, 93–4
Milosevic, Slobodan 146
Milton Friedman School of economics 81
Mohanty, Chandra 136, 153, 211
Mujahedin/warlords in Afghanistan 162–3,
    168, 169–70, 173–4
multidimensional understanding of space 50,
    55, 56, 61–2
multiplicity of space 52–4, 60, 62–8

Nakaya, Sumie 27
naming causes 102

nation building *see* Afghanistan,
    state-building in; state-building
Nazi concentration camps, bare life in 79
neoliberalism 167
Nesiah, Vasuki 8, 67, 133–6, 164
Neuwirth, Jessica 169
New Approaches to International Law 18
non-discrimination *see* equality and non-
    discrimination
non-governmental organisations (NGOS)
    advocacy 20, 73, 97–105, 108
    Anti-Terrorist Financing Guidelines:
        Voluntary Best Practices for US
        charities 107
    blind spots 73, 98, 101–5, 108
    co-option of 9/11 agenda 72
    crisis, language of 72, 85, 88
    empowerment of women 97
    equality of States 99–100
    financial support, Executive Order
        on 106
    framing 73, 101–2
    freezing of assets 106
    hegemonic international law 100–1
    hegemonic states 100–1
    human rights 98–9, 102, 105–6
    Initiative for Inclusive Security (formerly
        Women for Waging Peace) 103–4
    International Criminal Court,
        participation in 58
    international NGOs 99
    Iraq, post-conflict state-building in 85
    language of counter-terrorism 102–3, 105
    monitoring and recording 100
    nation states, importance of 99
    North, advocates from the 97–8, 105
    Ottawa Convention Banning
        Landmines 59
    PATRIOT Act 106
    polarisation 105
    post-9/11 security agenda 73, 97–108
    regulatory bureaucracy, increase
        in 105–7
    resistance/compliance binary 108
    road blocks 105, 108
    rules of the road 99–101
    sanctions 106–7
    scholars and activists, divide between 20
    security agenda 73, 97–108
    Security Council 101, 103
    security sector, desirability of joining the
        103–4
    South, advocates from the 98, 105
    spaces of international law 59
    Special Rapporteur on Violence against
        Women (UN) 98–9
    speed bumps 99, 105–7, 108
    surveillance 106
    terrorism, countering 99, 102–3, 105–7

transitional justice and international crimes 138
UN conferences on women 98–9, 108
United States 99, 102, 105–7
Vienna Declaration and Platform for Action 98–9
violence against women 98
Women, Peace and Security SC resolution 103
women's advocacy NGOs 103
North *see also* West
advocates from the North 97–8, 105
transnational justice institutions 155–6
Northern Ireland 26
Northern Territory, Australia, reduction of rights of Aboriginals in 80, 83
Nowak, Manfred 109, 111–12
Nuremberg Military Tribunal 143, 144

Obama, Barack 73, 80, 101, 104
object of feminist inquiry, law as 15
objective, law reform as 15
occupation and possession 35–6
oppression
Afghanistan, state-building in 134, 161, 164–5, 175
agency theory 123–4
inevitability, politics of 74, 121
liquid feminism 74
resistance 7
sex as locus of oppression 19
Orford, Anne 4, 14, 36–7, 40–1
organs, trafficking for 184–5
orientalist mythologies 94
other 4, 36, 41, 43–4, 188
Otomo, Yoriko 7, 13, 15–16
Ottawa Convention Banning Landmines 59
Otto, Dianne 4, 7, 64–5, 71–2, 125, 126, 135, 211
overreaching of feminism 116–17, 129

Packer, George 101
Pahuja, Sundhya 93
Palestine, bare life in 79
paradoxical spaces 15
parallel universe of international law 93
participation of women 25, 86–8, 93–4, 134, 138, 167–76
Pashtun 163, 165
PATRIOT Act 105, 121
patronage 174, 176
Patterson, Orlando 124
Pearson, Zoe 7, 13–16
Peru 147, 149
Philips, Ann 134
pimps 186–8
Pinochet, Augusto 81, 141

politics
Afghanistan, participation of women in 86–8, 93–4, 134, 167–76
aims 24
Argentina, debt crisis and takeover of factories by workers in 201–3
binaries, resistance to 51
civil and political rights 28
colonisation 72, 83
crisis, language of 79, 82–3, 85–6, 88, 91, 93–5
distinct from politics, international law as being 18
equality, political conflicts as springboard for 26
feminism 18–19
inevitability, politics of 8, 74, 82, 91, 95, 120–1, 127–9
Iraq, post-conflict state-building in 85–8, 93
Other 41
participation and representation of women 85–8, 93–4, 134, 167–76
revolution 39–40
spaces of international law 51, 53
speaking for women 134
state-building 26
transitional justice and international crimes 139
United States financial and political dominance, dissatisfaction with 92
post-9/11 era
advocacy 73, 93–105, 108
Afghanistan, state-building in 134, 160, 165–76
Anti-Terrorist Financing Guidelines: Voluntary Best Practices for US charities 107
blind spots 73, 98, 101–5, 108
co-option of feminist agenda 72
crisis, language of 71–3, 77–8
critical legal theory 20, 33
empowerment of women 97
equality of States 99–100
financial support, Executive Order on 106
framing 73, 101–2
freezing of assets 106
hegemony 71–2, 199–1
human rights 72, 98–9, 102, 105
Initiative for Inclusive Security (formerly Women for Waging Peace) 103–4
international NGOs 99
language of counter-terrorism 102–3, 105
liquid feminism 129
monitoring and recording 100
nation states, importance of 99
non-governmental organisations 73
North, advocates from the 97–8, 105
PATRIOT Act 106

polarisation 105
post-9/11 security agenda 73
rape as torture, criminalisation of 128
regulatory bureaucracy, increase in 105–7
resistance/compliance binary 108
road blocks 105, 108
rules of the road 99–101
sanctions 106–7
Security Council 101, 103
security agenda 6, 72–3, 77–8, 103–4
South, advocates from the 98, 105
Special Rapporteur on Violence against
    Women (UN) 98–9
speed bumps 99, 105–7, 108
state of exception 79–80
surveillance 106
terror and anxiety 110, 120
terrorism 99, 102–3, 105–7, 128
UN conferences on women 98–9, 108
United States 99, 102, 105–7
Vienna Declaration and Platform for
    Action 98–9
violence against women 98
Women, Peace and Security SC
    resolution 103
women's advocacy NGOs 103
postcards 213–19
post-colonial scholarship 4, 93, 114–15
post-modernism 19, 114–15
post-structural scholarship 4, 34
poverty 161–2, 164–5, 179, 181, 188, 190
power
    agency theory 111–12
    asymmetrical power relations 26
    disempowerment 112
    feminism, of 21–4, 31
    local power 112
    politics of inevitability 127–8
    rape as torture, criminalisation of 74,
        111–12, 115, 127–8
    self-expression 127
    trafficking 178–82, 190
pre-emptive self-defence 78, 80
private law
    Argentina, debt crisis and takeover of
        factories by workers in 194, 197, 203–12
    commonsense 194, 197, 203–12
    sanctity, private law doctrine of 204–5, 207
    sovereign debt market 194, 197, 203–12
privatisation, disaster capitalism and 81
privileged subject of transnational justice,
    feminist critique of 142–3, 144
processes of law 56, 58, 60
prostitution 177, 186–8
psychoanalytical theory 14–15, 35–8, 40
publications on international law 2–4
public/private dichotomy 28, 57, 59–60,
    195–6, 214

queer theory 21–2
quotas 173

race *see* ethnicity and race
Rajagopal, Balakrishnan 211
rape and sexual violence
    Afghanistan, state-building in 163
    agency theory 111–13, 115, 117–18,
        120–8, 149–50
    autonomy 136, 182
    bodily injury crimes 143, 149–50
    children, rape of 115–17, 119–20
    consent to rape 73, 113–17, 119–21,
        127–9, 182–3
    criminalisation 7–8, 73–4, 94, 109–29,
        182–4
    crisis, language of 89
    decontextualisation 73–4, 112, 120
    definition of rape 182–3
    disempowerment 112
    ethnic differences 113
    ethnicity determined by biological father
        94–5
    genocide 141, 149
    feminism 111–21, 126–9
    force requirement in Sweden 182–3, 185
    free choice of women to have sex with
        guards 74, 111–12
    heterosexual matrix 184
    human rights 111, 119
    inevitability, politics of 8, 74, 129
    International Criminal Tribunal for
        Rwanda 150
    International Criminal Tribunal for the
        former Yugoslavia 4, 19, 111–17,
        119–21, 126–7
    international humanitarian law 111–12,
        116, 119, 126
    interpretation 123–4
    liquid feminism 7–8, 74, 129
    local power 112
    male-centredness of international
        humanitarian law 112
    minimising of injury 150–1
    moments of exception 112
    murder, classification of rape as being as
        serious as 150
    Muslims, rape of 117, 126
    neo-Conservative Bush doctrine 74
    open and accessible bodies 183–4
    oppression of women 8, 74, 123–4,
        126, 129
    overreaching 116–17, 129
    post-9/11 era 128
    post-colonial critiques 114–15
    post-conflict peace-keeping 87–90
    post-modernist critiques 114–15
    power 74, 111–12, 115, 127–8

privacy of rape locations 116
privileged subject of transnational justice, feminist critique of 142–3, 144
purpose, torture must have a 117
self-expression 118, 120, 127–8
severe or intense pain and suffering 119, 127
subject of criminal protection 184
Swedish discourses on rape 182–4
terror and anxiety 74, 111
torture 74, 109–29, 148–9
transitional justice and international crimes 109–29, 143, 148–51, 157
victimisation, accentuating 150–1
vulnerability of subjects 182–4
war crimes 4, 19, 73–4, 89, 94–5, 109–29, 150, 163
will and resistance 182–3
women, war on 25, 91–2
rationality 134, 178, 190
Réaume, Denise 24
regulatory bureaucracy, increase in 105–7
rehabilitation and recovery 135
relationality 135, 200–1
relativism 18
religion
    Afghanistan, state-building in 162, 165, 176
    Christian fundamentalism 77
    East Timor, state-building in 14
    Iraq, post-conflict state-building in 27, 87–8
    rape as torture, criminalisation of 117, 126
    September 11, 2001 terrorist attacks on the United States 77
reparations 138, 145, 148, 155
resistance 6, 13, 15–16, 49–51, 54–6, 60–3, 65, 68
resistance/compliance binary 71–4
    crisis, language of 73
    feminist scholarship 4–6, 9, 17, 34, 48, 213
    hegemony 73
    location of women being interpreted 118
    non-governmental organisations 108
    silenced women, interpretation for 117–18
    spaces of international law 49, 56, 60, 62, 65, 68
    state-building 31
    terror and anxiety 74, 118, 121
restructuring of debt 208
revolutions 34–5, 38–40, 43
road blocks 105, 108
Robespierre, Maximilien 34
Robertson, Pat 77
Rose, Gillian 15, 54–5, 60, 65

Ross, Fiona 152
Rousseau, Stephanie 143
Rwanda 4, 143, 149, 150

sacrifice 36, 39–42
Saddam Hussein 26, 156
sanctions 106–7
sanctity, private law doctrine of 204–5, 207
Sartre, Jean-Paul 181
saved, Afghan women as needing to be 94, 167, 175
Schreiner, Olive 38
Scott, Joan Wallach 153, 179–80, 182
second wave feminist approaches 34
security agenda
    crisis, language of 72–3
    decontextualised feminist notion of agency 72
    hegemony 72–3
    human rights 77–8
    inclusive security 92
    institutionalisation 72
    post-9/11 era 6, 72–3, 77–8, 103–4
    security sector, desirability of joining the 103–4
    torture 118
    Women, Peace and Security resolution 85–6, 93
Security Council (UN)
    Afghanistan, state-building in 84
    anti-terror legislation 82
    crisis, language of 76–8, 80, 82, 85–6, 93, 95
    dominance 76–8
    gender mainstreaming 85
    hegemonic States 101
    Iraq, post-conflict state-building in 85
    non-governmental organisations 101, 103
    terrorism 80, 82
    Women, Peace and Security resolution 85–6, 93, 103
self-defence 78, 80
self-determination 28–9
self-expression 118, 120, 123, 127–8
self-reflection 6, 17
September 11, 2001 terrorist attacks on the United States *see also* post-9/11 era
    Christian fundamentalism 77
    crisis, language of 75–7
    hegemony 71
    male heroism 165–6
    masculinity, two types of 166
    state-building 25
    United States financial and political dominance, dissatisfaction with 92
    victims, women as 166
    war on women 25, 91
seriality, gender as 181–2

sex and gender, distinction between 30
sexual services, trafficking for 177, 184–5,
    186, 189–90
sexual violence *see* rape and sexual violence
sexuality
    anti-sex 21
    cross-ethnic sexual relations as
        criminal 150
    cultural feminism 21
    oppression, sex as locus of 19
    queer theory 21–2
Sharoni, Simona 26
shock therapy stabilisation programmes 81
Showalter, Elaine 38
Sierra Leone 140, 144, 149, 156
silenced women, interpretation for
    117–18, 123
slavery 124–5, 126
Smith, Sidonie 150
social costs of debt crisis 197, 198, 203–6,
    209–11
social death argument 124–5
social practices 49–50, 56–7
Soja, Edward 50, 56, 58, 60–1
South
    advocates from the South 98, 105
    transnational justice institutions 155
South Africa
    internal displacement and forced
        removals 149
    rape 152
    Truth and Reconciliation Commission
        145, 146, 147–8, 152, 155
sovereign debt market and Argentina 193–7,
    201–12
    bankruptcy 194–7, 202–3
    collective action clauses 205–6, 207
    contract 193–4, 201, 204–9
    convergence 202–4, 207, 210
    creditor codes of conduct 208
    feminist scholarship 207–12
    good faith 208–9
    governance 194–7, 201, 203–12
    information 208
    International Economic Law 195
    market failure 197, 201
    modification of contracts 205, 207–8
    neo-liberal convergence 207
    private law commonsense 194, 197,
        203–12
    repayment, contractual right to 204–7
    sanctity, private law doctrine of
        204–5, 207
    slippage between doctrinal and real
        209–12
    social contexts 208, 209
    social costs 197, 198, 203–6, 209–11
sovereign state relations, masculinist
    constructions of 35

sovereign subjectivity, masculinist
    constructions of 35–7
spaces of international law 47–68
    binaries 49, 51, 54–62, 65–8
    blind spots 62
    civilising mission of international law 57
    contestation 51–2, 56
    conversation between spaces 54
    counter-spaces 50–1
    critical legal geographies 14, 49–57,
        61–2
    diversity and difference 63–6
    exclusion of women 50
    fluidity 53, 55, 56, 62–5, 67–8
    gendered nature of space 49–52, 54
    global or international 53, 59–61
    hegemony 51–2, 54–6, 59, 61–2, 66, 67
    inclusion, process of 59–61, 65
    insider/outsider binaries 54–5
    knowledge creation 54, 62
    law and space 56
    lived spaces 50–1, 55, 62–3, 66–7
    local 53, 59, 61
    masculinist discourse 35
    multidimensional understanding of space
        50, 55, 56, 61–2
    multiplicity of space 52–4, 60, 62–8
    national 53, 59
    non-governmental organisations 57–9
    openness of space 51–2, 53–5, 62–5
    organisation of space, how law and legal
        institutions shape and control 57
    paradoxical space 54–6, 61–3, 65–7
    physical world, how law and legal
        institutions shape and control 57
    political resistance to binaries 51
    politics 51, 53
    processes and substance of law 56, 58, 60
    production of space 49–51
    public/private binary 57, 59–60
    racial hierarchies, creation and utilisation
        of 57
    reflection 16
    regional 53, 61
    regulation 57–8
    representations of space 50, 59, 61
    resistance 15–16, 49–51, 54–6, 60–3,
        65, 68
    resistance/compliance binary 49, 56, 60,
        62, 65, 68
    shaped by international law, space as
        60–2
    shaped by space, international law as
        57–60
    social practices 49–50, 56–7
    spaces of representation 50
    spatial practices 50
    symbolism 15
    transnational actors 57–8

violence of international law 59
visibility and invisibility of spaces of
    international law 60
where of international law 48–51, 56
speaking for women 134
Special Rapporteur on Violence against
    Women (UN) 98–9
speed bumps 99, 105–7, 108
Spivak, Gayatri Chakravorty 117, 123,
    147, 157
stabilisation programmes 81
state-building 25–32 *see also* **Afghanistan,**
    state-building in
asymmetrical power relations 26
civil and political rights 28
Cold War 25
decision-making tables, women's presence
    at 25
democratisation 14, 17
domestic labour, unequal balance of 28
East Timor 14
economic, social and cultural rights 28
ethnic partitions model 27–8
feminist scholarship 17
forgetfulness and insouciance about
    women 27
funding, lack of 27
gender mainstreaming 29–31, 35, 135
global and local, tension between 14
human rights standards 25, 27–9
international institutions 25, 27, 29–30
Iraq 14, 25–7, 78, 80–1, 85–9, 91–4
policy neglect 28
political conflicts as springboard for
    equality 26
procedural non-discrimination 27–8
public and private life, traditional
    structures of 28
resistance and compliance 31
revolution 35
self-determination 28–9
September 11, 2001 terrorist attacks on
    the United States 25
sexual exploitation 87–90
transitional justice and international
    crimes 139
UN Development Fund for Women 25
women's organisations 26, 88–9,
    163–5, 169
state of exception 70–80, 82–3
statutes of limitations 141
stereotypes 82, 91, 214
structural and systematic injustice 24
subjects
bias in subject constituted by international
    crimes 140–4, 148–9
privileged subject of transnational justice,
    feminist critique of 142–3, 144
rape in Sweden 184

trafficking 186–91
two-dimensional subjects of international
    law, perpetrator and victim as 142
vulnerability 182–4
subordination theory 20–1
substance of law 56, 58, 60
subversion 38
surveillance 106
Sweden
autonomy 182
consent and force 182–3
definition of rape 182–3
force and exploitation 182–3, 185
heterosexual matrix 184
incapacitation 183
open and accessible bodies 183–4
rape 182–5
subject of criminal protection 184
trafficking 184–90
vulnerability of subjects 182–4
will and resistance 182–3
symbolism 15, 180
synonym for women, gender as 31

Taliban 84, 87, 135, 160, 163–6, 169, 175
territorial sovereignty 35–6
terror and anxiety 33, 34–5
academic institutions 121–3
decontextualisation 74, 123
facts, war against 121
feminist scholarship 121
inevitability, politics of 120–1
interpretation 118
neutral interpreters, influence of 74
PATRIOT Act 121
post-9/11 110, 120
rape as torture, criminalisation of 74, 111
resistance/compliance binary 74, 118, 121
revolution 34–5
sovereign subjectivity, masculinist
    constructions of 35
terrorism 128
torture 109–10, 121–2, 128
United States 109–10, 121
virtue 34
terrorism
Afghanistan, state-building in 165–6
Anti-Terrorist Financing Guidelines:
    Voluntary Best Practices for US
    charities 107
binaries 128
clash of civilisations 1
framing 102–3
language of counter-terrorism 102–3, 105
non-governmental organisations 99,
    102–3, 105–7
PATRIOT Act 106
post-9/11 era 128
sanctions 106–7

Security Council 80, 82
terror and anxiety 128
war on terror 1, 53, 91–2, 128
war on women 91–2
testimony 145–8, 152–3, 156
third wave feminist approaches 34–7
Third World feminism 19
Thomas, Dania 8, 135–6
time limits 141
Timor Leste, post-conflict state-building in 14, 26–7, 140
tokenism 14, 18, 168
Tokyo Military Tribunal 143
torture
  academic institutions 121–2
  agency theory 72
  bodily injury crimes 143
  consent 119
  crisis, language of 78
  decontextualisation 120
  definition 118–20
  enhanced interrogation measures 118
  Harvard Law School 122
  legalisation 121–2
  memos 110
  mirroring 118–19
  national security 118
  purpose of torture 117, 119
  rape 74, 109–29, 148–9
  self-expression 118
  severe or intense pain and suffering 119–20
  terror and anxiety 109–10, 121–2, 128
  transitional justice and international crimes 148
  United States 109–10, 118–22
trafficking, vulnerability of victims of 177–91
  age of victims 185, 187
  agency 134, 180–1
  autonomy 134, 136, 177, 190
  children 185–8
  consent 134, 185
  contextualised or relationship subjects 179–80, 190–1
  criminal law 177–9, 184–90
  criminal responsibility 178
  definition 179
  demand 185–9
  discursive conditions 180–2, 189, 190
  distancing techniques 186, 187–9
  'domestic' women, recruitment of 188–9
  Eastern Europe 177, 189, 191
  elements of crime 184–5
  ethnicity 186, 187–9
  European Union Framework Decision 184, 186–7
  factors affecting practice of trafficking 185–6

force and exploitation 185
gender, aspects of 180–2
gender neutrality 186–7
human rights 178, 187, 190
individuals 179–82, 186–8, 190
inequality 179, 181, 188
international law 177–8
labour, trafficking for 185
organs, sale of 184–5
other 188
pimps 186–8
poverty 179, 181, 188, 190
power 178–82, 190
prostitution 177, 186–8
rational, women as 134, 178, 190
rule of law 178
seriality, gender as 181–2
sexual services 177, 184–5, 186, 189–90
structural factors 179–82, 188–90
subjects of trafficking 186–91
Sweden, criminalisation in 184–90
symbolic aspects of gender 180
Third World feminism 19
unemployment 179, 181, 188, 190
United Nations 184, 185
victimisation rhetoric 19
violence 178
transgressions 15–16, 39–40, 47–8
transitional justice *see* transitional justice and international crimes; transnational justice institutions
transitional justice and international crimes
  accountability 137, 140–1, 144
  ad hoc criminal tribunals 138, 140
  amnesties 140–1, 144
  biases 133–4, 139–44, 148–9, 151
  bodily injury crimes 141–2, 143, 149–50
  conservative feminism, consolidation of 134, 139
  crimes against humanity 140–1, 143, 149
  definition 137
  disappearances 141
  feminism 137–44, 148–51
  gender impunity gap 143
  gender mainstreaming 138
  genocide 141, 149
  human rights 137–8, 140, 143, 148
  institutions
    bias in how institutions describe, condemn and rectify abuses 144–8
    legalistic institutions, practices and discourses 144–5
    reforms 139
  internal displacement and forced removals 149
  International Criminal Court 138, 140–1, 156
  International Criminal Tribunal for Rwanda 143, 150

International Criminal Tribunal for the former Yugoslavia 143
international humanitarian law 138
legalistic institutions, practices and discourses 144–5
lobbying 138
Lome Accords 140
mainstreaming 138, 139
male perpetrators and victims 142–3
non-governmental organisations 138
participation of women 138
politics 139
post-conflict human rights 137
post-conflict state-building 138
privileged subject of transnational justice, feminist critique of 142–3, 144
rape and sexual violence 126, 143, 148–51, 157
rehabilitation and recovery 135
reparations, lobbying about 138
statutes of limitations 141
subject constituted by international crimes, bias in 140–4, 148–9
subjectivity of women 143
torture 148
two-dimensional subjects of international law, perpetrator and victim as 142
United Nations 138, 140
United States 156
victim, definition of 141
war crimes 156
transnational justice institutions
amnesties 144
bias in how institutions describe, condemn and rectify abuses 144–8, 152–4
bodily injury 147–53
comfort women 145
courts
cross-examination 146, 148
prioritisation of 144–5
testimony 145–8
victims, trauma of 145–7
cross-examination 146, 148
essentialism 155
experiences of women 147–8, 152–3, 155
feminist critique 145–8, 152–7
guilt or innocence model 144–5
human rights 156–7
legalistic institutions, practices and discourses 144–5
non-governmental organisations 155–6
North-South trajectory 155–6
perpetrators, focus on 145–6
reforms 139, 154
reparations 145, 148, 155
South, impetus from the 155
testimony 145–8, 152–3, 156
trauma, testimony regarding 147

truth and reconciliation commissions 137, 138, 139, 144–8, 152–3, 155
victims, alienation of 145–8
truth and reconciliation commissions
amnesties 144
bodily injury 152–3
context, exclusion of 146
courts 144–5
experiences of women 147–8, 152–3
forensic speech acts 146
forensic truth 145
gender mainstreaming 138
guilt or innocence model 144–5
investigative units 145
public hearings 145, 152
rape 152
reparations 145, 148
South Africa 145, 146, 147–8, 152, 155
standard of proof 144–5
testimony 146–8, 152–3
transnational justice institutions 137, 138, 139, 144–8, 152–3, 155
victim/perpetrator determination 145
Turkey, amnesties for Kurds in 140

undervaluation, language of 28
United Nations (UN) *see also* **Security Council (UN)**
Afghanistan, state-building in 84
Charter of UN 99–100
conferences on women 98–9, 108
Declaration on the Elimination of Violence against Women 3–4
Development Fund for Women 25
Economic and Social Council (ESOSOC) 29–31
equality of States 99–100
gender empowerment measures 26
General Assembly 84
Iraq, nation-building in 26
Lome Accords 140
Special Rapporteur on Violence against Women (UN) 4, 98–9
trafficking 178
transitional justice and international crimes 138
United States *see also* **September 11, 2001 terrorist attacks on the United States**
Afghanistan, intervention for women in 8, 25, 78, 84, 87–9, 94, 156, 160, 164–7, 175–6
agency theory 121
Anti-Terrorist Financing Guidelines: Voluntary Best Practices for US charities 107
counter-terrorism, language of 102, 105
disaster capitalism 81
factory, seizure by workers of 193
freezing of assets 106

Guantanamo Bay, bare life in 79
human rights 105–6
Latin America 81
non-governmental organisations 99, 102, 105–7
PATRIOT Act 106
regulatory bureaucracy, increase in 105–7
surveillance 106
terror and anxiety 109–10, 121–2
terrorism
  Anti-Terrorist Financing Guidelines 107
  counter-terrorism, language of 102, 105
  freezing of assets 106
torture 109–10, 118–22
transitional justice and international crimes 156
Treasury Department 106–7
universal jurisdiction 137

veiled women needing rescue, orientalist mythologies about 94
victims
  alienation 145–8
  cross-examination 146, 148
  definition 141
  disappearances 141
  genocide 141
  human rights movement 19
  International Criminal Tribunal for Rwanda 146
  International Criminal Tribunal for the former Yugoslavia 145–6
  males as perpetrators and victims 142–3
  minimising of injury 150–1
  rape, accentuating victimisation and 150–1
  September 11, 2001 terrorist attacks, women as victims of 166
  Third World feminism 18
  trafficking 19
  transnational justice institutions 145–8
  violence 19
Vienna Declaration and Platform for Action 98–9
violence *see also* rape and sexual violence
  Afghanistan, increase in violence against women in 87, 91–2
  international law, violence of 59
  Iraq, increase in violence against women in 87–8, 91–2
  non-governmental organisations 98
  psychoanalytical theory 40
  trafficking 178
  UN Declaration on the Elimination of Violence against Women 3–4
  UN Special Rapporteur on Violence against Women 4, 98–9
  victimisation rhetoric 19

virtue 34–5, 43–5
vulnerability
  rape 182–4
  trafficking 134, 177–81

war crimes
  ad hoc tribunals 111–17, 120–1, 127, 140, 143
  Afghanistan Parliament, perpetrators in 173–4
  International Criminal Tribunal for Rwanda 4, 143
  International Criminal Tribunal for the former Yugoslavia 4, 111–17, 120–1, 127, 143
  rape and sexual violence 4, 19, 73–4, 89, 94–5, 109–29, 150, 163
  statute of limitations 141
  transitional justice 156
  universal jurisdiction 137
wars and conflicts *see also* Afghanistan, state-building in; state-building; war crimes
  Afghanistan 161–4
  agency 19–20
  crimes 4, 19, 89, 94, 109–29, 150, 163
  cross-ethnic sexual relations as criminal 150
  father, ethnicity determined by biological 94–5
  International Criminal Tribunal for Rwanda 4
  intersectional analysis 94–5
  sexual agency during conflicts, denial of 19–20
  terror, war on 1, 53, 91–2, 128
  women, war on 25, 91–2
warlords in Afghanistan 162–3, 168, 169–70, 173–4
Washington Consensus 197–8
water 80
West *see also* Sweden; United States
  Afghanistan, intervention for women in 8, 25, 78, 84, 87–9, 94, 156, 160, 164–7, 175–6
  binaries 51
  blind spots of feminism 4
  clash of civilisations 1, 6, 165
  European Union 48, 163–4, 169, 175, 184, 186–7
  hegemony 2
  international law scholarship, invitation of feminists into 4–5
  North, advocates from the 97–8, 105
  Others, Western feminism speaking for 4
  patriarchy 2
West, Robin 21
'where' of international law 48–51, 56

'who' of international law 48
will and resistance 182–3
Women, Peace and Security resolution 85–6,
    93, 103
Women Waging Peace (now Initiative for
    Inclusive Security) 76–7, 85, 86, 103–4
Women's International League for Peace and
    Freedom 85
women's organisations
    Afghanistan, state-building in 88–9,
        163–5, 169
    culture 27
    East Timor 26–7
    gender mainstreaming 29
    Iraq 26
    local women's groups, failure to engage
        with 88–9

non-governmental organisations 103
    state-building 26, 88–9, 163–5, 169
Wordsworth, Anne 174
World Conference for Human Rights 1993 3
World Conference for Women 3
World Trade Organization (WTO) 23
workers *see also* Argentina, debt crisis and
    takeover of factories by workers in
    equal pay 28
    trafficking for labour 179, 181, 185,
        188, 190
Wright, Shelley 3

Yoo, John 122
Young, Iris Marion 179, 181
Yugoslavia *see* International Criminal
    Tribunal for the former Yugoslavia

www.ingramcontent.com/pod-product-compliance
Lightning Source LLC
Chambersburg PA
CBHW071417290326
41932CB00046B/1910